Veröffentlichungen des Ostasien-Instituts
der Ruhr-Universität Bochum

Band 63

2013

Harrassowitz Verlag · Wiesbaden

Gad C. Isay

The Philosophy of the View of Life
in Modern Chinese Thought

2013

Harrassowitz Verlag · Wiesbaden

Herausgegeben von der Fakultät für Ostasienwissenschaften
der Ruhr-Universität Bochum

Schriftleitung: zur Zeit Stefan Köck

Bibliografische Information der Deutschen Nationalbibliothek
Die Deutsche Nationalbibliothek verzeichnet diese Publikation in der Deutschen
Nationalbibliografie; detaillierte bibliografische Daten sind im Internet
über http://dnb.dnb.de abrufbar.

Bibliographic information published by the Deutsche Nationalbibliothek
The Deutsche Nationalbibliothek lists this publication in the Deutsche
Nationalbibliografie; detailed bibliographic data are available in the internet
at http://dnb.dnb.de.

For further information about our publishing program consult our
website http://www.harrassowitz-verlag.de

© Otto Harrassowitz GmbH & Co. KG, Wiesbaden 2013
Kreuzberger Ring 7c-d, D-65205 Wiesbaden,
produktsicherheit.verlag@harrassowitz.de
This work, including all of its parts, is protected by copyright. Any
use beyond the limits of copyright law without the permission of
the publisher is forbidden and subject to penalty. This applies
particularly to reproductions, translations, microfilms and storage
and processing in electronic systems.
Printed on permanent/durable paper.
Printed in Germany
ISSN 0340-6687
ISBN 978-3-447-06883-3

Acknowledgements

Writing this book on the Chinese 'view of life' has been rewarding beyond expectation. I convey my gratitude to the many persons and the institutions that were involved. Professor Irene Eber rendered me invaluable support. In addition to her profound and sound erudition, I benefited from her meticulous attention to detail, her perceptive criticism, her dedication, and her sense of humor. She has been, and still is, a constant source of inspiration and a stimulus to formulate new solutions to old problems. In addition, I am deeply grateful to Professor Harold Zvi Schiffrin for years of encouragement and help, for his enlightening remarks, and for his critical reading of large parts of an early draft manuscript. Professors Ben-Ami Scharfstein and Gabriel Motzkin read parts of the manuscript and kindly shared their scholarly expertise.

The extent of my research of the 'view of life' problem in the history of modern China evolved while studying, collecting source material and conducting interviews with academics at Peking (Beijing) University for several months during 1995 and 1996. For this I am indebted to the Exchange Program of the Hebrew University of Jerusalem and the Peking University. Wang Shouchang, among others, played a decisive role in helping me to find my way among the vast sources of East-West intellectual relations. My special thanks are due to my foreign friends at Beida: Professor Fujii Shozho, and Leo Leeb, Gregory Lloyd, and Lewis Mayo, who all in time achieved scholarly distinction. Each of them contributed a great deal to my life and my work. Professors Fujii and Chan Kwok-kou Leonard were instrumental in arranging a meeting with Lin Geng whom I interviewed on his father Lin Zaiping (Zhijun). Gregory Lloyd helped with the Huang Xuanmin interview about Hou Wailu. Leo, helped with the interviews with professors Shi Jun and Hu Weixi. I wish to express my deep gratitude to these scholars, as well as to the friends who helped to make those fruitful interviews possible.

During the academic year of 1998–1999 I went to Ohio State University to study with Professor Chang Hao whose works I had been admiring for many years. I profited immensely from my conversations with him, and from his lectures. Professor Chang was much more to me than a teacher. I shall always treasure his distinguished personality, and the warm friendship that he and his wife extended to me while staying at OSU. My deep gratitude also goes to Professor Richard Torrance who gave of his time beyond the call of duty. I also owe a debt of gratitude to Professor Christopher Reed. Likewise, I recall my friends at OSU, Wu Mingying, Wang Tianyi, Ed and Susan Weil, Jessica Torres, and Autumn. During my stay at Ohio I was privileged to visit Professor Julia Lin. The imprint of her personality will remain with me forever. This crucial period of study and research at OSU would not have been possible without the Fulbright grant awarded to me by the United States – Israel Educational Foundation. I am also indebted to the Faculty of Humanities at the Hebrew University of Jerusalem. The scholarship they awarded, in the name of the late Professor Nathan Rotenstreich, supported three years of research and writing, together with thought provoking discussions, encouragement, and financial aid.

With time, my interest in nineteenth century Protestant Missionaries in China coincided with the work and the personality of Professor Lauren Pfister. He became to me a great source of inspiration and support, for much more than the present project. Later, at the Academia Sinica in Taipei, I met Professor Yap Key-chong (Ye Qizhong), a leading authority on issues relating to the view of life controversy in modern Chinese history. I thank him for his encouragement, and for his efforts to provide relevant sources.

Eventually it was Professor Raoul David Findeisen who read an early draft of the book. He offered his comments and suggestions for revision. The extent of his contribution to the materialization of this book is matched only by the weight of his friendship. To his credit I add many vistas that recently opened in my life. Gratitude is due to the people at Harrassowitz Verlag, Dr. Barbara Krauss and Mr. Reinhard Friedrich. Recently I benefitted from the kind assistance of Zeev Raphael and Reut Pelleg. Regardless of all the support, I take full responsibility for the limitations of this study.

And finally, all this would not have been possible without my friends and my family. I thank my wife Lilah and my daughters Niva and Daphna, for their love, patience and support. In addition, I extend my deep gratitude to my brother Amnon and his family, as well as to my parents Aviva and Jurgen. Without the love and devoted co-operation of my late father, this work would not have materialized. It is to his memory that I dedicate this study.

February 2013

Gad C. Isay
Haifa

Contents

Acknowledgements	V
Introduction	1
Chapter One:	
The Philosophy of the View of Life in Traditional Chinese Thought	9
Background	11
Early and Mid-Qing	16
The Nineteenth Century	22
Conclusion	28
Chapter Two:	
Two Interpretations of Kant's 'View of Life': Ernst Faber and Liang Qichao	31
A. Ernst Faber and the Idea of Autonomous Individuality	33
B. Liang Qichao's Early Excursions in Kantian Philosophy	42
Conclusion	50
Chapter Three:	
Prelude to the 1923 Controversy	53
A. Resistance to Scientism in China: Foreign Sources	53
Henri Bergson and Rudolf Eucken	55
John Dewey and Bertrand Russell	59
Hans Driesch	63
B. Resistance to Scientism in China: First Chinese Attempts to Reconcile Chinese and Western Ideas	65
The Reflections of Liang Qichao	65
The Cultures of Liang Shuming	69
Conclusion	73
Chapter Four:	
Arguments against Scientism	75
The Problem	76
Views on Mind-Reality Correspondence	79
The Sphere of Science	86
Conclusion	91
Chapter Five:	
The View of Life Based on Metaphysics	93
The Age of New Metaphysics	94

The 'View of Life' Arguments	96
The Question of Culture	104
Conclusion	107

Chapter Six:
Philosophical Continuities 109
    Xiong Shili 110
    Hou Wailu 113
    Qian Mu 117
    Conclusion 120

Conclusion 123

Bibliography 131
    Chinese Sources 131
    Western Sources 135

Index 141

Introduction

Twentieth century Chinese intellectuals have probably been preoccupied with nothing so much as the question of the modern transformation of Chinese culture. With many and shifting variations the debate on the question of culture, in the sense of the nature of Chinese living, has continued to the present day. Views have ranged from the complete rejection of the tradition of that culture to its careful preservation. The entire spectrum of intellectuals has been involved: from those who first were exposed to missionary views to their converts in the 1920s; from Marxists to the "New Confucians" (*xinrujia* 新儒家); and more recently the New Leftists (*xinzuopai* 新左派) and others who seek a Chinese alternative to Western forms of living. Using the controversy about the 'view of life' (*rensheng guan* 人生觀) of 1923 as a basis, this study investigates the philosophical discussion that the question of culture involved, taking it beyond the period that became associated with the May Fourth Movement (1915–23).

The 'view of life' is originally a German philosophical term (*Lebensanschauung*) that China borrowed from modern Japanese.[1] It denotes a philosophy which asks after the meaning, value and purpose of life, turning away from purely theoretical knowledge towards the undistorted fullness of lived experience. In the second half of the nineteenth and the early twentieth century German philosophers used the concept of 'life' to oppose rigid abstractions with a philosophy based on feeling and intuition. They sought to establish the priority of 'life' as an all-encompassing whole. The central claim underlying this current of thought is that life can be understood only from within.[2] Simply said, the 'view of life' concerns what it means to be human.

To be sure, the concern for what it means to be human engaged Chinese thinkers since antiquity. Yet, as the traditional order transformed in the beginning of the twentieth century, the applicability of traditional ideas in the context of a dialogue across cultures was intensely questioned. Equally questioned was the comparability of Chinese traditional ideas to foreign ideas in the efforts to reconstruct Chinese culture to make it fit modern needs. The idea of "new culture" was anticipated well before the revolution of 1911 by such intellectuals as Liang Qichao and other Chinese students in Japan who questioned and opposed Confucian morality and advocated a scientific world view. The establishment of "New Youth" magazine in 1915 well in-

---

1 Lydia H. Liu, *Translingual Practice: Literature, National Culture, and Translated Modernity – China, 1900–1937*. Stanford: Stanford University Press, 1995, 352 (Appendix E).
2 *Routledge Encyclopedia of Philosophy*. Gen. ed., Edward Craig. London: Routledge, 1998, vol. V, 487.

dicated the radicalization of a student generation. The May Fourth Movement, on the other hand, began with a specific political event: the student demonstrations of 1919 against the Versailles Peace Treaty. The movement soon spread to encompass other than anti-imperialist ideas, including those of the new culturalists, language and literature. Were traditional ideas comparable to foreign ideas and applicable for the reconstruction of modern Chinese culture, the continuity of Chinese culture would have been guaranteed. But during the New Culture Movement and throughout the ascendance of communism in China, the possibility of such continuity was highly contested.

In 1968 Joseph R. Levenson associated his view about the break in Chinese culture in the course of the encounter with modern changes with disrespect for the content of the 'view of life' controversy. He concluded in his *Confucian China and Its Modern Fate* that "Confucius [...] might be kept as a national monument, unworshipped, yet also unshattered."[3] In an earlier volume of the same work he wrote:

> Anyone interested in Chinese history can profit from [D. W. Y.] Kwok's discussion of the 1923 debate on "Science and Metaphysics" [the 'view of life' controversy]. Anyone interested in science and metaphysics need not give it another glance.[4]

Kwok, however, paid attention almost exclusively to the arguments of those who supported science, neglecting the metaphysics' advocates who attempted to reconcile foreign and traditional ideas and whom he considered defeated in this debate.[5] Since the publication of Levenson's and Kwok's works, researchers have assumed a more "China-centered approach." Still, the arguments of the 'view of life' of the metaphysics advocates have not been considered worthy of philosophical analysis. Accordingly, the historical and philosophical significance of their ideas has remained unrecognized. In attempting to correct this inattention, the present investigation offers an analysis of the philosophical foundations underlying their views and their relation to the discourse of modern change in China.

It is assumed here that one of the stimuli of the modern discourse about culture in China must be located in the encounter with missionaries as purveyors of philosophical ideas from the West. Then came translations, study abroad, and visiting philosophers. But the intellectuals' readiness to question long held assumptions about Chinese culture and tradition must also be sought in the Chinese intellectual scene. Inasmuch as foreign sources enriched the discussion of the 'view of life' proponents, Chinese tradition, more specifically, the body of ideas transmitted since Confucius and Mencius, emerged in this controversy as remarkably resourceful.

---

3 Joseph R. Levenson, *Confucian China and Its Modern Fate: A Trilogy*, vol. III, *The Problem of Historical Significance*. Berkeley: University of California Press, 1968, 79.
4 Ibid., vol. I, *The Problem of Intellectual Continuity*, XVI. For Kwok, see D.W.Y. Kwok, *Scientism in Chinese Thought, 1900–1950*. New Haven: Yale University Press, 1965.
5 Kwok, *Scientism in Chinese Thought*.

What were the origins of the 'view of life' in the intellectual heritage of past Confucian masters? How were the arguments of the 1923 'view of life' debaters connected to their tradition? To respond to these questions and provide a reference for the discussion that follows, chapter one studies the 'view of life' in Confucian thought. Granted that the traditional masters were, like others, concerned with what it means to be human, the discussion follows the development of Confucian thought, selectively focusing only on the issues that are relevant to the 'view of life' problem. A full-scale study of this problem is still needed. The argument here is that Confucian thought was primarily, and, more importantly, continuously concerned with the 'view of life' problem. Furthermore, from Confucius and Mencius, through the Song and Ming masters, to the evidential scholars and the scholars of Song learning of the Qing period, the 'view of life', far from standing still, was continuously discussed and was regarded from varying perspectives. How to relate Confucian thought to the discussion of the 'view of life'? How did the views develop through different thinkers and periods? These questions are treated in chapter one.

Toward the end of the nineteenth century, scholars in China recognized that there were things the foreigners had that could be used by the Chinese. Nevertheless, they regarded controlling the foreign influence and checking its inward flow as a major responsibility on their part. Since the Tongzhi 同治 restoration in the 1860s, the formula that became standard in cultural dealings with foreigners, was most authoritatively proclaimed by Zhang Zhidong 張之洞 (1837–1909) who said in 1898: "Chinese learning for [spiritual] substance, Western learning for [material] function" (*zhongxue wei ti, xixue wei yong* 中學為體, 西學為用).[6] "Spiritual substance" (*ti*) was to him "[...] our human relationships and fundamental principles [...] our sage's way [...] the principle of the mind."[7] "Material function" (*yong*) stood for material products and technology, which were synonymous with science. This formula said that in cultural matters the classical sources were the authority. Philosophically, the *tiyong* formula said something about what it means to be human: it emphasized the priority of the spiritual and morally valued over the material. This approach indicates that toward the end of the nineteenth century Chinese scholars thought that the discussion about what it means to be human should be confined within the limits of their culture. The foreign ideas regarding this question represented a potential threat

---

6 Zhang was by no means the first to proclaim this idea. The tiyong dichotomy may be philosophically traced back to Wang Bi (226–149) and later to Zhu Xi (1130–1200). See discussion in Levenson, *Confucian China and Its Modern Fate*, 59–78. According to Xiong Yuezhi 熊月之 the formula was first mentioned in the pages of the missionary magazine Wanguo gongbao 萬國公報 (*The Globe Magazine*) in April 1895. See his *Xixue Dongjian yu wan Qing shehui* 西學東漸與晚清社會 (The dissemination of Western learning and late Qing society). Shanghai: Renmin chubanshi, 1994, 724.

7 Zhang Zhidong, "Exhortation to Study." In *China's Response to the West*. Teng Ssu-yu and John K. Fairbank, eds. Cambridge, Mass.: Harvard University Press, 1965, 171.

to the Chinese mode of life. Still, like other formulas invented during this period,[8] the substance-function approach accommodated a certain degree of change.

The *tiyong* formula sufficed for a while, and indeed, until towards the end of the nineteenth century China accepted foreign material products and technological knowledge while showing little concern for other aspects of the foreigners' culture. However, in early 1895 Japan defeated China in a naval war, and in late 1898 a reform movement started and after one hundred days collapsed. Thereafter the cause of change was openly proclaimed, and the forces working to accommodate new modes of government, education, economy and thought dramatically increased.[9] Chinese intellectuals, especially the thousands who went to Japan, were exposed to attractions of Western culture. Not only did the *yong* gain an unprecedented weight of attention and support, but also the *ti* was critically eroded.

Around the turn of the twentieth century Chinese intellectuals recognized their need to acquire new ideas in addition to what China had already borrowed from the West. Cultural bridges are naturally created where shared concerns meet one another. Like Chinese thought, the philosophy of Emmanuel Kant argues for the autonomy of the person's moral choices.[10] Regardless of the differences between the two worlds of thought, this shared concern was essential to the 'view of life' discussion. Kant thus offered a starting point for an East-West synthesis of ideas about what it means to be human. To examine this beginning of philosophical relations across cultures in the 'view of life' discussion, chapter two concentrates on aspects of the introduction of Kant into China. This study will show how two pioneer thinkers, one a German missionary, the other Chinese, worked in this direction. Both emphasized Kant's ethical message. Far from imposing a diversion, Kant was used to invigorate the spiritual substance (*ti*) of Chinese culture. By now, the question of what it means to be human was no longer confined to a purely Chinese context.

During the period of intellectual transition (roughly 1895–1920) Chinese intellectuals underwent a process of crisis and transformation. According to Chang Hao, those who shared despair over foreign imperialist attacks, at the same time had to appreciate and accommodate some of the values these same hostile sources repre-

---

8 One formula read: "Western learning originated in China" (Xixue Zhong yuan 西學中源). This claim was heard since the first contacts between Chinese intellectuals and Western astronomy and mathematics around the transition from Ming (1368–1644) to Qing (1644–1911). Xiong Yuezhi. *Xixue Dongjian*, 719. Another formula was Wei Yuan's (1794–1856) "Learn the barbarians' technology in order to control the barbarians" (師夷之長技以制夷 shi yi zhi changji yi zhi yi).

9 However far backwards studies extend the beginnings of 'modern' developments in Chinese history, there are ample reasons to regard 1895 as a watershed in this respect. See discussion and works cited in Chow Kai-wing et al, "introduction," in idem, *Beyond the May Fourth Paradigm: In Search of Chinese Modernity*. Lanham, MD: Lexington Books, 2008, 1–23.

10 Thomas Metzger observes that "[...] the ontological question of the relation between the cosmos and the flow of human consciousness was central to both Neo-Confucianism and German idealism." See his *Escape From Predicament: Neo-Confucianism and China's Evolving Political Culture*. New York: Columbia University Press, 1977, 8.

sented.¹¹ Yu Yingshi observes that the new generation of intellectuals, unlike their parents, inherited a past that was questioned as never before, and confronted unfamiliar problems.¹² They saw the abolition of the examination system in 1905 and the collapse of the imperial order, and were consequently cut off from the major sources of both their social status and their inherent obligation of concern for the culture of China. Intellectuals of different generations and diverse tempers were subject to various sources of influence, and all were engaged in a highly emotional, multi-faceted discourse. Historical perspective allows us to discern the mixture of ideas and to see continuities with the past. But most of the individuals who experienced that process from within evidently sensed at the time a break with their history.

Conditioned by a strong sense of emergency, during the second decade of the twentieth century, intellectuals became extremely sensitive to the charm of the new, the speedy, the concrete and the apparently sweeping solutions. A ready-made concept that matched these requirements almost perfectly was at hand. Scientism – the attitude that science, in its function as an accurate natural discipline, as a total system of nature – was considered capable of informing physical existence, and of categorizing human life and society.¹³ This grand notion mixed science with all there is, elevating it to the status of the only valid and guaranteed explanation of life and the world. The unmistaken religious characteristic of scientism reflected the radical bent of the intellectuals' quest.

Scientism admittedly was attractive in that time and place. Its reputation was founded on concrete achievements, its tools were uniquely sharp and presumably accurate, and it was useful for the practical implementation of progress. Due to historical circumstances, these impressive attributes made scientism apparently suited to contemporary demands, beyond any rival. Moreover, the recent past had seen the distinct current of Qing learning's empirical research, which now readily suggested linking scientism with the past. Increasingly, broad support gathered around the ideas of scientism. Along with cultural iconoclasm, the two most outstanding slogans of the May Fourth incident of 1919, "Mr. Democracy" (*De xiansheng* 德先生) and "Mr. Science" (*Sai xiansheng* 塞先生), flourished as a kind of new saviors.¹⁴

Since the beginning of the New Culture Movement (1915) and throughout the May Fourth period (beginning with 1919) it was almost impossible to talk about the concerns of Chinese culture without using foreign ideas, and support of the latter

---

11 Zhang Hao (Chang Hao) 張灝, "Zhongguo jindai sixiangshi de zhuanxing shidai" 國近代思想史的轉型時代 (The age of transition in modern Chinese intellectual history). *Ershiyi shiji* 二十一世紀, vol. 52 (April 1999), 36.
12 For the radicalization of Chinese intellectuals during that period see Yu Ying-shih, "The Radicalization of China in the Twentieth Century." In *China in Transformation*. Tu Weiming, ed. Cambridge, Mass.: Harvard University Press, 1994, 125–157.
13 Kwok, *Scientism in Chinese Thought*, 3, 21.
14 "Sai" refers to the first tone of the word "Science." But in translation it also suggests "competition." "De" similarly refers to democracy and also to moral virtue.

went hand in hand with criticism of the former. Critical attacks against the Confucian tradition by intellectual leaders like Chen Duxiu (1879–1942) and Hu Shi (1891–1962) were inseparable from their support of scientism. A broader historical perspective allows however, that later developments in what is called today New Confucianism owed to these and other critics as much as to their rivals. On the one hand, scientism became acceptable to the extent that the *yong* almost completely took the place of *ti*. But the human capacity for moral autonomy, so essential to the old *ti* concept, was non-arguable in terms of scientism with its positivist claims for materialism, mechanism and heredity. Eventually, the arguments of the iconoclasts reached a point where they melted the philosophical foundations of their own ambition to nurture a new specie of autonomous individual who will propel China into modern times. On the other hand, along with the positivist ideas that nourished scientism came also rival idealist ideas which, on the contrary, were conducive to the discussion of a person's moral autonomy. The first part of chapter three studies the appearance and reception of relevant foreign currents of thought in China. The discussion traces the contribution of five different foreign philosophers, of whom three held lecture tours in China, to the question of individual autonomy. Their ideas became inseparable from the Chinese discussions of the 'view of life' problem.

Once Chinese intellectuals acquired a basic knowledge of Western philosophy, and in conjunction with the World War I destruction in Europe, a minority among them began to readdress the question of what the spiritual substance (*ti*) of Chinese culture is. Recognizing the proximity between idealist ideas and Chinese thought, in 1919 and 1921 two leading intellectuals attempted to reconstruct the *ti*. Though they were not systematic, they prepared the ground for later syntheses. The second part of chapter three arranges their arguments to show the underlying philosophical basis. Liang Qichao (1873–1929) and Liang Shuming (1893–1988) refrained from completely rejecting science, but concerned as they were with the *ti* and ultimately with the question of what it means to be human, they also saw that science had its limitations. To answer the challenges of scientism they formulated philosophical arguments against logical reason. In their attempts to reconcile idealist and traditional ideas with modern needs, they were in the forefront of modern Chinese thought.

During 1923 the 'view of life' problem became the center of discussions on the Chinese intellectual scene. The questions that were raised were evidently not new to Chinese thought. As distinct from the late nineteenth century, the question was not one of cultural origins, but concerned the need to preserve what it means to be human. The debaters who had received their formal education still within imperial China and its traditional educational system,[15] were, more than any of their predecessors, familiar with foreign philosophical currents. Working to reconstruct the Chinese *ti* they used ideas both from their tradition and from the West. The discussions involved two fundamental philosophical questions: What is human

---

15 Lin Yu-sheng, *The Crisis of Chinese Consciousness: Radical Anti-Traditionalism in the May Fourth Era*. Madison: University of Wisconsin Press, 1979, 154–156.

nature and what is the nature of the context of human relationships? The debaters asked how the individual should behave in order to live a moral life that would accord with the reality of human relationships. This brings forward epistemological questions: How does one know that he knows, and what are the relations between knowledge and reality? Although human nature is a major topic in Chinese thought and epistemological issues were also part of the philosophical quest, the joining of these to the question of Chinese culture in conditions of modern change is a new departure.

This study of the 1923 controversy focuses on the opinions of the 'view of life' supporters, whose arguments were mostly marginalized in studies of the debate ever since. They argued simultaneously against scientism and for the 'view of life'. Their arguments are divided into two chapters. Chapter four concentrates on the arguments against scientism. Acknowledging the benefits that science confers in many areas, they differentiated between the sphere of science and the sphere beyond it. To rationally explain their arguments, which were not rational in the same way as scientism was felt to be, they focused on the problem of knowledge, attacking the epistemological assumptions of scientism to provide knowledge that corresponds to objective reality, especially as far as mental phenomena are concerned. Following the philosophical message of the *tiyong* differentiation between material function and spiritual substance, they sought to isolate science from the discussion of what it means to be human.

The next chapter discusses the 'view of life'. To the advocates of the 'view of life' in the 1923 controversy, the problem at issue was the extent to which Chinese culture could preserve its Chinese character. To counter the view that their rivals based on scientism, they based their view on what they referred to as 'metaphysics'. Chapter five systematizes their unsystematic ideas and demonstrates how they associated the sphere beyond science – the sphere of the 'view of life' – with a philosophical structure that contained a center and attributes that were both moral and humanistic. With few exceptions, the emphasis was on the internal processes of the person. Associating ideas from varied sources that still accorded with what they conceived as the spirit of Confucian thought they established a reconstructed version of the former spiritual substance that attempted to reconcile Eastern and Western ideas. The discussion shows the changes in the traditional concept of *ti*, and how the 'view of life' supporters regarded it best adapted to modern change. Philosophically, this 'view of life' created a new Chinese individual. It presented what it means to be human in a context that also accommodated modernity. Chapter five concludes with a discussion of the changes that the spiritual substance concept underwent from the *ti* of the *tiyong* formula to the 'view of life' based on metaphysics.

After 1923 the debate over the 'view of life' continued, though less intensively, until around 1928. At the same time, the debate about Chinese culture and Western civilization that started around 1922 continued until 1935.[16] Calls for total West-

---

16 Irene Eber, "Hu Shih and the Controversy on Chinese Culture and Western Civilization." In

ernization (*quanpan xihua* 全盤西化) were suggested by leading intellectuals.[17] During the thirties the controversies over dialectical materialism[18] and the nature of Chinese society were on center stage.[19] During the forties Chinese intellectuals engaged in a controversy over "The role of art and the formation of a people."[20] These controversies as well as other intellectual milestones such as the Yan'an Talks in 1942 have all been dealt with in the literature and I shall not go into them here.

As an epilogue to this study, chapter six discusses three modern Chinese philosophers who continued to reflect on the 'view of life' problem during the 1940's. As in other parts, the focus is on specific men because they connected their new ideas with their background in Chinese tradition. From their more distant time-perspective, yet under pressing new conditions, and, aware of World War II, these three philosophers took the 'view of life' problem further, each in a different direction. During the forties they reinforced the foundations for a modern-era Confucian thought, Chinese Marxism and the broader framework of culture and history, which eventually became the ground for ensuing discussions about what it means to be human through the rest of the twentieth century and into the next one.

The 'view of life' problem is at the core of the philosophical meeting of Eastern and Western cultures. The search for the 'view of life', the philosophical framework that would allow for modern change and still preserve what it means to be human has been continuously pursued by Chinese thinkers during the twentieth century. Twenty first century intellectuals in China and elsewhere will surely continue to offer new answers to this question. The following investigation attempts to clarify the philosophical issues inherent in the arguments heard in the past and to establish a framework for making these relevant to contemporary discussions.

East Asian Occasional Papers (II). Harry, J. Lamley, ed. Honolulu: University of Hawaii Press, 1970, 29–45.

17 According to Chow Tse-tsung, slogans such as 'wholesale Westernization' were adopted in 1929 and 1934 by Chen Xujing and Hu Shi. See his *The May Fourth Movement: Intellectual Revolution in Modern China*. Cambridge, Mass.: Harvard University Press, 1960, 332n.

18 Werner Meissner, *Philosophy and Politics in China: The Controversy over Dialectical Materialism in the 1930s*. Trans. Richard Mann. London: Hurst and Company, 1990.

19 Li Zehou 李澤厚, *Zhongguo xiandai sixiangshi lun* 中國現代思想史論 (Discussion of modern Chinese thought). Anhui: Anhui wenyi chubanshe, 1994, 53–90.

20 Ibid.

CHAPTER ONE

The Philosophy of the View of Life in Traditional Chinese Thought

Although the phrase 'view of life' (*rensheng guan* 人生觀) was not used by Chinese philosophers before the 1920s, the issues that Western philosophers discussed under this title were certainly not foreign to Chinese thought. In both the West and China a crucial underlying question was what it means to be human. The Judaic religion suggested that man was created in the image of God and in His likeness. Greek philosophers proposed 'reason' to be the distinctive characteristic of being human.[1] But notably, both the presumed relatedness to God and the reliance on reason presuppose a common human capacity: a person can make choices, and freely, or autonomously, conduct his life. Personal autonomy thus plays a decisive role in determining what it means to be human.

Autonomy can have several forms. Freedom of choice is one, and the sense of having no mental barriers is another. This, in turn, might be attained either through a release from the flux of the natural order, or through an integration with that order. The thinkers of China who asked what it means to be human, were particularly attracted to the latter form of autonomy, the integration with an all-encompassing whole. They accordingly saw the self as having the capacity to shed one's mental barriers, and to experience integration with heaven and earth, with the whole of humanity and, eventually, with the myriad things. They aspired to form one body with the universe.

Confidence in the attainability of this integration was based on a view of the universe which saw a consistent linkage between heaven and man. Heaven, within this formula, functions as the ultimate context of existence. Integration consists of realizing linkage with that context. Being human, therefore, depended predominantly on the autonomy enjoyed by the person in realizing the linkage.

During the classical period of Chinese thought this linkage had a twofold structure.[2] One channel was the link through the imperial order by means of the three bonds (*sangang* 三綱) system: ruler-subject; father-son; husband-wife. A person

---

1 Reinhold Niebuhr, *The Self and the Dramas of History*. New York: Charles Scribner's Sons, 1955, 3.
2 Chang Hao, "Some Reflections on the Problems of the Axial-Age Breakthrough in Relation to Classical Confucianism." In *Ideas Across Cultures: Essays on Chinese Thought in Honor of Benjamin I. Schwartz*. Paul A. Cohen and Merle Goldman, eds. Cambridge, Mass.: Council on East Asian Studies, Harvard University, 1990, 17–31.

relied on his relationship to the emperor – who functioned as a linchpin connecting the realms of heaven and earth – to realize the linkage with the larger context. Whereas this route remained relatively intact throughout most of China's imperial history, another, alternative channel, evoked continuously changing views and conceptions.[3] This other linkage was more individualized, in claiming that the person's mind sustained the relatedness to heaven. In order to achieve the linkage, the mind was required to meet certain conditions, which depended on self-cultivation.

Most thinkers saw no contradiction between the two channels and regarded them as complementary. This chapter focuses on the history of the views concerned with how the human mind relates to the ultimate context of existence. The capacity to integrate with the whole that the individual thought to derive from this linkage, together with the autonomy involved in realizing this goal, was precisely what being human meant in Chinese thought. The ultimate context of existence, the linkage, the individual's autonomy, and the integration ideal, this nexus of ideas, I propose, forms the foundations of the 'view of life' in Chinese thought.

The first section of this chapter will discuss major ideas up to the Song and Ming periods, followed in the second section by early Qing thinkers, who, in contrast to their predecessors' emphasis on the inner life, sought ways to return to the reality of human relationships. Included here are the late eighteenth century scholar, Dai Zhen (1724–1777), the leading Qing philosopher, who applied the critical spirit of the preceding two centuries to the heaven-earth linkage and its realization. A scholar who challenged Dai Zhen's notion of linkage is the much less well known Peng Shaosheng (1740–1796). The ideas of Dai Zhen's followers, Ruan Yuan (1764–1848) and Jiao Xun (1763–1820), will be also considered.

During the nineteenth century the concept of linkage underwent further development, which will be discussed in the third section. One group of philosophers representing Confucian learning on the eve of the intellectual impact of the West, included Tang Jian (1778–1861), and Zeng Guofan (1810–1872). Chen Li (1810–1882), who shared many of their views, was among the few whose work and learning survived the Taiping destruction. This great Confucian scholar was remarkable for carrying confidence in the Chinese heritage into the early eighties of the nineteenth century. Assuming that throughout the history of Chinese thought until the twentieth century the concept of the ultimate context of existence remained the same, the aim in this chapter is to analyze the idea of personal autonomy resulting from the concept of linkage in relation to the ideal of integration. With this as background, the twentieth century concern with the problem of the 'view of life' philosophy should become more apparent.

---

3 Chang Hao, "Confucian Cosmological Myth and Neo-Confucian Transcendence." In *Cosmology, Ontology, and Human Efficacy*. Richard J. Smith and D.W.Y. Kwok, eds. Honolulu: University of Hawaii Press, 1993, 11–33.

Background

The difference between the human order and a higher, ideal normative order appeared already among pre-Confucian thinkers. Their ideas about human life and its problems reflected awareness of a gulf between the human order as it is and as it ought to be.[4] Hence they sought the means to bridge it. Benjamin I. Schwartz observes: "[Confucius] already finds a full exposition of the fundamental problem – why does the human reality fall away from Heaven's norms? How is the normative order to be restored?"[5] According to A. C. Graham the crucial question was "Where is the Way?" the way to order the state and conduct personal life.[6] The Chinese intellectual tradition of the Way (*dao* 道), was in fact the quest to reinstate the normative order of the world. Starting with the *Analects* and especially the *Mencius*, correct moral conduct was regarded as a means to elevate the individual's life and make it correspond to the ideal normative order. Moral standards were sought as means to achieve correspondence between human existence and the *dao*. Insofar as a linkage between the two was believed to be attainable, moral conduct made possible the relation between human life and the ultimate context of existence. Morality became the vehicle of realizing what it means to be human because of its function in restoring the normative order to the world.

According to the *Analects*, Confucius 孔子 (551–479 B.C.E.) engaged in the quest to improve human life. He considered it possible to recover the linkage between the human community, on the one hand, and the ultimate context of existence – the *dao*, on the other.[7] The profile of the gentleman (*junzi* 君子), emphasizes his concern to seek *dao*: he seeks the Way and not profit;[8] the fundamental is his duty;[9] above all he is devoted to humanity.[10] The six-stage account of Confucius' own life illustrates how he attained his goal:

> At fifteen I was intent on learning. At thirty I was established. At forty I was no longer confused. At fifty I knew the decree of heaven. At sixty I heard exactly what was said. At seventy my mind's desires corresponded to the norms.[11]

---

4 Benjamin I. Schwartz, *The World of Thought in Ancient China*. Cambridge, Mass.: Harvard University Press, 1985, 51–55. Chang Hao, "Axial-Age Breakthrough," 17–31.
5 Schwartz, *World of Thought*, 55.
6 Angus C. Graham, *Disputers of the Tao: Philosophical Argumentation in Ancient China*. La Salle: Open Court, 1989, 3.
7 Lunyu 論語 (Analects), 16:2, 18:6, in *Sishu duben* 四書讀本 (Basic reader of the Four Books). Taibei: Sanmin shuju, 1988, 258, 282.
8 Ibid., 15:31, 252.
9 Ibid., 1:2, 65–66.
10 Ibid., 4:5, 98.
11 Ibid., 2:4, 75.

The mind, the last to be mastered, is the pivot in this process; the accumulated effort culminates in the mind where the person overcomes his mental barriers and becomes one with all that there is. The sixth stage would then mean that Confucius had already internalized the former stages – he hears exactly what is said, knows the decree of heaven, is no longer confused, and integration with the whole is realized.

With Mencius 孟子 (372–289 B.C.E.) the individual's integration had profounder implications, and Confucius' earlier incipient linkage between heaven and man became a basic assumption. The gentleman transforms (*hua* 化) and preserves sacredness (*cunshen* 存神); above and below he shares in the flow of heaven and earth (*shangxia yu tiandi tongliu* 上下與天地同流).[12] According to Mencius, human nature is realized in the mind, and heaven is realized in human nature.[13] The capacities for actualizing the linkage are internal because of the innate moral capacity (*liangneng* 良能), the innate knowledge of the good (*liangzhi* 良知), as well as the so-called four beginnings of virtues.[14]

This innate moral capacity in Mencius' scheme which makes possible the integration with heaven might be termed subjective autonomy. Material things act on the material senses and lead them astray.[15] Therefore, the conditions of a person's life are objectively determined from the outside. But the capacity to react, to activate thought, is innate, and in this regard the person is autonomous.[16] The Mencian person who has innate moral capacity can establish the linkage by means of which he is able to integrate with the whole and thus assert his autonomy.

In contrast to Mencius' innate moral capacities, Xunzi 荀子 (300–215 B.C.E.) based his concept of morality on externally imposed rules of propriety (*li* 禮).[17] His sage is capable of integrating with the ultimate context of existence by finding his place with heaven and earth (*can yu tiandi* 參與天地).[18] The autonomy of Xunzi's person is more pragmatic because the integrative morality is suggested to him by utilitarian intellectual considerations based on the prevailing social order.

These ideas of linkage, autonomy, and integration were metaphysically elaborated by the Song-Ming neo-Confucian masters. To them, the goal in life was the quest for sagehood and the achievement of moral clarity, together with a comprehensive cognitive grasp of human existence and the cosmos as a coherently linked whole. This would lead to the realization of unity with the ultimate context of existence, and the ability to set the whole world in order. The link between the human

---

12 *Mencius* 孟子, 7A:13, ibid., 619.
13 Ibid., 7A:1, 613.
14 Ibid., 7A:15, 620; 2A:6, 377.
15 Ibid., 6A:15, 584–85.
16 For a short discussion of the self who lives between autonomy and heteronomy, see Calvin O. Schrag, *The Self after Postmodernity*. New Haven: Yale University Press, 1997, 59–60.
17 Xunzi, "On the rules of decorum"; chapter 19. In Schwartz, *World of Thought*, 301.
18 Xunzi 荀子, "Xingwu" 性惡 (The nature of man is evil; chapter 23). In *Xunzi yuezhu* 荀子約注 (Xunzi). Taibei: Shejie shuju, 1958, vol. II, 334.

being and his ultimate context was thus based on the idea of a preexistent universal coherence.

Three different views can be distinguished regarding the ordering of this coherence. It was either the vital force (*qi* 氣), the physical existence of all things, according to Zhang Zai 張載 (1022–1077); or principle (*li* 理), the ordering pattern of reality, according to Cheng Yi 程頤 (1033–1107) and Zhu Xi 朱熹 (1130–1200); or the mind, for Lu Xiangshan 陸象山 (1139–1193) and Wang Yangming 王陽明 (1472–1529). Each of them held that the all-encompassing coherent reality was charged with humaneness (*ren* 仁), conceived as both an affective virtue of integration and a metaphysical seed of growth. *Ren* was, moreover, closely associated with the working of the mind, and was considered as that which communicates and integrates the individual with the whole.[19]

The three versions represent efforts to accommodate the Mencian theory of human nature to the structure and function of the mind, the idea of the linkage included. They most urgently wanted to explain why moral practice is so elusive. If moral knowledge is accessible to the person from within himself, and is supported by a linkage with heaven, how is evil to be explained? The answers can be classified according to their advocates' tendency to base the linkage on internal, subjective capacities, or on more verifiable sources. That is, by making a synthesis between internal capacities and external knowledge.

Zhang Zai represented the innate moral endowment as the original and ideal, pure vital force (*qingqi* 清氣), which forms one part of human nature. He distinguished this from its counterpart, the turbid vital force (*hunqi* 昏氣) which makes for less favorable tendencies. To Zhang, what is original in nature is endowed with innate moral knowledge: "The knowledge of the moral nature (*dexing suozhi* 德性所知), does not originate from hearing and seeing."[20] Conversely: "In the physical nature there is that which the superior man denies to be his original nature."[21] According to Irene Bloom, this distinction between original or ideal nature and physical nature, and the acceptance of its epistemological corollary, discounted the importance of sense experience.[22]

---

19 See discussion in Irene Bloom, "On the Matter of the Mind: The Metaphysical Basis of the Expanded Self." In *Individualism and Holism: Studies in Confucian and Taoist Values*. Donald J. Munro, ed. Ann Arbor: University of Michigan Center for Chinese Studies, 1985, especially, 314–316.
20 Zhang Zai 張載, "Daxin pian" 大心篇 (On expanding the mind). In *Zhongguo zhexueshi jiaoxue ziliao zaoji* 中國哲學史教學資料造輯 (Selected sources for the study of the history of Chinese philosophy). The Philosophy Department at Beijing University, ed. Beijing: Zhonghua shuju, 1982, vol. II, 35–36. Hereafter *Ziliao zaoji*.
21 Wing-tsit Chan, trans. and comp., *A Source Book in Chinese Philosophy*. Princeton. N.J.: Princeton University Press, 1973, 511 (article 41).
22 Bloom, "On the Matter of the Mind," 307.

Cheng Yi and Zhu Xi were uneasy, to say the least, with this implication. To Cheng Yi, "The internal Way and the external Way are identical."[23] Zhu Xi too, as Yu Yingshi observes, did not recognize any division between innate knowledge and knowledge acquired through sense perception.[24] Both were dissatisfied with the dichotomy, but nonetheless contended that human nature is uniformly good by virtue of its being the same as principle, which is analogous to the virtue of heaven. On the other hand, the capacity (*cai* 才) of the mind is variable in quality, owing to its association with a clear or turbid vital force. Accordingly, the disharmony between inner endowments and their application derives from inconsistencies between human nature and mind.

Wang Yangming's vision of human life emphasized the inseparability of human nature both from the external things and from their ordering principle which he equated with the mind. No distinction between the internal human nature and external things for him.[25] Likewise, human nature cannot be separated from the vital force which is the ground of its expression: "Material force is also nature and nature is also material force."[26] In his later years Wang argued that "innate knowledge of the good" (*liangzhi* 良知), incorporated the "everything is mind" of Lu Xiangshan with the Mencian notion of a built-in disposition toward the good. *Liangzhi* specified that element in the mind, whether obscured or not, which was harmonized with the heavenly order. The *liangzhi* linkage now associated with the moral quality of "good," functioned as the subjective and intuitive compass in everything a person did.

These three interwoven strains of ideas all concerned themselves with the problem of how to realize the linkage connecting the person and the ultimate concept of existence. But doubts about innate moral capacities motivated Cheng Yi, Zhu Xi, and their followers to view the person's autonomy as dependent also on knowledge of objective reality. On the other hand, Zhang Zai and Lu Xiangshan and Wang Yangming, and their followers regarded innate moral knowledge as trustworthy, thus supporting the more subjective autonomy that Mencius had referred to. In either case the linkage with the ultimate context of existence presupposed the existence of autonomous persons.

Self-cultivation became a program of lifetime self-improvement for these men.[27] The central concern was how to remove whatever prevented the extension of the mind through study of principle, according to Cheng-Zhu, or distorted the working of the mind, according to Lu-Wang. The goal of self-cultivation was to eradicate or

---

23 Cheng Yi 程頤, "Yulu" 語錄 (Selected sayings), *Ziliao zaoji*, 83.
24 Yu Yingshi 余英時, *Zhongguo sixiang chuantong de xiandai quanshi* 中國思想傳統的現代詮釋 (Interpretation of the tradition of thought in modern China). Taibei: Lianjing chuban shiye gongsi, 1987, 436–37.
25 Wing-tsit Chan, trans., *Instructions for Practical Living and other Neo-Confucian Writings by Wang Yang-ming*. New York: Columbia University Press, 1963, 221.
26 Ibid., 208.
27 Munro, *Individualism and Holism*, 12.

remove obstacles, such as selfish thoughts that prevent an individual from following his natural predisposition of proper relations with other people.²⁸ The person was instructed to cultivate himself. After removing all the mental barriers, he was expected to arrive at a state of integration with all the people and the universe as a whole. The Great Learning (*Daxue* 大學) paradigm that universal order begins with cultivation of the self was well established in neo-Confucian philosophical circles.

What was it like to be a sage? When they incorporated the notion of self realization with integration with the whole, the Song-Ming masters associated the realized self with a somewhat reduced personal uniqueness. Quoting from the *Classic of Changes* (*Yijing* 易經), Zhou Dunyi 周敦頤 (1017–1073) characterized the sage as someone who,

> [...] is virtuous (*de* 德) with heaven and earth; is bright (*ming* 明) with the moon and the sun; is orderly (*xu* 序) with the four seasons; and is fortunate and unfortunate with demons and spirits (*guishen* 鬼神).²⁹

As Zhu Xi's sage experienced and understood the nourishment and transformation of the universe, he was marked by psychic equilibrium and harmony.³⁰ In this state he was honest and free from falsehood; his mind and heart became like a bright mirror, reflecting all things.³¹ The highest achievement of the sage is associated with lack of individualizing traits. To Zhang Zai integration with the universe involved an intimate relationship of all people:

> That which fills the universe I regard as my body and that which directs the universe I consider as my nature. All the people are my brothers and sisters, and all things are my companions.³²

Each of these masters identified integration with a reduced sense of personal uniqueness.

Perhaps the statement about the state of forming one body with the universe is clearest in Wang Yangming:

> The great man regards Heaven, Earth, and the myriad things as one body. He regards the world as one family and the country as one person. As to those who make a cleavage between objects and distinguish between self and others, they are small men. That the great man regards Heaven, and Earth, and the myriad things as one body is not because he deliberately wants to do so, but because it is natural to the humane nature of his mind that he does so.³³

---

28 Ibid.
29 Zhou Dunyi 周敦頤, "Taiji tushuo" 太極圖說, *Ziliao zaoji*, 4.
30 Chiu Hansheng, "Zhu Xi's Doctrine of Principle." In *Chu Hsi and Neo-Confucianism*. Wing-tsit Chan, ed. Honolulu: University of Hawaii Press, 1986, 124.
31 Julia Ching, "Chu Hsi on Personal Cultivation," ibid., 276.
32 Chan, *Source Book*, 497.
33 Chan, Practical Living, 272. See also in Wing-tsit Chan, "The Concept of Man in Chinese

The last sentence refers to an effortless integration that does not require individual will.

The state of integration thus demands that the person shed his personal uniqueness. Is this valuable? According to Wolfgang Kubin, Zhu Xi's account of sagehood is nothing but the conscious effort to erase all possible (individualizing) features of the self,[34] a process Kubin contrasts with the Western understanding of individuality. Irene Bloom insists that integration does not involve dissolution of the natural boundaries separating the individual self from others. She argues that to "enlarge and complete [the self] where once there were boundaries" is not to obliterate the distinction between self and others but to recognize the implications of human interrelatedness and interaction and to perceive that the self is actually realized in responsiveness rather than in isolation.[35]

Kubin and Bloom are alluding to different forms of autonomy. The former contrasts Zhu Xi's sage with the individual who, by means of rational introspection, overcomes the flux of natural and social order.[36] The latter refers to autonomy within that order. Both forms, however, characterize the essence of what it means to be human, essential for the discussion of the 'view of life' problem. What Kubin sees as erasing all features of the self can also be described, as Bloom suggests, as the removal of those mental barriers that prevent the realization of human interrelatedness. After integration into the all-encompassing whole, personal autonomy is no longer a release from the flux of the natural and social order, but is experienced as autonomy within that order.

Early and Mid-Qing

The neo-Confucian ideal of integration of the twelfth century reached a new stage by the seventeenth. According to W.T. de Bary:

> From the inner enlightenment of the sage had emerged the new 'enlightenment' of critical scholarship and thought in the seventeenth century. In this process a crucial transformation had taken place in the original unifying conception of the sage.[37]

Thought." In *Neo-Confucianism, Etc.: Essays by Wing-tsit Chan*. Hong Kong: Oriental Society, 1969, 152–153.
34 W. Kubin, "On the Problem of the Self." In *Confucianism and the Modernization of China*. Silke Krieger and Rolf Trauzettel, eds. Mainz: Hase and Koehler Verlag, 1991, 63–95, esp. 70–75.
35 Bloom, "On the Matter of the Mind," 316.
36 Kubin refers to "the subject who liberated himself from church and nobility, 'places itself', and is autonomous." Kubin, "On the Problem of the Self," 69.
37 Wm. T. de Bary, "Neo-Confucian Cultivation and the Seventeenth-Century Enlightenment." In *The Unfolding of Neo-Confucianism*. de Bary, ed. New York: Columbia University Press, 1975, 203.

One aspect of this transformation is represented by the followers of Wang Yangming, known as the Taizhou 泰州 school, who during the second half of the Ming period radicalized the idea of innate knowledge of the good and its implications. Wang Ji 王畿 (1498–1583) contributed to this trend when he interpreted his teacher's concept of mind beyond good and evil, to beyond mind (*wuxin* 無心).[38] His *liangzhi* was something that exists autonomously in the mind, and transcends the state of being. Provided with individual intrinsic transcendence, Taizhou scholars sought new ways to close the gap between what they saw as the real and the ideal modes of existence. As they shifted their views from prevailing moral rules to the dictates of *liangzhi*, natural and impulsive behavior replaced accepted, moral norms. They tended to reduce the distance between the notion of *liangzhi* and human emotions and desires by equating them as synonymous. Another, not unrelated, trend, was the pursuit of enlightenment (*wu* 悟). Wang Gen 王艮 (1483–1540) and others discussed the concept of an inborn enlightenment. In due course, the combination of uncritical trust in innate capacities and enlightenment led some of these scholars to a radical individuality with few precedents in the Confucian tradition. Li Zhi's 李贄 (1527–1602) straightforward statement – perhaps during one of his more radical moments – that it is all right for a person to act on his selfish desires, implied that responsible social participation is not required for the purpose of forming one body with the universe as a whole. Although the Taizhou scholars preserved the Mencian idea of subjective linkage, they discarded its corollary of moral content.

These late Ming views tended to break away from the ethics of the three bonds, of family, social, and political order, daring to reject the institutionalized linkage through the imperial institution. Concomitantly, they marked a shift in the nature of the neo-Confucian concept of integration. The longed for goal of life no longer concerned other people, nor was it associated with the good of society. Seen from a self interest perspective, it rather involved the dissolution of the individual's relations to others. Contrary to their predecessors, these radical followers of Wang Yangming sought autonomy from the natural and the social order rather than within it. They were later accused of holding empty discussions while allowing the polity and the social order to disintegrate. Yet they bequeathed to future generations a critical spirit that led to new ways of thinking about linkage, autonomy and integration.

Underlying the philosophical discourse of late Ming and early Qing thought lay the shift of priorities from principle (*li* 理) to the vital force (*qi* 氣).[39] Several scholars of this period viewed *qi* as the essential substance that fills the universe. *Qi* was

---

38 Willard J. Peterson, "Confucian Learning in Late Ming Thought." In *The Cambridge History of China*. Denis Twitchett and Frederick W. Mote, eds. Cambridge: Cambridge University Press, 1998, vol. VIII, 721.

39 Bloom argues that the philosophy of qi was in the fullest sense a Ming product. Irene Bloom, "On the Abstraction of Ming Thought: Some Concrete Evidence from the Philosophy of Lo Chin-shun." In *Principle and Practicality*. Irene Bloom and Wm. Theodore de Bary, eds. New York: Columbia University Press, 1979, 106.

not solidly material and not immaterial either. Yet, compared with the abstract notion of *li*, it was considered more concrete.

How did this transformation affect the ideal of integration? Was the idea of linkage, as some contemporary researchers argue, altogether discarded?[40] Ng On-cho, in his paper, "Toward an Interpretation of Ch'ing Ontology," seems to affirm that linkage with the transcendent was no longer an issue. He associates the profound change he finds in late Ming and early Qing thought with a sort of "vitalism." This vitalism, he observes:

> [...] refers to a philosophy of life that restricted attention in large part to the evidence provided by life grasped from within the body, the self, or external thing. This evidence [...] [was] composed of concrete tendencies that were not readily dissolved by metaphysical speculation. This life grasped from within the actualities of the self and the external world was finite. Thus [this] vitalism was opposed to the mysticism of the overarching *dao* and the immutable *li*, which pointed to the limitless and infinite.[41]

Ng further defines this vitalism as a dynamic monism:

> [...] it was dynamic in that it rejected the existence of an immutable *dao* bearing unchanging and infinite truths in favor of a relativized *dao* embodying transient and finite truths; it was monistic in that it repudiated the neo-Confucian dichotomy of the superior *li* (belonging to the metaphysical and spiritual realm), and the inferior *qi* (belonging to the perceptual and experiential realm), in favor of a monistic reduction of all reality to *qi*. Life, within this vitalistic framework [...] was also individualized by, and expressed in, the external signs of the self's contingency, frailty, and finitude. Life was the synthesis of the functions that related it to its circumstances, including sensory perceptions, feelings, desires, emotions, and so forth.[42]

Finally, Ng implies that this transformation reflects the disintegration of the Song-Ming metaphysical context of meaningful life.[43]

Ng's depiction of late Ming and early Qing *qi* philosophers as vitalists – their conceptions of inner resources grounded in concrete experience alone – seems to miss much of their intellectual world. He portrays these scholars favorably as proto-scientists and possibly also individualists, who tended to trust their conceptions of life and the world, concrete and finite evidence, rather than abstract speculation. But

---

40 Benjamin Elman gives an affirmative answer to this question: "Personal achievement of sagehood, by now an unrealistic aim for serious Confucians, was no longer their goal." In Benjamin Elman, *From Philosophy to Philology: Social and Intellectual Aspects of Change in Late Imperial China*. Cambridge, Mass.: Harvard University, Council on East Asian Studies, 1984, 6.
41 Ng On-cho, "Toward an Interpretation of Ch'ing Ontology." In *Cosmology, Ontology, and Human Efficacy*, 37.
42 Ibid.
43 Ibid., 37, 54–55.

in fact, their vitalism co-existed with the ideal of integration. Several prominent late Ming and early Qing scholars, explicitly mentioned in Ng's article, by no means abandoned the linkage with the ultimate context of existence.

Already in 1603 Liu Zongzhou 劉宗周 (1578–1645) recognized that preserving heaven's coherence in his nature and restraining his human desires were his life goals.[44] Although he shifted the focus of moral effort exclusively to the will, he did so within the context of these goals. "Taking care of the absolute good will in solitude" as well as in one's relations with others,[45] meant that even when alone, a person had to be watchful (*shendu* 慎獨). By practicing deep knowledge of the self a person had the capacity to transcend his own mental barriers and yet still remain himself in his union with the whole.

According to Wang Fuzhi 王夫之 (1619–1692), "To know one's nature is to know that the Way of Heaven is completed by one's nature," and "The [human] nature and the Way of Heaven achieve ultimate unity." This is why the operations and manifestations of the vital force (*qi*) "are all my concern, and their cultivation my proper role."[46] Ian McMorran believes that "The concept of a unity which consists of a dynamic harmony is one which pervades all of Wang's thinking."[47] Wang Fuzhi further said:

> As he [the sage] views the world there is in it not a single thing which is not his own self. This is what Mencius means when he says that through fully exploiting one's mind (*jinxin* 盡心) one can come to know one's nature and Heaven.[48]

Again, McMorran comments that to Wang,

> [...] the life of man ought ideally to accord with its own moral Way, which was itself a vitally important part of the Way of the universe which comprehended all the Ways of everything within it.[49]

Another prominent seventeenth century philosopher, Yan Yuan 顏淵 (1635–1704), who was renowned for stressing practical matters,[50] also wrote:

> Integrate the inner and the outer, this is the making of a human being, relating life and world into one fragment, this is working as a whole.[51]

---

44 Peterson, "Confucian Learning in Late Ming Thought," 767.
45 Tang Jun-i, "Liu Tsung-chou's Doctrine of Moral Mind and Practice and his Critique of Wang Yang-ming." In de Bary, ed., *Unfolding*, 324.
46 Wang Fuzhi, "Zhangzi zhengmeng zhu" (Commentary on Zhang Zai's "Correcting Youthful Ignorance"). Cited in Ian McMorran, "Wang Fu-chih and the Neo-Confucian Tradition." In de Bary, ed., *Unfolding*, 448.
47 Ibid.
48 Wang Fuzhi, "Zhangzi zhengmeng zhu," quoted, ibid., 452.
49 Ibid., 447–448.
50 Donald J. Munro, *Images of Human Nature*, A Sung Portrait. Princeton, N.J.: Princeton University Press, 1988, 222–223.

These three seventeenth century philosophers obviously preserved their predecessors' belief about universal coherence and the correspondence between mind and the ultimate context of existence. Personal autonomy was seen in terms of integration. No matter how emphatically they stressed the concrete nature of human experience, their assertion of the individual coexisted with the integration ideal.

The ideal of integration remained alive in the seventeenth century, and was in fact still a major concern throughout the Qing period. Dai Zhen 戴震 (1724–1777) based his idea of individual autonomy on intellectual capacity, rejecting the notion that people are born with innate moral norms. His vision of the linkage between heaven and man was based on his belief in the individual's access to sacred intelligence (*shenming* 神明), and the ensuing capacity to follow what he called the necessary pattern (*biran* 必然), and attain perfection.[52] Dai Zhen's follower of *biran* has his desires and emotions correspond to the final unchanging norm (*bu yi zhi ze* 不易之則). The essence of his view of the idea of integration is that the individual's emotions and desires conform, by way of intellectual considerations, to a recognizable pattern.

Peng Shaosheng 彭紹升 (1740–1796), was critical of Dai Zhen's disregard of innate, subjective moral autonomy. They engaged in a letter debate during the latter's final year of life (1777). According to Peng, moral norms must have an inner source, and the view that "The moral capacity, when aided by inquiry and study, advances into sagely wisdom," is incorrect, since it implies that the innate capacity has to be aided by scholarship before it can exhaustively probe the Way.[53] If this is indeed the case, then moral norms are not worth honoring.[54] Because he believed that moral norms are derived from Heaven, Peng argued that scholarship adds nothing to them; however, at the same time he rather modified Lu-Wang when he added that what learning does is enable moral capacity to realize its full potential.[55]

Around the turn of the nineteenth century, two Yangzhou scholars, Jiao Xun 焦循 (1763–1820) and Ruan Yuan 阮元 (1764–1848), followed Dai Zhen in elaborating *qi* philosophy. This initiated a new direction concerned with the person's relation to the context of his existence by means of concrete action. Accepting the latter's

---

51 Yan Yuan,顏元 "Cunxing bian" 存性編 (On dwelling in human nature). In Qian Mu 錢穆, *Zhongguo sixiangshi* 中國思想史 (History of Chinese Thought). Taibei: Xuesheng shuju yinxing, 1995, 261.

52 Qian Mu 錢穆, *Zhongguo jin sanbainian xueshu shi* 中國近三百年學術史 (Chinese Learning in the Recent Three Hundred Years). Taibei: Taiwan shangwu, 1995, vol. I, 379.

53 Peng Shaosheng 彭紹升, "Yu Dai Dongyuan shu" 與戴東原書 (A letter to Dai Dongyuan). In Hu Shi 胡適, *Dai Dongyuan de zhexue* 戴東原的哲學 (The philosophy of Dai Dongyuan). Taibei: Taiwan shangwu yinshuguan, 1996, 339–342.

54 Richard Shek, "Testimony to the resilience of the mind: the life and thought of Peng Shaosheng (1740–1796)." In *Cosmology, Ontology, and Human Efficacy*, 104.

55 Judith A. Berling, "When They Go Their Separate Ways: The Collapse of the Unitary Vision of Chinese Religion in the Early Ch'ing." In *Meeting of Minds: Intellectual and Religious Interaction in East Asian Traditions of Thought*. Irene Bloom and Joshua A. Fogel, eds. New York: Columbia University Press, 1997, 226.

intellectually based autonomy, they replaced his "final unchanging norms" with the system of the rules of propriety (*li* 禮). The individual's humaneness (*ren* 仁), they argued, cannot be divorced from its application. Ruan Yuan said that the mind's humaneness is only a beginning:

> [...] what is complete in the mind is [only] the beginning of *ren*. It must be enlarged and filled so that it will be manifested in actions and human affairs, before it can be called *ren*.[56]

Applying *ren* consisted of self-control (*keji* 克己) which Ruan Yuan and Jiao Xun associated with ritual-propriety in matters of seeing, hearing, speaking, and movement. A state of *ren* brings about relations with others.[57] Significantly, Ruan Yuan favored an approach that stressed the reality of the here and now. Jiao Xun shared this attitude, calling for reversing the victory of the learning of principle over the system of ritual-propriety.[58] In appointing ritual-propriety at the center of their programs, both saw the realization of the integration ideal in terms of intellectual comprehension of recognizable social norms.

Jiao Xun's writings reveal that he associated the integration ideal with the attribute of transpersonal interrelatedness (*tong* 通). Referring to the one thread (*yiguan* 一貫) in Confucius' teaching, he declared that a person must conquer the self to the point of losing his individuality (*keji ze wuwo* 克己則無我). Having no self he is impartial toward all things in the world.[59] Moreover, Jiao Xun understood the capacity to interrelate emotions with those of others as the virtue of human goodness.[60] His sage realizes his own nature in order to realize the nature of others. Connecting and relating (with all beings and things), he forms a linkage with spirituality, and harmonizes the emotions of all things.[61] He wrote:

> The meaning of the one thread is the union of the inner and the outer, everywhere nothing is not interrelated (*chuchu erwu butong* 出處而無不通).[62]

Thereafter the 'view of life' concepts of linkage, autonomy and integration, which were previously marked by their appeal to the inward dimension of individual existence, underwent a major process of change. Practical activity, or *praxis*, with its direct influence on social life and on developing the future in the realm of concrete activity gradually predominated.[63] Whereas in the past the correspondence between

---

56 Qian Mu, *Jin sanbainian*, 539. Benjamin Elman, "The Revaluation of Benevolence (Jen) in Ch'ing Evidential Research." In *Cosmology, Ontology, and Human Efficacy*, 68.
57 Chow Kai-wing, "Purist Hermeneutics and Ritualist Ethics in Mid-Ch'ing Thought," ibid., 195.
58 Elman, "Benevolence (Jen) in Ch'ing," ibid., 74.
59 Qian Mu, *Jin sanbainian*, 512.
60 Ibid., 507.
61 Ibid., 512.
62 Ibid., 513.
63 Richard J. Bernstein, *Praxis and Action: Contemporary Philosophies of Human Activity*. Philadelphia: University of Pennsylvania Press, 1971, xi.

the principles of things and inborn principle had been important, now concrete actions and emotions were emphasized. To Dai Zhen's autonomy, a result of access to recognizable reality, Ruan Yuan and Jiao Xun added the familiar rules of propriety. Autonomy for social and political action would be the next step.

The Nineteenth Century

The beginning of the nineteenth century saw the emergence of three interrelated currents of thought which further transformed the idea of personal autonomy into practical activism. The New Text (*Jinwen* 今文) tradition pictured Confucius as author of the Six Classics and reformer of ancient institutions, crediting the Classic of the *Spring and Autumn Annals* with the systematic record of his message. This position was charged with political as well as religious implications. Politically, the New Text portrayed Confucius as a reformer who was practically involved in the affairs of his day. Religiously, it saw Confucius as a genuine visionary prophet recalling Catholic models.[64] The New Text learning opened new avenues for the interpretation of the Confucian tradition in terms of practical activism.

At the same time, Song learning (*Songxue* 宋學) which came into vogue was in fact a modified doctrine, quite different from its earlier origins. The early nineteenth century scholars associated with Song learning sought to reverse the tendency of uncritically accepting externally imposed moral norms. They thus called for reestablishing the role of subjectivity when arriving at moral decisions. Fang Dongshu's 方東樹 (1772–1851) defense of the Cheng-Zhu doctrine of principle *li*, is illustrative:

> Whereas the rules of ritual-propriety (*li* 禮) are secondary and external, the principles (*li* 理) that activate them are primary and internal; all occurring affairs and things have their specific principles. Unlike ritual-propriety [...] principles determines true and false, [while] the rules of ritual-propriety are the civilized appearance; if the principles are not fulfilled, how can the rules of ritual-propriety flourish, how can people recognize the meaning of the rules of ritual-propriety without their principles?[65]

On the one hand, Fang proposed that moral principles must be the foundation of social norms. On the other, by emphasizing that principle and the rules of ritual-propriety are inseparable he recognized the need and the standard for principles to be practically implemented.

Song learning became inseparable from another ideal that gained prominence during that period, that of 'setting the world in order' (*jingshi* 經世). In his study of

---

64 Benjamin Elman, *Classicism, Politics and Kinship: The Ch'ang-chou School of New Text Confucianism in Late Imperial China*. Berkeley: University of California Press, 1990, 87–92, 141–43.
65 Qian Mu, *Jin sanbainian*, 575.

this current, Chang Hao points out that while *jingshi* was anchored in the transcendental belief centered on the idea of "the way of Heaven" (*tiandao* 天道), it was, nonetheless, concerned with the fulfillment of humanity in this world.[66] As an ideal it entailed the Confucian process of self-cultivation and an effort at personal moral transformation. Since it "… combined a transcendentally grounded selfhood with a sense of social rootedness and commitment, the vocational ideal of *jingshi* crosscuts the individualism/collectivism dichotomy."[67] Eventually, while the notion of integration was still central to the *jingshi* program, it also gave prominence to moral fulfillment as an end in itself, as long as the political good of society was considered.

The emphasis on praxis was contained in the teachings of leading statesmen and scholars in the second half of the nineteenth century, such as Tang Jian 唐鑒 (1778–1861), and Zeng Guofan 曾國藩 (1811–1872), from Hunan, and the Cantonese scholar Chen Li 陳澧 (1810–1882). All three followed the philosophical tradition of Cheng-Zhu neo-Confucianism. In their view, since human nature is identical with principle (*li*), the process of self-cultivation which emphasizes learning may lead to realizing the linkage with heaven.[68] Concurrently they emphasized the framework of the rules of propriety. The principal pillar of Zeng Guofan's ethical thought was the doctrine of propriety (*lixue* 禮學), which he used to synthesize the schools of Han and Song learning. Like Ruan Yuan, Zeng considered *li* an integrative factor in the personal inner and outer realms;[69] the outer rules of ritual and propriety in the human community were a balance to *ren*, the inner world of individual morality. The "inner sagehood outer kingship" (*neisheng waiwang* 內聖外王) concept, which Zeng associated with the *jingshi* ideal, particularly well reflected this view.[70]

A particular contribution of these scholars was their application of practical self-cultivation methods. Practices of self-examination were combined with following the rules of propriety and with practical, social and political action. The moral praxis of Song learning scholar-officials in mid-nineteenth century is nowhere better exemplified than by Zeng Guofan. His confession-like remarks, notes and writings express his radical, yet concrete sincerity. He wrote, "Each day I struggle with anger and desire. I well know their existence but just simply cannot get rid of them."[71] Elsewhere: "While composing a poem, I was always in a mood to surpass others and

---

66 Chang Hao, "The Intellectual Heritage of the Confucian Ideal of Ching-shih." In *Confucian Traditions in East Asian Modernity: Moral Education and Economic Culture in Japan and the Four Mini-Dragons*. Tu Wei-ming, ed. Cambridge, Mass.: Harvard University Press, 1996, 73.
67 Ibid., 75.
68 Tang Jian 唐鑒, "Zhiyu shuo" 窒欲說 (On the control of desires), in *Tang Queshen gongji* 唐確慎公集 (A collection of Tang Jian), *Sibu beiyao* 四部備要. Taibei: Zhonghua shuju, 1972, book 2, pp. 24–26.
69 For the synthetic nature of Zeng Guofan's system of *li* see Qian Mu, *Jin sanbainian*, 647–53.
70 Chiu Wei-chun. *Morality as Politics: The Restoration of the Ch'eng-Chu Neo-Confucianism in Late Imperial China*. Ph.D. dissertation, Ohio State University, 1992, 261.
71 Ibid., 217.

to achieve fame."⁷² Another hindrance on the road to self-realization was sexual desire.⁷³ Qian Mu, a modern scholar, discussed in chapter 6, highlighted Zeng's saying: "Transform your personal inclination to mundane practices (*xisu* 習俗) and to mold (*taozhu* 陶鑄) the capacity of the people of the world," as indicating Zeng's lifelong message of learning and practice. Zeng characterized this program of self-cultivation by uprightness (*gangzhi* 剛直) and sincerity (*zhongcheng* 忠誠), the former meaning that there is nothing that cannot be done by effort, the latter meaning to master oneself and to love others.⁷⁴

Hellmut Wilhelm noted two methods of self-cultivation used by Song learning scholars such as Tang Jian and Zeng Guofan.⁷⁵ One was to keep a self-reproaching diary, a daily examination and criticism of personal attitudes and actions, composed of guiding maxims which might be quotations from the Classics, appended words of teachers and friends, or personal formulations.⁷⁶ It was customary to circulate this diary among friends, and ask them to add comments. Another was the reading list, to which a scholar added critical notes and asked his friends to correct these and add their own observations.

To be sure, by complementing autonomy with action and practice these nineteenth century scholars significantly contributed to the traditional discourse on human nature. Was their idea of personal autonomy based on subjective moral norms or on knowing the real through learning? According to Wilhelm, Tang Jian and Zeng Guofan's 'self realization' "[...] amounted to a rediscovery of the human mind along psychological rather than philosophical lines and on this basis [they] approached establishing the autonomy of the human mind within the framework of responsible orthodox thought."⁷⁷ Wilhelm found, however, that at some point their concern for overcoming the self (*keji* 克己) turned into an intimacy with its deepest reaches. "[...] they were not far any more from an understanding of the autonomy of the self and together with it the autonomy of the human mind."⁷⁸

Wilhelm's analysis led him to identify the Song learning scholars' self-realization ideal with the Western notion of individual autonomy. This, in turn, led him to substitute the Western goal of mental progress for the integrative goal of Confucian self-cultivation. What Wilhelm seemed to disregard is that the personal striving of these scholars was to form one body with all things and not apart from all things. His analysis stipulates a mixture of goals. What he interprets as their capacity to reach a deeper level of self-realization was rather their ability to associate their self-

---

72 Ibid., 219.
73 Ibid., 220.
74 Qian Mu, *Jin sanbainian*, 640–41.
75 Hellmut Wilhelm, "Chinese Confucianism on the Eve of the Great Encounter." In *Changing Japanese Attitudes toward Modernization*. Marius Jansen, ed. Princeton, N.J.: Princeton University Press,1965, 283–310.
76 Ibid., 292–93.
77 Ibid., 290.
78 Ibid., 303.

cultivation with concrete and practical reality. To these nineteenth century scholars, to be human had come to signify a state far more complex than it had been in the seventeenth century. Infusing Song learning's moral teaching with practical activism, they indeed accomplished a significant attainment in the development of this school.

Inasmuch as 1895 signifies acceleration of the modern process in China, and around 1920 foreign views were already relatively established on the intellectual scene, the period that stretches between these years was a period of intellectual transition (1895–1920).[79] At the beginning of the period the ideal of integration still dominated the thought of leading scholars, such as Tan Sitong 譚嗣同 (1865–1898) and Zhang Taiyan 章太炎 (1869–1936). Chang Hao characterizes Tan's perception of reality as an image of organic oneness.[80] "Tan, then, holds that the world is ultimately made up of a primordial substance believed to permeate everywhere to form an all-encompassing whole. In this whole, all existences, through the medium of the primordial substance, interpenetrate and fuse."[81] Organic oneness is moreover charged with *ren* 仁. In Tan's words: "Within heaven and earth *ren* alone exists, that is all."[82] *Ren*, according to him, was all-pervasive because it existed in the various media,[83] like ether (*yitai* 以太), electricity (*dian* 電), and mental power (*xinli* 心力), all of which he identified with *ren*.

As it was for Jiao Xun, the foremost characteristic of *ren* is that it interrelates (*tong* 通) all people and things, thus it functions as a linkage integrating the individual with the ultimate context of existence. It is a formless nerve fiber with the power to connect heaven, earth, the myriad things, others, and the self as one.[84] *Ren* is also: love without discrimination as argued by Mozi; the sea of nature and compassion advocated by the Buddha; and the soul and moral principle, "you shall love your neighbor as yourself," of Jesus.[85] Being all-pervasive, *ren* is primarily a moral virtue of the self. When exercising love and compassion, and other qualities of *ren*, the person is morally autonomous.

Integration was imbued with new foreign political ideas. Since all creatures and objects consisted alike of chemical elements and occupied the same space suffused

---

79 For more information see Zhang Hao (Chang Hao) 張灝, "Zhongguo jindai sixiangshi de zhuanxing shidai" 國近代思想史的轉型時代 (The age of transition in modern Chinese intellectual history). *Ershiyi shiji* 二十一世紀, vol. 52 (April 1999), 29–39.
80 Chang Hao, *Chinese Intellectuals in Crisis: Search for Order and Meaning, 1890–1911*. Berkeley: University of California Press, 1988, 88.
81 Ibid.
82 Tan Sitong 譚嗣同, Renxue 仁學 (An Exposition of Benevolence), section 5. In Chan Sin-wai, trans., *An Exposition of Benevolence: The Jen-hsueh of T'an Ssu-t'ung*. Hong Kong: The Chinese University Press, 1984, 242. Hereafter, *Renxue*. My translation from the original Chinese text in this book.
83 Luke S.K. Kwong, *T'an Ssu-t'ung, 1865–1898: Life and Thought of a Reformer*. Leiden: E.J. Brill, 1996, 155.
84 *Renxue* 3, 241.
85 Ibid., 1, 239.

by ether and electric energy, there were no intrinsic differences among them. Implying a holistic tendency, for Tan, even the distinction between body and soul, matter and spirit, would eventually cease to exist.[86] This aspect of his thought was compatible with liberal ideals, such as the idea that everyone has the right of self-determination, which Protestant missionaries like Alexander Williamson (1829–1890), and Ernst Faber (1839–1899), were advocating in China at the time.[87] Tan thus stipulated the oneness of individual and society and the equality of all human beings and things.

Self-cultivation accordingly consisted of removing all mental constraints, such as: national, between China and foreign countries; political, between ruler and ruled; sexual, between male and female; and personal, between self and others;[88] a Chinese world without the rules of propriety and the imperial institution. According to Chang Hao, Tan launched an unreserved, frontal attack on the doctrine of the three bonds. He called on people to muster the courage to rip apart and burst the ropes that the doctrine had created around them.[89] Nevertheless, joined with this iconoclastic stance was integration with the whole. In fact, in one place Tan radicalized (and perhaps one can say Buddhicized) his position stating that the person who achieved integration has no self, is non-existent, and is non-mortal.[90]

Activism was the message of Tan's holistic vision. Autonomy was now implemented not with the rules of propriety but in social involvement:

> [...] the Buddha, Confucius, and Christ deserved praise because they exemplified dynamism and activism. The Christian missions' world-wide outreach, the Confucian motto of "daily renewal" (*rixin* 日新) in the *Changes*, and, especially, the Buddhist call for valor and courage [,..] all exhibited a commitment to action and change.[91]

Tan criticized contentment and praised the willingness to spend, to invest, to enjoy, and to live life to its fullest.[92]

The late Qing Buddhist revival was likewise obvious in Zhang Taiyan's writings soon after his release from prison in 1906. According to him,[93] the outside phenome-

---

86 Kwong, *T'an Ssu-t'ung*, 156.
87 Chang Hao, *Chinese Intellectuals in Crisis*, 98–99. Williamson is explicitly mentioned in *Renxue*, chapters 13, 39. In addition, John Fryer was in touch with Tan. See Tan Sitong 譚嗣同, "Shang Ouyang Banjiangshi shu" 上歐陽瓣疆師書 (Letter to Ouyang Banjiang), *Tan Sitong quanji* 譚嗣同全集 (Complete works of Tan Sitong). Beijing: Xinhua shuju, 1954, 316–29. Especially p. 317–18. For Faber see chapter two below.
88 Kwong, *T'an Ssu-t'ung*, 156.
89 Chang Hao, *Chinese Intellectuals in Crisis*, 101.
90 *Renxue*, 26, 268.
91 Quoted in Kwong, *T'an Ssu-t'ung*, 156–57.
92 Chang Hao, *Chinese Intellectuals in Crisis*, 90–95.
93 The enigmatic character of Zhang's personality has to be considered. My discussion refers to his writings around 1906. Philosophically, he was at that period strongly influenced by Buddhist ideas.

nal world as well as the ego-self, are nothing but the false projections of consciousness:

> All the myriad things have no nature of their own (*wanwu jiewu zixing* 萬物皆無自性). The world of sentient beings (*qingjie* 情界) and the world of inanimate things (*qijie* 器界), are all subject to constant change [...]. [All phenomena] are the shadows of the mind.[94]

Nonetheless, according to Zhang's interpretation of the Yogacara teaching, in the final analysis there is an ultimate spiritual reality beyond the present reality.[95] This reality is an organic oneness, and within it all things are equal. As Chang Hao observes, the burden of the whole Yogacara teaching is to demonstrate the possibility of transforming false consciousness into transcendental insight.[96] The linkage between the individual and that ultimate spiritual reality is represented through the pure, as distinguished from the impure, seeds of consciousness. Enlightenment consists of transcending the effect of the impure seeds and activating the pure seeds. According to Zhang, it essentially involved the ethics of the Bodhisattva ideal.

Whereas Tan Sitong based his message of social and political activism on the idea of humaneness, Zhang based it on the Bodhisattva ideal, involving a natural disposition of mutual concern among all human beings. "One is directed to give up seeking his own accomplishment in order to assist others."[97] In a passage of his essay *Jianli zongjiaolun* 建立宗教論 (On establishing religion), Zhang alludes to the Boddhisattva ideal, to highlight the accountability of human beings toward each other in the ordinary, though illusory, world:

> Talking about worldly truth (*sudi* 俗諦) [where everything is illusion] [...]. [Humanity may be likened to] the leaking boat in the midst of large waves, which is about to sink. Who among the people on board, is not alarmed and concerned for their fellow men; [they] search for a wooden raft (*mufa* 木筏) to share with the other people on the boat, so that all together would avoid drowning. Certainly, their being alarmed is not for the leaking boat but for their fellow travelers on it.[98]

---

94 Zhang Taiyan 章太炎, "Bianxing" 辨性 (On human nature), in *Zhangshi congshu* 章氏叢書 (The collected writings of Zhang Taiyan). Hangzhou: Zhejiang tushuguan, 1919, 2:15, 148.
95 Chang Hao, *Chinese Intellectuals in Crisis*, 131.
96 Ibid., 128.
97 Zhang Taiyan 章太炎, "Jianli zongjiao" 建立宗教 (On establishing religion), in *Zhangshi congshu*, 3:2, 26a.
98 Ibid., 25b. The raft image is an allusion to Buddhist teaching as a conveyance to release from suffering.

Conclusion

In traditional Chinese thought being human implied abandoning all mental barriers, thus allowing the person to form one body with the universe as a whole. This ideal was thought to be attainable, on the assumption that human beings are capable of making autonomous choices in setting the course of their lives toward such a goal. The individual's mind was the key that could link heaven and man. All the relevant connections and processes involved the workings of the mind. Autonomously choosing to form one body with the whole offered to the individual a way to realize himself and to be human.

However, though most thinkers agreed on the mind's autonomous self determination, they differed regarding the nature of the linkage and the course that the required action should take. The Song-Ming neo-Confucian masters used metaphysical explanations to substantiate the Mencian theory of human nature. With the late Ming and early Qing *qi*-philosophers, the implication was accepted that the world being real, to be human was to act in it. By the eighteenth century, the changing world demanded new answers about taking action in order to be human. Ruan Yuan and Jiao Xun answered the increasing nineteenth century demand for active participation by setting up ritual propriety (*li*), as an objective set of rules to balance the inner subjective capacities. Concern for applying philosophical understanding by practice was at the center of early nineteenth century intellectual movements such as the New Text school, Song learning, and setting the world in order (*jingshi*). A new generation of Confucian scholars active during the middle and later half of the nineteenth century further developed the earlier synthesis between innate moral capacities and external counterbalances, relying heavily on the system of rules of propriety. But for Tan Sitong and Zhang Taiyan this system was no longer acceptable; these turn of the twentieth century scholars combined their belief in innate capacities with a message of political and social activism.

Throughout these periods it was impossible to escape metaphysics, because subjective, inwardly directed tendencies, persisted. Dai Zhen needed the spiritual source for his intelligence.[99] Peng Shaosheng questioned the value of morality which is not innate. Ruan Yuan talked about the beginnings of *ren*. Jiao Xun presented the virtue of interrelatedness, as a subjective capacity for attaining integration. Tang Jian, Zeng Guofan, and Chen Li, reaffirmed the Song learning concept of principle. Like their predecessors they assumed that the universe was coherent and the individual's capacity to form one body with the whole. The integration ideal still figured in the thought of Tan Sitong and Zhang Taiyan, whose ideas also reflected Buddhist theories and confidence in internal resources leading toward achieving integration.

---

99 Here I differ from Hu Shi who defined Dai Zhen as a materialist. Hu Shih, "Jige fanlixue de sixiangjia" 幾個反理學的思想家 (A few thinkers who opposed the Learning of Principle). In *Hu Shi Wencun* 胡適文存 (Collected essays of Hu Shih). Taibei: Yundong, 1953. vol. III, 74.

Autonomy, with its source in the mind, became a problem in the twentieth century when the institutional linkage through the imperial system ceased. The abolition of the institutional linkage was the decisive blow which led to a feeling of abandonment on the part of individual Chinese thinkers and to an ominous sense of disintegration. Now they had only their own mind to support the quest for meaning in life. Obviously, alternative ideas arriving from foreign sources became part of the confusion, when doubts about the nature of the ultimate context of existence began to appear. Nonetheless, the *Great Learning* paradigm continued to hold sway. World order begins with the individual's self-cultivation and with the notion of human nature as the starting point for world order.

The question of the 'view of life' continued to be asked in traditional Chinese thought. New ideas constantly appeared, modifying existing formulations and suggesting new syntheses. The Song masters' emphasis on principle and the Qing scholars' stress on the rules of propriety were no longer valid for late Qing thinkers. From the Song to the late Qing the 'view of life' philosophy had underwent changes as metaphysical and subjective ideas were combined with more practical and dynamic views about what it means to be human. Among the various questions that remained open to debate at the beginning of the twentieth century two of the most crucial were what a life of activism was to be like, and what is innate and what is not.

CHAPTER TWO

Two Interpretations of Kant's 'View of Life': Ernst Faber and Liang Qichao

Around the turn of the twentieth century the foreign impact with its onslaught of ideas became inseparable from the emerging intellectual discourse in China. At first, the transitional period intellectuals, who were imbued with a sense of crisis, tended to underestimate the foreign philosophical agenda. The formula, "Chinese learning for substance, Western learning for function" (*zhongxue wei ti, xixue wei yong* 中學為體, 西學為用), represented the still current confidence in traditional wisdom as far as cultural values and philosophical assumptions were concerned.

Until around 1895 the Chinese scholars' appreciation of Western material products and technological knowledge far exceeded their concern for whatever else the West had to offer. Still firmly grounded in familiar tradition, they considered the affirmation of "wealth and power" (*fuqiang* 富強) a sufficient concession on their part. Under intensifying external and internal pressure, strengthening the *yong* with foreign aid seemed to satisfy their commitment to setting the world in order (*jingshi* 經世). Only gradually did a minority of intellectuals realize that some aspects of Western learning did not fit into the *yong* alone. As Western political, social, humanistic, and philosophical knowledge gained respect in the eyes of leading scholars like Yan Fu, Cai Yuanpei, Liang Qichao, and others, the *ti* was directly challenged, and so was the balance that the *tiyong* formula represented.[1]

On closer examination, some of the Western ideas were not entirely foreign to the Chinese *ti*. Like Chinese thought, German idealism in particular entertained a belief in the internal spiritual and moral capacities of man, and associated these capacities with moral practice. Being human essentially involved such capacities and their application. Foreign ideas offered new perspectives on questions of human nature and what it means to be human which continued to be discussed in Chinese scholarly circles, even if not as major issues. This chapter focuses on the initial acquaintance in China with the Kantian idea of individual autonomy. I propose to explore this process by juxtaposing the German Protestant missionary-philosopher, Ernst Faber (known in China also as Hua Zhi-an 花之安 1839–1899), and Liang

---

1 Yan Fu suggested an original version on the tiyong formula, saying that freedom should be the substance and the people's democracy the function (yi ziyou weiti, yi minzhu weiyong 以自由為體，以民主為用). Quoted in Benjamin I. Schwartz, *In Search of Wealth and Power: Yen Fu and the West*. Cambridge, Mass.: Harvard University Press, 1964, 62.

Qichao 梁啟超 (1873–1929). Both were closely involved with the journey of German idealism in China. Faber transmitted Kant's ideas in his Chinese texts by recourse to Christian argumentation. Liang learned about Kant from Japanese translations, and transmitted Kant's ideas by resorting mainly to Buddhist and Wang Yangming concepts.

Though never before discussed in scholarly research as such,[2] Faber was probably the first scholar of Kantian and post-Kantian German philosophy to dwell on Chinese soil. His knowledge of both Western philosophy and Chinese thought qualified him, I would suggest, to occupy a unique position within late nineteenth century Sino-Western discourse. The present study focuses on four works containing his intellectual and philosophical views[3] (hereafter: *Education*, *Civilization*, *Theories*, and *Classics*), which aimed to present to the Chinese the value of the Christian mode of living in its practical, cultural, and philosophical aspects.

Liang Qichao, an exile in Japan since 1898, was during the early 1900's a leading voice for transforming Chinese thought. He was the first modern Chinese intellectual to introduce the philosophy of Kant to Chinese readers, in an essay that tended to advocate a Buddhist 'view of life'. The present chapter will focus on Liang's essay on Kant (1903–1904) and his annotated collection of moral sayings (1905), where he further developed his critique of Kant, from a Wang Yangming perspective.[4]

---

2 He Lin and other scholars who studied the introduction of Kantian ideas in China have so far failed to check missionary sources. One example is, He Lin 賀麟, "Kangde Hei-ge-er zhexue dongjianji" 康德黑格尔哲學東漸記 (The introduction of Kant and Hegel's philosophy in the East). *Zhongguo zhexue* 中國哲學, vol. II (April 1981), 343–387.

3 Hua Zhi-an 花之安 (Ernst Faber). *Taixi xuexiao* 泰西學校 (Western schools). Shanghai: Shangwu yinshuguan chengyin, 1897 (first published in 1873). Hereafter *Education*. *Zi Xi cu Dong* 自西徂東 (From West to East) (English title: Civilization, East and West: The Fruits of Christianity Compared with Those of the Chinese Religion). Hong Kong: Zhonghua yinwu zongju, 1884. Hereafter *Civilization*. *Xinghai yuanyuan* 性海淵源 (Inquiry of theories of human nature). Shanghai: Guangxuehui yin, 1893. Hereafter *Theories*. *Jingxue bu yan jing* 經學不厭精 (The classics are not contrary to Christianity) (English title: An Examination of the Thirteen Classics and the Development of Confucianism). Shanghai: American Presbyterian Mission Press, 1898. Hereafter *Classics*. Parts of the first two were published earlier as articles, the former (Education) in *Jiaohui xinbao* 教會新報 (Church News) between 1871–1878, the latter (Civilization) in *Wangguo gongbao* 萬國公報 (*Globe Magazine*) in 1881–1883, prior to their publication in book forms.

4 Respectively, Liang Qichao, "Jinshi diyi dazhi kangde zhi xueshuo" 近世第一大哲康德之學說 (The doctrine of Kant, the greatest philosopher of modern times). In *Zichan jieji xueshu sixiang pipan cankao ziliao* 資產階級學術思想批判參考資料 (Reference material for criticizing capitalist thought). Beijing: Shangwu yinshuguan, vol. VIII, 1960. Hereafter *Essay*. The Kant Essay was published in several issues in Liang's journal *Xinmin congbao* 新民叢報 (The new people journal). It was interrupted during his America trip (1903), and resumed publication with the last part in early 1904. "Deyujian" 德育鑑 (Mirror for moral cultivation). In *Yinbingshi zhuanji* 飲冰室專集 (Collected works of the Ice-Drinker's Studio). Shanghai: Zhonghua shuju, vol. XXVI, 1936. Hereafter *Mirror*.

This comparison brings together two complementary early facets of Kantian philosophy in China. Whereas Liang Qichao depended on his understanding of foreign ideas in their Japanese translation, Faber knew the original sources but still needed to adapt them to the Chinese language. Reading both men's texts we gain a singular insight into the initial phase of the meeting between Chinese and Western ideas. Faber and Liang convey a perspective that we in the twenty-first century can no longer have. How did these two thinkers view the relevance of Kantian ideas to the Chinese philosophical discourse of their day? In what way did each man's reading of Kant within a Chinese philosophical context lead to the advocacy of a different 'view of life'? What kind of syntheses did Faber and Liang create?

A. Ernst Faber and the Idea of Autonomous Individuality

Until the beginning of the twentieth century a major channel of intellectual communication between China and the West was activated by Jesuit and other Catholic missionaries since the sixteenth century, and of Protestants, since the nineteenth. Not unlike their predecessors, the latter combined their religious concerns with fields of learning such as medicine, education, science, history, and geography. Aware of the power of the written word in Chinese culture, they published books and periodicals that fused Western knowledge with Christian values. The German Protestant missionary Ernst Faber came to China in 1865 and before long was involved with the already existing missionary intellectual infrastructure.[5] His missionary training had begun around 1857 and in the early 1860s he studied, among other subjects, Christian theology, hermeneutics and philosophy. As he became increasingly familiar with the Chinese people, their culture and conditions of living in China, Faber determined to reform Chinese beliefs about life and the world.[6]

An examination of four of Faber's Chinese works shows that the first three, *Education*, *Civilization*, and *Theories*, attempted to introduce Western knowledge to his Chinese readers and to convey an overall critique of Chinese civilization. The fourth, the *Classics*, suggested a synthesis of Chinese and Western views which accommodated neo-Confucian beliefs about human nature, the linkage between man and transcendence, autonomy, and the ideal of integration.[7] One may critically indicate that Faber's synthesis derived the sense of spirituality exclusively from the Judeo-Christian concept of God, failing to recognize the Chinese sense of spirituality that derived from the sense of integration with the whole.

---

5 For a more detailed study of Faber's thought see Gad C. Isay, "A Missionary Philosopher in Late Qing: Ernst Faber (1839–99) and his Intercultural Synthesis of Human Nature," *Sino-Western Cultural Relations Journal*, 23 (August 2001), 22–49.

6 For Faber's personal transformation during his mission see, Gad C. Isay, "Religious Obligation Transformed into Intercultural Agency. Ernst Faber's Mission in China," *Monumenta Serica*, Vol. 54, 2006, 273–287.

7 Isay, "A Missionary Philosopher," 22–49.

From Faber's perspective, the ultimate context of existence was interchangeable with God. Similarly, he viewed Creation as a personal and intentional act of God, as compared with the Chinese view which conceived of an impersonal and unintentional evolutionary process. His human being, who dwells in God's world, is created in the image of God: "The Bible says that man was created in the image of God" (*ren wei Shangdi zhi xiang* 人為上帝之像).[8] Man was not only created in the image of God, he was, moreover, created with a purpose in this world, to reflect God's glory.[9] Man, therefore, is essential within the scheme of Creation; his capacities position him in a meaningful context.

The Chinese idea of the linkage between heaven and man was transformed into the linkage between God and man. Faber's first three works, *Education*, *Civilization*, and *Theories*, suggested the image of the soul (*linghun* 靈魂) as the link, but later, in the *Classics*, he stipulated human nature for that purpose. The spiritual quality of this linkage derives from its being of the same substance as God: "Man and God are related" (*ren yu Shangdi xiangyun* 人與上帝相運).[10] And, "[...] both participate with each other (*erzhe canguan* 二者參觀)."[11] Reminiscent of Zhu Xi's famous maxim, "human nature is principle" (*xing ji li* 性即理), Faber declared in his *Classics*: "God is imprinted into the system of the human mind" (*Shangdi mingyu renxin zhifa* 上帝銘於人心之法).[12]

Faber based his view of the individual self on a set of philosophical dichotomies: mind and body; spirit and matter; reason and emotions. The core of the self is in the mind and, owing to the inherent linkage with God, the individual's mind is endowed with both spirituality and reason. Material qualities and emotions, on the other hand, are of mundane origin, and are generated by the body. Due to their association with matter, the material qualities and emotions affect the mind from the outside. But it is specifically mind and its reason that humanize the individual's nature.

This mind, according to Faber's account, associates the individual with the qualities of will, autonomy, and uniqueness. These qualities were predominantly based on the individual's ability to rationally dominate the emotions. Considering Faber's background, the insistence on the application of the mind-body dichotomy could hardly be avoided. Although indeed, both Confucians and German idealists dichotomized reason and emotions, the Kantian pure reason which legislated rules to subdue the emotions to its will, was foreign to Confucian thought. Faber's assumptions differed here from neo-Confucian views.

Faber presents will as the capacity to make choices between moral (good-evil) alternatives. Another function of the will is to correspond to and to accord with orig-

---

8 *Theories*, 76a, concluding remark no. 9.
9 *Classics*, Renjuan 仁卷, 2a.
10 *Theories*, 77a, concluding remark no. 14.
11 Ibid., 76a, concluding remark no. 9.
12 *Classics*, Renjuan, 2a. Here Faber referred to Romans, where one finds statements such as "[...] because love of God is shed abroad in your hearts by the Holy Ghost which is given unto us." *Romans*, 4:5.

inal human nature in the sense of having reverence (*mu* 穆) for God. Accordingly, the individual is self-determining, not only because one transcends natural processes and is able to choose between various alternatives presented by these processes, but because one can also transcend oneself and choose one's ultimate life goal.[13]

The will-possessing self is of course autonomous. The idea of personal autonomy was first explicitly introduced by Faber in his *Theories* where he discussed the distinction between the individual and the universal (common-to-all) nature of man: "In each person's human nature," Faber wrote:

> [...] there are both the individual nature (*jizhixing* 己之性) and the universal nature (*renzhixing* 人之性). Universal nature is that which all human beings share. Where they are not individuals (*ren bu yu ji tong* 人不與己同), this is the universal nature. Where the individual differs from others (*ji bu yu ren tong* 己不與人同), this is the individual nature. What is common to both the individual and the universal is [the capacity for] self-knowledge (*zizhi* 自知) and autonomy (*zizhu* 自主), the foundations of human nature which inform the specificity of being human.[14]

Self-knowledge and autonomy should be understood as an appeal to reason. According to *Theories*, the authority (*quan* 權) of man's self-knowledge and autonomy originate from God.[15] Therefore, the beginnings of a person's self-knowledge and autonomy are the same in everyone. People differ according to capacity.[16] Faber followed the same reasoning in the *Classics*, where he declared that luminous (*ming* 明) self-knowledge and authority of autonomy, "[...] define the foundation of human nature, and distinguish mankind from other living beings." Continuing the Kantian connection between reason and morality, Faber associated these capacities with a higher goal of life (discussed later), namely, the ability to put the self aside and be ultimately concerned for other people.[17]

Self-knowledge also leads each person toward his or her true nature and determines each person's individual uniqueness.[18] Faber discussed uniqueness by distinguishing the true self from other people's selves, on the one hand, and the true na-

---

13 To Faber, reverence (mu 穆) for God is the natural disposition of man. *Classics*, 4a. For a discussion of self-determination, see Reinhold Niebuhr, *The Nature and Destiny of Man, Human Nature*. New York: Charles Scribner's Sons, vol. I, 1964, 163.
14 *Theories*, 76a, concluding remark no. 6.
15 Ibid., concluding remark no. 7.
16 Ibid., 77a, concluding remark no. 15.
17 *Classics*, 10a.
18 Donald Munro argues that uniqueness as a value does not have a history in China. This claim should be treated cautiously as it ignores late Ming and Qing thinkers like Li Zhi. Nevertheless, Munro acknowledges, "Although in their philosophical writings Neo- Confucians never exalted uniqueness [...] their ranks were peopled by unique individuals." Donald J. Munro, ed., *Individualism and Holism: Studies in Confucian and Taoist Values*. Ann Arbor: University of Michigan Center for Chinese Studies, 1985, 4–5.

ture or essence and emotions, on the other. The uniqueness of the true self among other selves is grounded in a person's true nature. He wrote:

> Because my mind has luminous self-knowledge, I differ from other people. I am different from other things and I also have tensions within myself. When I contemplate where I differ from and resemble other people, things, and myself, what then is my true self (*zhenwo* 真我)? Admittedly, I have the seven emotions (*qiqing* 七情), and cannot avoid happiness, anger, sorrow, joy, love, hate, desire. But emotions are emotions and I am me. My seven emotions should not be confused with my own true nature (*zhenxing* 真性).[19]

The true self is distinguishable from others due to the capacity to cast off emotions; the individual's uniqueness thus consists in asserting his own rational resources.

Faber's account of the individual's qualities of will, autonomy, and uniqueness resorted to arguments and terms found in Kant and German idealism generally, together with their mind-body and reason-emotions dichotomies. By successfully engaging these qualities with spirit and reason exclusively, his individual was capable of following the right course of life and of being in accord with his appointed role in the universal scheme. In his discussion of these notions Faber resembled others who sought emancipation from the authority of the church, as well as post-enlightenment individuals who were no longer subordinated to aristocratic authority.

Faber's account is noteworthy for his efforts to complement the 'view of life' with a theory of knowledge, joined, however, to the subjectivity of knowledge. Already in his work on *Education* (1873), he emphasized the subjectivity of knowledge:

> Because the pattern of thought emanates in the faculty of spiritual mentality (*fu yifa, naiyou lingfu suoqi* 夫意法乃由靈府所起), therefore each idea has to adapt to this pattern (*guge yisi xucong qifa* 故各意思須從其法). All words and actions are likewise intrinsic to this pattern.[20]

This was the first time that the Kantian distinction between *noumenal*, the world of things-in-themselves, and *phenomenal*, the world of appearance, was formulated in Chinese.

Later, in his *Civilization* (1884) Faber again wrote, "People have one-sided perspectives (*yipian zhijian* 一偏之見) and cannot capture reality."[21] For this reason, he stated, in order to discuss philosophical matters, we ought to gather all the principles (*li*) and unite them. Only then can we grasp the ultimate foundation and have the knowledge that stops at nothing (*zhiwu buche* 知無不撤).[22] Yet this absolute

---

19 *Civilization*, 255a–255b. For more on uniqueness see discussion of subjectivity below.
20 *Education*, 5b.
21 *Civilization*, 253b.
22 Ibid., 252b.

knowledge is impossible. Nor can we really know whether something is true or false (*zhenjia* 真假): "The principle of mystery is everywhere in this world."²³

Faber's discussion in *Civilization* of the problem of knowledge once again stressed his view of the linkage between God and man:

> The spiritual luminous [essence] of my mind (*wuxin zhi lingming* 吾心之靈明), is originally endowed with true knowledge (*benzi you zhenzhi suozai* 本自有真知所在). The true knowledge of my mind issues from the sequence of the following three phases: from observing the principles of the myriad things outside [myself]; from the stirring (*yan* 驗) of the soul inside my body; and from the effortless God above.²⁴

In *Theories*, the presence of a divine quality in man's mind informs the ground of knowledge:

> The Lord's purpose (*Shangdi zhizhi* 上帝之旨) is hidden in the [subjective] view of the self (*zijian* 自見) and in spoken words. How is that? God's sacred [element] (*Shangdi zhishen* 上帝之神) inhabits the mind, therefore it is possible to fathom God's mind (*keyi ming Shangdi zhixin* 可以明上帝之心).²⁵

Dealing with the question of knowledge, in *Education* Faber also introduced epistemology, referring to a philosopher he calls Luxi 路隙, who could be R.H. Lotze (1817–81), or more likely, John Locke (1632–1704). Luxi, wrote Faber, studied the pattern of thought (*yifa* 意法); how the soul (*linghun* 靈魂) produces ideas (*fachu yisi* 發出意思), and how there are many types of ideas.²⁶ He also interpreted how true (*shi* 是) and false (*fei* 非) are confirmed and distinguished from each other. He (Luxi) discussed how perception (*zhijue* 知覺) enters via the five sense organs, stimulating (*suoqi* 所起) the faculty of spiritual mentality (*lingfu* 靈府), and the interaction between perception and stimulation. Such discussions about the problem of understanding (*ming* 明), Faber noted, are absent in China.²⁷

The epistemological issues merely touched on in *Education* were more extensively discussed and further supported with new information in *Civilization*. According to Faber, intelligence (*zhi* 智) is bestowed by God (implying the idea of revelation), and is revealed in the mind by means of the soul. God knows everything; There is nothing He cannot do. He bestows on man the spiritual luminous essence, and creates human intelligence. Nonetheless, the extension (*kuochong* 擴充) of this intelligence necessarily involves the knowledge of the individual's mind (*wuxin*

---

23 Ibid., 252b.
24 Ibid., 257b. Note Faber's usage of ling (spiritual) in Civilization (1884) and shen (sacred) in *Theories* (1893) for a similar philosophical purpose.
25 *Theories*, 1.
26 *Education*, 5a. For Locke's five types of ideas, see John Locke, *An Essay Concerning Human Understanding*. P.H. Nidditch, ed. Oxford: Oxford University Press, 1975, Book II.
27 Education, 5b. Faber mentioned Gong Sunlong 公孫龍, in this connection, but, "[...] definitions of names are not enough."

zhizhi 吾心之知).[28] Much as the role of revelation is essential to the process of knowledge, the importance of its interaction with an inborn capacity for reason cannot be overstated. The following discussion shows that in his later work on the *Classics* Faber used *daoli* (道理) for reason while the content of the following quote and the discussion that follows reveal that already in his earlier work on *Civilizations* his usage of the term for thought *si* (思) appeals to the rational aspect of thought rather than the emotional aspect or a mixture of both:

> The formation of intelligence depends on the capacity to perceive (*jue* 覺) through the five senses. But perception comes from the thought in the mind (*xinsi* 心思). Where do the seeing of the eye, the hearing of the ear, the capacity of the mind to memorize (*jiyi* 記憶), and to meditate (*jingsi* 靜思) what it saw and heard in the past all come from? Thought (*si* 思) is therefore indispensable. Thought is required first in order to activate intelligence.[29]

Faber's motive for discussing the problem of knowledge belongs in the context of his religious concerns. For him there were two relevant questions: how can God be known; and how can the idea of God be communicated to different peoples and cultures? He found the answer in Kant's assumption that all human beings are equally endowed with *a priori* categories of knowledge. We know God because we have the inborn capacity for such knowledge, and we can communicate this knowledge because we all have these same categories.

According to Faber, thought is the application of inborn conceptual categories to the act of knowing, or, the association between inborn capacities and outer objects:

> Within us there are innate [Faber uses the character (*xiong* 胸) which can be the breast] *a priori* conceptual categories (*xianzang shijian* 先藏識見), so that when we see an object we know the pattern that it necessarily follows.[30]

He shared this view of knowledge with other nineteenth century scholars, according to whom the miracle of knowledge consists of sense perception, internal sensation, and God's intervention. Indeed,

> God had so arranged our bodies and minds that upon receipt of a certain stimulus, our bodies feel a given sensation, and our minds conceive a particular perceptual belief.[31]

The capacity to know does not guarantee, however, a worthwhile life. Unless the individual finds the way to the Lord, wrote Faber, he will always confront an exis-

---

28 *Civilization*, 252a.
29 Ibid., 252a.
30 Ibid., 252b.
31 Edward S. Reed, "The Separation of Psychology from Philosophy: Studies in the Sciences of the Mind 1815–1879." In *Routledge History of Philosophy: The Nineteenth Century*. Ed. C. L. Ten. London: Routledge, vol. VII, 1994, 299.

tential predicament which is loss of direction and purposelessness. The *Classics* presents images of loss of direction and instability. People are likened to a ship; God, or faith in God, is the anchor.[32] In the sixth section, Faber discusses the faithless mind losing direction and not knowing where to go.[33]

The proposed solution to the human predicament is the life of faith. Faber's life of faith was the culmination of his self realization program and consisted in reliance on God. By oneself one cannot break through the idleness of the mind and eliminate the internal complexity.[34] A person must fix his mind on God, have him constantly in mind, like the ship's anchor. When the mind is fixed on God, His direction is accepted and the moral nature (*dexing* 德性) is established, nourished (*hanyang* 涵養), maintained (*jianxing* 踐行), and controlled (*kezhi* 克治). This is the subtle art of ordering the mind (*zhixin* 治心).[35]

The life of faith, the Way, according to Faber, is nowhere discussed more deeply than in the Bible.[36] The Bible suggests man's capacity to aspire to attain the level of the image of God (*yi cheng Shangdi zhi xiang* 以成上帝之象), as the goal of life.[37] By the same token, the image of the Savior (*Jiuzhu* 救主) qualifies each human being to embrace the grace of God. "Rely on the savior, believe he is the loved child of the heavenly father [...] forms one body with him (*yu zhi he wei yiti* 與之合為一體)."[38]

The life of faith together with the aspiration to attain the level of the image of God and reliance on the image of the savior, will reinforce the individual's will to union with the transcendent purpose of the universe. Faber's notion of faith, to use Paul Tillich's definition, consists of being ultimately concerned.[39] He who wishes to make his thoughts complete, has to seriously examine himself and always be cautiously alarmed.[40] A person has to be:

> Attentive, ready, respectful and devoted, then the self [will be led] toward the Way. Cease your hesitations; put an end to feelings of doubt. Do away with the empty, revere the real; quit the false, return to truth. Courageously enter the Way of exhausting the capacities of human nature. Revere God's teaching always and absolutely.[41]

---

32 *Classics*, Renjuan, 4b. Compare usage of ship and anchor metaphors to Liang Qichao's *Reflections*, discussed below in chapter 3.
33 Ibid..
34 Ibid., 3b.
35 Ibid., 5a.
36 Ibid., 5b.
37 Ibid., 6a.
38 Ibid..
39 Paul Tillich, *The Dynamics of Faith*. New York: Harper and Brothers Publishers, 1957, 1–4.
40 *Classics*, 6b.
41 Ibid., 6a.

The life of faith is the highest level in a person's existential journey between three spheres of existence. The first and most basic is the sphere of the senses, the transient world (*yushi* 寓世), where a person is concerned merely with emotional happiness (*qingfu* 情福).[42] The second, the ethical sphere, concerns the overcoming of selfish desires and not losing the original nature. The third sphere concerns the self's religious appeal to the transcendental, turning to the divine source and reaching for divine happiness. These spheres correspond, Faber says, to the individual's concern, first only with himself, then with what is outside himself (*shenwai* 身外), his fellow man, and finally, with God (*xiang Shangdi* 向上帝).[43] These spheres of existence and the call to find the meaningful life by transcending finite concerns, remarkably correspond to the aesthetic, ethical, and religious spheres of existence and the idea of the 'leap of faith' advocated by Søren Kierkegaard (1813–1855) in his philosophical writings.[44]

In the third sphere, where the individual is ultimately concerned and lives the life of faith, his life integrates with the whole. The idea of the individual who integrates with society and with the whole world is not exclusive to any particular culture. It was therefore available to Faber in both his non-Confucian and Confucian sources.[45] Christianity teaches that all people equally share the brotherhood of love for Christ, and are able to transcend the self and form a union of transcendental individuals who tread on earth but have their hearts in heaven.[46] The following characteristic neo-Confucian sentences, however, show that Faber recognized a corresponding idea in Chinese sources. He wrote: "He who cultivates the Way loves others as he loves himself." "Sagehood consists of the responsibility to involve self realization with caring for the rest of the world. Self renewal [correlates with] renewal of the people (*zixin xinmin* 自新新民)."[47]

Faber also explained the notion of integration as emulating the virtue of Heaven, and he conveyed his ethical message in words reminiscent of Mozi's 墨子 chapter on Universal Love (*jianai* 兼愛, chapter fifteen), writing:

> [...] as heaven regards the five continents as one family, likewise, the follower of the Way who embodies the mind of heaven (*xiangdaozhe zeti*

---

42 *Education*, 5–6, sec. 6.
43 Ibid.,.
44 In this specific text, Faber emphasizes the 'leap' from the first to the second and third. But an examination of his later writings indicates the third level as the ultimate goal.
45 For Faber's knowledge of the thought of Karl Marx, see E. Faber, *Socialismus oder die Lehre des Philosophen Micius* (Socialism or the teaching of the philosopher Mo Zi). Elberfeld: R.L. Friderichs, 1877. 20. For his familiarity with the ideas of Arthur Schopenhauer, as well as other European philosophers, see his *Introduction to the Science of Chinese Religion. A Critique of Max Muller and other Authors*. Hongkong: Lane, Crawford and Co., 1879.
46 Louis Dumont, "A Modified View of Our Origins: The Christian Beginnings of Modern Individualism." In *The Category of the Person: Anthropology, Philosophy, History*. Eds. M. Carrithers, S. Collins, and S. Lukes, Cambridge: Cambridge University Press, 1985, 99.
47 *Classics*, 9a.

tianxin 向道者則體天心), pacifies (*hemu* 和睦) the five continents like one family. As heaven wishes there to be no poverty and pain (*qiongkun* 窮困), likewise, the follower of the Way [...] deliberates to find methods to save the poor. As heaven wishes people to have no transgressions (*zuiguo* 罪過) [...] the follower of the Way [...] seeks ways to correct the faults, directs the community (*qun* 群) toward knowing the good. Heaven wants nobody to be deprived of knowledge, likewise, the follower of the Way [...] labors so that everyone can accumulate knowledge and entertain present and future happiness. As heaven unselfishly loves all people, likewise, the follower of the Way [...] seeks ways to help. He loves everyone equally, and views the whole world like one family (*wanguo yijia* 萬國一家).[48]

But, as distinct from Mozi, faith challenged Faber's insistence on integration, for faith demands complete non-attachment except to faith itself and its object. Faber advocated, however, that in caring for people one should be totally unselfish and regard only the equality and the brotherhood of man. No matter how people differ from one another in their natures, all are also the same.[49] Everyone's nature is endowed with the potential for autonomy and self-knowledge and, therefore, every human being has the beginnings of goodness. He who can be forgetful of the self and only concerned with others, the goodness of all the people is his own. Those who are only concerned with their own goodness heedless of others, are deficient as human beings.[50]

Not divorced from China's reality Faber's 'view of life', stressing individual autonomy and emphasizing faith, raised issues that were debated later in the 1920s. He considered the increasing appeal of material progress as threatening to what he would have called the authentic human life, and advocated weighing material progress against spiritual values. Without humanity and love (*renai* 仁愛), Faber wrote, progress is empty,[51] warning pointedly:

> If the teachers do not have the mind of love and humanity, teaching is not real teaching, [if] the students will not have the mind of love and humanity, learning is not learning. Teaching and learning are thus aborted, they carry the name but have no real content. Humanity should be the foundation, otherwise order in society and the world cannot be established.[52]

In his *Classics* (1898) Faber achieved a Sino-Western philosophical synthesis in two major areas. First, he dropped his previous concept of the soul, now using human nature instead. This substitution considerably reduced the distance between his position and the neo-Confucian views on linkage. Second, he discussed the ideal of inte-

---

48 Ibid., 9a-9b.
49 Ibid., 9b.
50 Ibid., 10a.
51 Compare with Liang Qichao on the weaknesses of science in chapter 4.
52 *Classics*, 136a.

gration, characteristic of Western, Christian, and neo-Confucian philosophies, using both Confucian terms and a Mozi-like perspective. He also discussed autonomy, but there he referred to the capacity to use reason (*daoli* 道理),[53] arguing in terms new to Chinese discourse. His self-cultivation program with its emphasis on religious faith further diverged from the customary Chinese view.

Like Kant, Faber based his view about life and the world on epistemological arguments. Knowledge, according to Faber, is the sequence of revelation, human capacities, and the objects of perception. His theory of knowledge was crucial in substantiating human nature and relating it to the context of existence. Between things as they appear and things as they are in themselves, between *phenomena* and *noumena*, each person functions as an independent source of knowledge. The linkage with God informs the act of knowledge with a transcendent source. At the same time, thought or, rather, rational thought or reason, is equipped with *a priori* conceptual categories by means of which the person attains and communicates the knowledge of this world.

From the perspective of Chinese philosophy one may critically observe that Faber's individual corresponded to the mind-body dichotomy. He contrasted the mind, which sustains the linkage between God and the individual, with the body, representing the more mundane inclinations of man. The major import of this dichotomy involves the superiority of spirit and rational thought (or reason) over matter and emotions. The individual is directed to associate himself with spirit and rational thought, and in this way to realize his humanity. Reason is the overriding quality underlying individual capacities for self determination (will), autonomy, and uniqueness.

B. Liang Qichao's Early Excursions in Kantian Philosophy

In the spring of 1890 the young Cantonese scholar Liang Qichao passed through Shanghai on the way home from Beijing. There, he first encountered 'Western learning' when he read *Haiguo tuzhi* 海國圖志 (Outline of world geography), compiled by Wei Yuan's (1794–1856) during the 1840's.[54] The following year Liang enrolled in Kang Youwei's (1858–1927) school, the *Wanmu caotang* 萬木草堂 (Thatched hall of myriad trees), where 'Barbarian Affairs' (*yiwu* 夷物) was one of the seven categories of study. Thereafter, Liang's association with Kang and the reform movement brought him into contact with missionary writings and with missionaries who were involved with the movement, as well as with the intellectual

---

53 Ibid., 2b.
54 Chen Chi-yun, "Liang Ch'i-ch'ao's 'Missionary Education': A Case Study of Missionary Influence on the Reformers." *Papers on China*, vol. XVI, 1962, 72. Wei Yuan 魏源, *Haiguo tuzhi* 海國圖志 (Outline of world geography). A fifty-volume version was first published in 1842, sixty-volume in 1847 and one hundred-volume in 1852.

B. Liang Qichao's Early Excursions in Kantian Philosophy 43

currents of late Qing China.⁵⁵ Indeed, we know that Liang did have some direct contacts with people like Timothy Richard (Li Timotai 李提摩太 1845–1919) and Young J. Allen (Lin Yuezhi 林樂知 1836–1907).⁵⁶ Although in Liang's reading list of Western books, published in late 1896, he characterized Faber's *Civilization* as "crude and shallow,"⁵⁷ this judgment should not be taken at face value. Liang, like other contemporary scholars, was for various reasons, though not unconditionally, inclined to deny the value of missionary works.⁵⁸

A new phase in Liang's – and indeed a whole generation of Chinese scholars' – contact with foreign learning, opened in Japan, to which he escaped after the collapse of the Hundred Days Reform Movement in late 1898. Compared to China, since the Meiji reforms of 1868, Western learning was already far advanced. German philosophy began to be known in Japan through scholars who studied in Europe starting in the 1860s, and then through foreign teachers. Ludwig Busse (1862–1907) came to Japan in 1887 and in 1893 Raphael von Koeber (1848–1923) took his place. Both delivered lectures at Tokyo University on Kantian and neo-Kantian philosophy, and German Idealism, among other topics. In Japan Liang found reading material and translations as well as interpretations in addition to his conversations with Japanese intellectuals.⁵⁹

Gino K. Piovesana observes that from the beginning a tension between naturalist, materialist, and positivist approaches, on the one hand, and idealist tendencies on the other, marked the introduction of Western philosophy into Japan. Spencerian Social Darwinism was widespread, but there were critics too.⁶⁰ Others, like the eminent Inoue Tetsujirō 井上哲次郎 (1855–1944) advocated Lu-Wang concepts in his criticism of prevalent utilitarian and individualistic ethics.⁶¹ According to Piovesana, the foremost nineteenth century Japanese expert on Kant, Onishi Hajime 大西祝 (1864–1900), thought that conscience (良心, *liangxin* in Chinese) "[...] was derived from

---

55 Kang himself recorded that in 1883 he bought copies of the *Wanguo gongbao* 萬國公報 (*The Globe Magazine*). Chen Chi-yun, "Liang Ch'i-ch'ao," 72. The 1883 volume of the *Wanguo gongbao*, as well as earlier ones, contained chapters from Faber's *Civilization*.
56 Liang was associated with Richard in 1895–96. In 1897 Liang reportedly conversed with Allen for a whole day in the Shanghai headquarters of the Society for the Diffusion of Knowledge (SDK), of which Faber was a leading member.
57 Chen, " Liang Ch'i-ch'ao," 112.
58 The anti-Christian current then prevalent in China is discussed in Paul A. Cohen, "Christian Missions and Their Impact to 1900." *The Cambridge History of China* Vol. X. John K. Fairbank, ed. Cambridge: Cambridge University Press, 1978, 543–90. For a specific reference to Faber's difficulties in this respect, see Leslie R. Marchant, *Ernst Faber's Scholarly Mission to Convert the Confucian Literati in the Late Ch'ing Period*. N.P.: University of Western Australia Center for East Asian Studies, 1982, 17–18.
59 Joseph Fass (pseudonym of Marian Galik), "The Introduction of Kant's Ideas into Japan and its Historical Prerequisites." *Asian and African Studies* (Bratislava), vol. XX (1984) 111–118.
60 Gino K. Piovesana, *Recent Japanese Philosophical Thought: 1862–1962*. A Survey. Tokyo: Enderle Bookstore, 1968, 10, 26.
61 Ibid., 40–41.

the human tendency to fulfil our ideal. This ideal must be realized to conform with the totality of which people were part."[62] Taking advantage of these favorable conditions in Japan during his years of exile (until October 1912), one of the tasks Liang assumed involved the study of foreign ideas and introducing these to his Chinese audience.[63]

During his years in exile, and especially between 1899–1906, Liang was at the height of his intellectual influence in China. He was relatively young, active, and had extraordinary literary skill.[64] According to Chang Hao, during the early 1900s Liang was the foremost and most widely read writer among Chinese intellectuals.[65] The journal he published, the articles he wrote, and his speeches attracted wide audiences and influenced a new generation of intellectuals.

In 1903–1904 Liang published his essay on Immanuel Kant, "the great Western sage" (hereafter *Essay*), and in 1905 his work on moral cultivation *Deyujian* 德育鑑 (hereafter *Mirror*).[66] The former used mainly Buddhist (Yogacara school) and also Wang Yangming arguments, and the latter was already predominantly disposed toward Wang's school. Both sources interpreted Kantian philosophy along different lines than Faber. In the following I will review Liang's 'view of life' ideas as they appeared in the *Essay* and in the *Mirror*.

Around 1903, the year that he visited North America, Liang was obviously deliberating how to divide his attention between the notions of individuality – meaning civil rights – and integrative collectivism, namely the individual's obligation toward the group. Before 1903, his concern centered on the civil rights of his New Citizen. At that time he still believed with Herbert Spencer[67] that competition among individuals would have positive effects on the well being of the whole. However, after 1903, Liang emphasized the concept of obligation (*yiwu* 義務). According to Chang Hao:

> Apparently frightened by the disruptive influence of the ideal of rights on many Chinese intellectuals who misunderstood it as a sanction for selfishness and licentiousness, Liang now reversed his emphasis and asserted the priority of obligations over rights.[68]

---

62 Piovesana, *Recent Japanese Philosophical Thought*, 47.
63 For the role of Japanese sources in Liang's study and work on Kant, see Huang Kewu 黃克武, "Liang Qichao yu Kangde" 梁啟超 與康德 (Liang Qichao and Kant). In *Zhongyang yanjiuyuan. Jindaishi yanjiu suojikan* 中央研究院, 近代史研究所集刊 Academica Sinica, Bulletin of the Institute of Modern History, vol. XXX (1998), 101–148.
64 Robert Scalapino and George T. Yu, *Modern China and Its Revolutionary Process*. Berkeley: University of California Press, 1985, 111.
65 Chang Hao, *Liang Ch'i-ch'ao and Intellectual Transition in China, 1890–1907*. Cambridge, Mass.: Harvard University Press, 1971, 133.
66 For a study of this neglected source see Chang Hao, *Liang Ch'i-ch'ao*, 272–295.
67 Herbert Spencer (1820–1903) introduced Darwin's idea of the struggle for survival into the realm of international politics.
68 Chang Hao, *Liang Ch'i-ch'ao*, 275.

B. Liang Qichao's Early Excursions in Kantian Philosophy 45

In the Kant *Essay*, writing about humanism (*rendao* 人道) as the foundation of philosophy (pp. 10–14), Liang analyzed the Kantian individual, suggesting the following differentiation. To Kant, he wrote, each individual possesses his own "true self" (*zhenwo* 真我) which transcends the categories of time and space, is governed by the principle of autonomy (*ziyou zhili* 自由之理), and is different from the selves of others. According to Liang, this "true self" complements the "phenomenal self" (*xianxiang zhiwo* 現象之我), which is subordinated to the principle of necessity (*bukebi zhili* 不可避之理). "In this respect, he observed, the Kantian teaching resembles *Huayan* Great Vehicle Buddhism."[69]

However, the Buddhists, Liang wrote (referring mainly to the Yogacara school), have a different "true self" in mind, the "major self" (*dawo* 大我),[70] which consists of all the "minor selves" (*xiaowo* 小我), of particular individuals. Associating the seeming multiple nature of the context of existence with the misleading function of consciousness, Liang contended that the differentiation of the phenomenal world resembles nothing but smoke, meaning, they are not real. Understanding the Buddhist doctrine, Liang assured us, we know not to trust in appearances (because they are partial).[71] Now, referring to the individual in Kant's works, Liang asked, should we divide the Buddhist "true self" (the "major self") into its particular components of "minor selves"? His answer was negative; we rather orient ourselves to face the reality of the "major self." At this stage of the *Essay* Liang contended that the Western sage failed to comprehend this one thing.[72]

According to Liang both Kant and the Buddhists speak about the "true self." The Buddhists name the "true self" as the "major self." However, the truth that Kant attributed to his notion of the "true self" was illusory. The fact is, asserted Liang, that what Kant really means by the "true self" is called by the Buddhists "thusness" (*zhenru* 真如, *bhutatathata*).[73] Liang added that what Wang Yangming called the innate knowledge of the good (*liangzhi* 良知) is also synonymous with "thusness".[74] On the other hand, what Kant calls the "phenomenal self" is comparable to the Buddhist non-enlightened (*wuming* 無明, *avidya*), the self who confuses the illusory for the real. In Liang's view, the Buddhist "true self" ranks above Kant's "true self." He

---

69 Liang Qichao, *Essay*, 12.
70 For a thought provoking article about the history and especially the political connotations of the Great Self in the history of republican China, see Thomas Fröhlich, "Das Grosse Ich: Religion, Evolution und Entpolitisierung bei Liang Qichao (1873–1929)" (The great self: religion, evolution and de-politization in Liang Qichao). *Oriens Extremus*, 41.1 (1998/99), 193–210.
71 Ibid., 12.
72 Ibid., 12.
73 The reader should bear in mind the critical remarks by Wang Guowei and He Lin, according to whom Liang took his misunderstanding of Buddhism to interpret his misunderstanding of Kant. Wang Guowei 王國維, "Lun jinnian xueshujie" (On the recent world of learning) 論今年之學術界. In *Wang Guantang quanji* (Collected works of Wang Guantang) 王觀堂全集, vol. V, 1767–1770. He Lin 賀麟, "Kangde Hei-ge-er zhexue dongjianji" (The Introduction of Kant and Hegel's Philosophy in the East). In *Zhongguo zhexue*, vol. II (April 1981), 343–387.
74 Liang Qichao, *Essay*, 18.

noted that within the store of consciousness of human nature (*xinghai shizang* 性海識藏), that is in this world, the individual has just "thusness," and non-enlightenment, to hold on to; at this level he remains wrapped in smoke. Transforming this level of consciousness – that is attaining the level of the Buddhist "major self," that is something the Buddhists associate with wisdom (*zhi* 智).[75]

Liang therefore thought that the practical consideration Kant associated with the individual should be applied to the "major self." The first step would be to recognize the "major self" which encompasses the numerous "minor selves." Two years later, in his *Mirror*, Liang proposed, now in an obvious Confucian tone, that the order of this recognition should follow from individual to family, and then to the whole country.[76] Eventually, Liang wrote – displaying a utopian vision – in the state of great unity (*datong* 大同) the "minor self" resolves the problems of selfishness and self profiting by applying himself to the "major self."[77]

The difference between the Buddhist (and Confucian) positions and Kant, according to Liang, seems to concern the nature of communal life. The Buddhist ideal involves social participation and mutual aid among all people, who jointly constitute the "major self." The "thusness" of the Buddhists, he wrote, is shared by all living beings, not just one. Hence, the Buddhists say that as long as a single living creature has not yet realized enlightenment (*buchengfo* 不成佛) – since all share the same body – none can attain enlightenment. This, wrote Liang, is the bodhisattva (*pudu* 普度) ideal of saving all with mercy.[78] To Kant, however, each individual forms a "true self" of his own. What mattered to Kant, Liang thought, was that the individual who aspires to goodness has the autonomy of his own body. Therefore, the Kantian self-cultivation program is simplistic and confined to the minor or true self.[79]

So far, Liang finds a weakness in the Western sage's concept of the individual, as compared to the "major self" in Buddhist thought. Yet, Liang seems to contradict himself, for in the same text he also presents a different position. Indeed, as indicated above, in the *Essay* Liang equated Kant's "true self" with Wang Yangming's innate knowledge of the good and with the Buddhists' "thusness." Eventually, he observed, however, in one respect the Kantian "true self" forms a synthesis of both. According to the Buddhists, whereas the "major self" stands for the accumulated souls of all living creatures, "thusness" fails to recognize this. Subsequently this consciousness differentiates the phenomenal world, falls into confusion, and regresses into evil. With Kant's "true self," the case is different. The association that Kant makes between the "true self" as he saw it and the ideas of moral duty (*daode*

---

75 Ibid., 14.
76 Liang Qichao, *Mirror*, 42.
77 Ibid., 43.
78 Liang Qichao, *Essay*, 14.
79 Ibid..

B. Liang Qichao's Early Excursions in Kantian Philosophy

zhi zeren 道德之責任) and moral effort (*gongfu* 功夫), made it possible for the individual to expand his concerns beyond himself to his fellow human beings.[80]

Liang's account of Kant's philosophy stipulated moral duty as a linkage between the individual and the whole of society. According to him, Kant's combination of the "true self" with the notion of moral duty implied the capacity to eliminate barriers among individuals in society. We note that while Faber discussed an integration of faith which established God at the center of all aspirations, Liang in his account of Kant referred to a transpersonal interrelatedness which involved persons realizing their moral duty. He dropped all cosmic implications that tradition attached to this ideal. To Liang, this linkage between moral duty and interrelatedness was the culmination of Kant's philosophy. In the final analysis, from this perspective, the philosophy of Kant has the same merit as the teaching of Wang Yangming and Buddhism.[81]

Liang recognized that in order to function as a linkage, interrelating the self with the social whole, the individual's moral duty must be associated with an autonomous element. As in Faber, a theory of knowledge provided the context for his discussion of autonomy. Liang tells his readers that for Kant, the world is perceived in terms of time and space; the properties belong not to the objects, but rather to our perception of them. Stating the *noumena-phenomena* distinction he claimed: since our perception is nothing but consciousness, the appearances, which are external to consciousness, cannot be known as they are in themselves.[82]

To prove autonomy Liang attempted a synthesis of the Kantian *noumena-phenomena* dichotomy with the substance-function (*tiyong* 體用) formula. Using the *tiyong* formula Liang interpreted that consciousness has the soul (*linghun* 靈魂) as its substance (*ti*) and knowledge as its function (*yong*).[83] The content of knowledge are perceptions of *phenomena* (appearances). According to Kant, he observed, the *phenomena* appear as constantly moving in space, they appear as changeable, they follow necessity, and cannot disappear; the substance of animate life (the soul) however, is synonymous with the *noumena*. It is not affected by time and space, is unchanging, autonomous, and imperishable. To know the shape and the movements of the soul within our body is impossible.[84] According to Liang, "The act of knowing [*phenomena*, function] and the soul [*noumena*, substance], are two things different in kind."[85] The involvement of the soul element in the process of knowledge led him to conclude that the individual is autonomous in his thought.

The appearances-substance dichotomy applies to human life. The body and the senses are appearances in time and space like other material things. The life of the

---

80 Ibid., 17.
81 Ibid., 16.
82 Ibid., 11.
83 *Essay*, 11.
84 Earlier Liang coupled the soul with the universe (shijie 世界) and God (shen 神), the Creator (zaohuazhu 造化主), who jointly constitute the ultimate ground of existence, that is, the Kantian noumena that cannot be accessed. Ibid., 10.
85 Ibid., 11.

body is not only an appearance in itself, it is also caused by one. Therefore, it cannot avoid the law of necessity and extinction. In the *Mirror* Liang said that each person has two levels of life. One is the bodily life, depicted as the soul's shell (*quqiao* 軀殼), which is perishable. This existence depends on food, drink, and sleep, in order to survive.[86] But we are not merely a physical body. Intertwined with the body and the senses, Liang continued, is the living, imperceptible substance of life, which transcends time and space. This substance is autonomous: "To infer from the body which is non-autonomous, that the substance too is non-autonomous, that is inconceivable."[87] The mind's soul (*xinhun* 心魂), he declared in the *Mirror*, is imperishable.[88] Liang's study of Kant led him to conclude that each individual contained a non-physical, spiritual mind substance, which is autonomous. But this substance coexists with the appearances. According to Kant, wrote Liang, in human life, "[...] the principle of autonomy and the principle of necessity coexist and are not antithetical."[89]

The autonomy of the knowing person is manifested, according to Liang's interpretation, in the sphere of morality. Outwardly, the spiritual substance of the mind, the autonomous substance of life, is manifested through the individual's moral choices.[90] Here Liang used the Confucian term *liangxin* 良心, which Mencius had used in the sense of "true heart,"[91] and Wang Yangming used as the innate mind.[92] Liang, however, suggested another meaning for this vital moral element. To Kant, he thought, *liangxin* equals the "true self,"[93] and to follow *liangxin* is to follow the categorical imperative (*daode zhi faling* 道德之法令).[94] This innate moral impulse, or "true self," *liangxin*, directs moral choices. In his *Mirror* Liang noted, referring to Wang's teaching, that the spiritual element in man's mind (*renxin zhiling* 人心之靈) informs the individual's knowledge. Regardless of external distractions, right and wrong are always distinguishable on first reflection.[95] In following the direction of *liangxin* and in assuming moral duties the "true self" realizes his autonomy.[96]

Apparently, Liang had managed to gather together the Confucian concepts of innate knowledge of the good (*liangzhi*) and *liangxin*, and the Kantian categorical imperative and "true self," as synonymous. But this intercultural equation glossed over a major difference that was basic to the two views. As indicated above, Liang's account of Kant's individual argued that thinking was sustained by a certain inner sub-

---

86 Liang Qichao, *Mirror*, 56.
87 Liang Qichao, *Essay*, 13.
88 Liang Qichao, *Mirror*, 56.
89 Liang Qichao, *Essay*, 12.
90 Ibid..
91 Benjamin I. Schwartz, *The World of Thought*, 268, 274. Original text see *Mencius*, 6A:8.
92 As mentioned above, to Onishi Hajime liangxin was conscience.
93 Liang Qichao, *Essay*, 17.
94 Ibid., 15.
95 Liang Qichao, *Mirror*, 27.
96 Liang Qichao, *Essay*, 15.

B. Liang Qichao's Early Excursions in Kantian Philosophy

stance. Liang combined the soul, and then the "true self," the categorical imperative, *liangxin*, and moral choice, as aspects of this inner substance – the core of the individual's autonomy. But to Kant, the transcendental element in man informed reason, and reason was inseparable from the individual's autonomy. A person is autonomous to the extent that he reasons. But whereas Kant presupposed the existence of God, Liang's concept of *liangxin* included no such source. Unlike Faber, who derived the authority for autonomy from noumenal transcendence and whose moral choice depended on God-given reason, Liang's moral choice relied on the individual's moral direction of *liangxin*.

The source of transcendence, within or without, significantly determined the status of reason. Indeed, as almost all critics indicate, Liang apparently failed to comprehend the underlying logic of Kant's moral philosophy.[97] Despite this justified criticism, it is worth noting that two years later, in the *Mirror*, Liang did associate free choice (*zhiyuan* 志願) with intellectual knowledge (*zhishi* 智識). Both, he believed, were interdependent.[98] However, it is wrong to rely on innate knowledge of the good (*liangzhi* 良知) alone: "When one is physically strong, nourishment is still indispensable. [Similarly,] Confidence in *liangzhi*, must not take over the need for self-cultivation."[99] Notwithstanding this clarification, to Liang, reason was neither specified as a quality of the human substance nor accepted as basis of autonomy.

The problem of reason thoroughly undermined Liang's interpretation of Kant. It became most visible in his criticism of science. Like Faber, Liang expressed reservations about science, but he formulated his concerns differently. Fearing the extent to which science can impinge on human life, Liang wrote that the problem of autonomy cannot be determined by either logicians (*lunlijia* 論理家) or scientists (*gezhijia* 格致家). Being themselves limited by the categories of causality the scientists cannot explain the direct experience of life; therefore they cannot be regarded as authoritative concerning autonomy.[100] In the *Mirror* Liang wrote that science cannot disown the learning of the body's mind as its foundation.[101] Subordinating scientific knowledge to the mind, Liang dissociated himself from reason that can be verified against the phenomenal world. Liang's claim that the autonomous moral substance of man is safeguarded from science, marked him as a true forerunner of the proponents of metaphysics in the 1923 controversy of the 'view of life'.

To Liang the goal of life was transpersonal interrelatedness among people, which he associated with the Buddhist "major self," in conjunction with the Bodhisattva ideal. Although he observed that Kant's stress on the individual clashed with Buddhist concepts, yet, considering the association that Kant had made between the au-

---

97 He Lin 賀麟, "Kangde Hei-ge-er zhexue dongjianji." Yu Yingshi 余英時, *Zhongguo jindai sixiangshi de Hu Shi* 中國近代思想史上的胡適 (Hu Shi and the history of modern Chinese thought). Taibei: Lianjing chubansheye gongsi, 1984, 56–57.
98 Liang Qichao, *Mirror*, 21.
99 Ibid., 56.
100 Liang Qichao, *Essay*, 14–15.
101 Ibid., 23.

tonomous individual and moral duty, he praised Kant and eventually credited his teaching with the goal of transpersonal interrelatedness. Unlike earlier Confucian thinkers Liang's integration was reduced to the area of human relationships. Traces of cosmic relatedness were removed. Moral duty became synonymous with the linkage for achieving this goal.

Explaining the autonomy of the person to apply this linkage Liang used Kant's *noumena-phenomena* dichotomy together with the *tiyong* formula. The substance corresponds to the *noumena*, function to the *phenomena*. Once the substance of knowledge, depicted as the soul, became associated with the *noumena*, relating this spiritual substance with innate morality, followed. *Liangxin*, the term he borrowed from Mencius and Wang Yangming, assumed the role of Kant's categorical imperative, guiding the individual's autonomous moral choices. But Liang failed to associate *liangxin* with reason as Kant had done. In the *Mirror* he implied that intellectual knowledge was inseparable from moral judgement. Yet at the same time he subordinated all knowledge exclusively to mind, thus dissociating rational thought from its grounds in objectivity.

Conclusion

Faber's and Liang's concepts of human nature started from different departure points. In his Chinese works Faber introduced a foreign theory which established a personal and an intentional God as the source and authority over all living beings and things. In fact he sought to change the entire perspective of his readers. Liang, on the other hand, avoided a clear statement about any sources of authority and their nature. Nevertheless, he was obviously transforming a number of traditional views. When he stipulated transpersonal interrelatedness rather than forming one body with the universe as a whole as the goal of life, it marked a significant departure from the traditional goal of life.

Both Faber and Liang were unable to appreciate the other culture's sense of spirituality. Inasmuch as Liang rejected the spirituality that Faber associated with God, Faber neglected the spirituality that the Chinese derived from forming one body with the whole universe, or as now suggested by Liang, from transpersonal interrelatedness. Seeking the purpose of life in the life of faith that consisted of his being in immediate relation to God beyond the mundane world, Faber's linkage concept, either of soul or of human nature, was to establish a connection between the individual and God. Liang's *liangxin* or moral duty removed barriers between people relating with each other.

Liang's failure to appreciate the role that reason played in Kant's concept of individual autonomy and morality, is possibly related to the absence of God from his ideas. Consequently, their definitions of the individual's autonomy differed considerably. Whereas Faber's individual derived his autonomy from God, to Liang, individual autonomy was innate and independent of any external source of transcendence. Whereas Faber referred to God to support a mind-reality correspondence, Liang was concerned almost exclusively with the role of the mind in interrelating people in society. Therefore, the concern for relations in society was more emphasized in Liang's thought. It also follows that being human was to Faber primarily to relate to God, and to Liang to relate in society.

To Liang, the *tiyong* appeared more as a philosophical formula than as a tool to differentiate between cultural origins, which it was for Zhang Zhidong, for example. Liang's readiness to absorb foreign ideas into his framework of what it means to be human is illustrated by his treatment of Kant. The noumena-phenomena dichotomy that for Faber explained individuality, namely, that each person subjectively sees things as they appear to him and not as they are in themselves, played a significant role in Liang's agenda. This is where the philosophical meeting, discussed in this study, of China and the West started. The philosophical argument which qualitatively distinguished appearances from substance that Liang discovered in Kant, enabled him to affirm the ideas of individual autonomy and humanness. He established the *noumena* within the person but not outside as well, as in Kant, and synthesized it with the *tiyong* formula, identifying the *noumena* with the substance (*ti*). The *noumenal* substance now became the substance of what it means to be human. This substance was, according to Liang, comparable to Kant's "true self" with its categorical imperative and moral duty and effort, which he associated with the linkage and its moral implications in traditional Chinese ideas. This formulation charged the individual with an innate moral impulse that interrelates him with other people.

Regarding the 'view of life' problem, Faber's synthesis raised issues that engaged Chinese minds in the 1920s and afterwards as well. His notions of individual autonomy and uniqueness preceded later arguments. The Christian concept of God also offered new grounds for a radically different context of all existence. As for Liang, both *Essay* and *Mirror* reveal that what he sought to defend by suggesting the various philosophical dichotomies was exactly that spiritual element responsible for moral choices by means of which interpersonal barriers are removed. Both Faber and Liang felt the threat of the materialistic and mechanistic explanations of the person's humanness. Faber emphasized that materialism must coexist with spirituality, and that humanness should be the foundation of all considerations about society. Establishing a *noumenal* substance within the individual, Liang differentiated between the causal sphere of matter and the living sphere of people who autonomously make moral choices.

CHAPTER THREE

Prelude to the 1923 Controversy

During the two decades before the 1923 'view of life' controversy, intellectual communications between Chinese and foreigners increased greatly. More Chinese intellectuals went abroad, Western philosophers came to visit, and Chinese translations and critical works appeared in print. During this period a view that leaned exclusively on science suggested a positivist picture of a world in which both man and the phenomenal world are materialistic, mechanistic and naturalistic. Later scholars referred to this view by the name 'scientism'. It challenged both Liang Qichao's revision of the traditional view and the religious view propagated by Ernst Faber, in their interpretations of Kant's philosophical ideas.

At the same time, intellectuals who associated mind with spiritual and moral values continued to be heard. This chapter discusses the early twentieth century split between those who considered personal autonomy in terms of innate morality, and those who applied positivist approaches to mental processes and life. The former used the ideas of Kant and other idealist thinkers together with traditional Chinese ideas. The first part of this chapter discusses the Western background and five Western philosophers, Henri Bergson (1859–1941), Rudolf C. Eucken (1846–1926), John Dewey (1851–1952), Bertrand Russell (1872–1970) and Hans Driesch (1867–1941), who were directly involved in the intellectual process that culminated in the 1923 controversy.

The second part will introduce two works by Liang Qichao (梁啟超 1873–1929) and Liang Shuming (梁漱溟 1893–1988). They were the first Chinese intellectuals to attempt a synthesis of Chinese and Western idealist ideas that aimed at redefining the essence of Chinese culture in view of the changing times. The two Liangs used different terms, but both addressed broad issues by raising questions of person and society and Chinese and Western cultures, in their attempts to point the way toward a sounder 'view of life' of Chinese and humankind.

A. Resistance to Scientism in China: Foreign Sources

Toward the end of the nineteenth century and the beginning of the twentieth, the status of determinism – the doctrine that advocates the causal and necessary relations of all processes – steadily increased in European intellectual circles. This side effect of the growing prestige of science gained strength by further concrete scientific achievements. Philosophers of science such as Thomas Huxley, Ernst Mach, and Karl Pearson, were leaders of this trend. The basic argument of this movement, generally labeled positivism, assumed an analogous correspondence between mind and reality. Positivism proposed to embrace all phenomena along with the mental faculties of man in one uniform system, suggesting that the phenomenal world is matter.

The positivist argument rests on three main currents: materialism, according to which reality is matter alone, with no other element beyond it; mechanism, which describes the world and all its constituents as a machine-like structure consisting of physical bodies, which are mechanical, and whose dynamic movements can be calculated. And also naturalism, which allows for evolutionary explanations, emphasizing the relations between antecedents and the struggle for survival. According to this sequence of assumptions, man, body and mind are material phenomena among other material phenomena. Applied to human life positivist ideas are synonymous with scientism.

For many, the fusion between the sciences with their deterministic explanations, and human mentality, created an artificial mixture that threatened the assumption of the autonomy of man. The consequences of this threat were of major importance to morality. Indeed, what is the value of a moral action that is not generated by free choice? The obvious critics of the positivists were idealist philosophers. They argued for a more-than-matter reality, claiming that the function of mind involved a spiritual element that was not subject to the rules of matter. In life there is a moral and autonomous element at the individual's disposal that defies mechanistic and materialist explanations. Affirming the internal spirituality of man, idealists argued that the determinist explanation is not applicable to human behavior and to the moral capacity of man.

As discussed in chapter one, traditional Chinese thinkers had also rejected determinism. Accordingly, those who challenged the deterministic claims of scientism in 1923, preserved the belief in the person's ability to "calm the mind and determine destiny" (*anxin liming* 安心立明),[1] of their own intellectual tradition while accepting foreign idealist trends. Throughout the controversy and thereafter they were identified by their association with metaphysics. During the May Fourth period however, they faced an unprecedented upsurge in the status of science, and of determinism which came with it. European idealism helped the Chinese supporters of human spiritual capacities to recognize the problem, and provided the argumentation and authority to resist it. Two philosophers in particular, Henri Bergson of France and Rudolf C. Eucken of Germany had an impact on Chinese metaphysics prior to and during the May Fourth period.

---

1 This Zen-Buddhist maxim was and is used to characterize the supporters of the Confucian tradition during the late nineteenth and the twentieth century.

Henri Bergson and Rudolf Eucken

Years before World War I, Henri Bergson became a forerunner of an increasingly skeptical attitude towards positivism in Europe. In four major publications between 1889–1907 he shifted intellectual attention from the isolated details that affect human life from the outside, toward the internal mental life of consciousness.[2] The central persuasion of Bergson's thought consisted of recognizing the gap between the flow of time in reality, and the perception of time by the intellect, which superficially divides time into well-defined measures. Bergson suggested solving this inconsistency by means of a dualistic differentiation. On the one hand, he divided reality between inanimate and living things. On the other, he split consciousness into intellect and intuition, arguing on this basis that the intellect is the proper medium for managing the inanimate material world by the methods of science. Intuition however, is the proper medium by means of which to access the sphere of internal life. At the same time he argued that the twofold structure of consciousness reveals its intrinsic pull to adjust to matter, and to simultaneously preserve its hold on the flow of life.

Once Bergson posited that "[...] the twofold structure of consciousness corresponds to the twofold structure of reality," he was able to stipulate a dependent relationship between knowledge and metaphysics.[3] Knowledge has to pass through metaphysical speculation, where intuition – as a kind of innate knowledge – occupies an authoritative position. A person, Bergson argued, is capable of exercising free will, making his life an unpredictable experience.[4] He used images of waves and flow to articulate his view:

> Life as a whole, from the initial impulsion that thrust it into the world, will appear as a wave which rises, and which is opposed by the descending movement of matter. On the greater part of its surface, at different heights, the current is converted by matter into a vortex. At one point alone it passes freely, dragging with it the obstacle which will weigh on its progress but will not stop it. At this point is humanity; it is our privileged situation. On the other hand, this rising wave is consciousness, and, like all consciousness, it includes potentialities without number [...]. Consciousness is essentially free; it is freedom itself; but it cannot pass through matter without settling on it, without adapting itself to it.[5]

---

2 *Essai sur les Données Immédiates de Conscince*, 1889 (*Time and Free Will*, 1910), *Matière et Mémoire*, 1896 (*Matter and Memory*, 1911), *Introduction à la Métaphysique*, 1903 (*Introduction to Metaphysics*, 1903), and *L'evolution Créatrice*, 1907 (*Creative Evolution*, 1911).
3 Henri Bergson, *Creative Evolution*. Trans. Arthur Mitchell. New York: The Modern Library, 1944, 196.
4 Henri Bergson, *Time and Free Will: An Essay on the Immediate Data of Consciousness*. Trans. F.L. Pogson. New York: The Macmillan Publishers, 1950, 140–221.
5 Bergson, *Creative Evolution*, 293–294.

Bergson sought to transcend the deterministic implications of positivistic explanations of behavior of the mind. His call for a synthesis of intellect with intuition and matter with spirit, was intended to secure the primacy of free will over necessity. The human capacity to exercise free will, leads to the association of spiritual attainments with a transcendental value. Like the Song neo-Confucians, Bergson's vision acknowledged individuality and yet depicted life as a whole as a great flowing river: "All the living hold together, and all yield to the same tremendous push."[6] Among its main ideas Bergson's philosophy highlighted a whole spectrum of humanistic ideas: the element of creativity in human life, freedom that includes compromise, the solidarity of life as a whole, and the hope for a valuable and meaningful existence.

At the university of Jena in Germany, at the same time, Rudolf C. Eucken lectured on the problem of human life. His explanations carried an obvious religious message. Whereas Ernst Haeckel (1843–1919), Eucken's coleague at Jena, supported a determinist explanation for the behavior of the mind, Eucken proposed to differentiate between material and spiritual life. At the center of Eucken's *Lebensanschauung* was activism, namely, a person's capacity to become involved in life and to resist determinism.[7] Anti-positivism marked his writings since before the turn of the twentieth century. Eucken criticized materialism, mechanism, and naturalism, and championed faith in a spiritual life. He highlighted the emptiness of material life:

> We would have expected, when life became so much richer, more plastic, and more pleasurable, and when unceasing progress was made in every direction, that an overflowing happiness would have filled men's hearts. How does it come about that the very opposite has occurred, that we have become depressed rather than elated?[8]

At the same time the mechanistic effects of progress worried him:

> It is obvious that the age of the daily newspaper and the machine must exert a peculiarly powerful pressure upon the individual; its influences, working in masses, stifle from the very beginning really personal activity and feeling; no other epoch has so reduced man to a mere cog in a great machine.[9]

Regarding the Naturalist approach underlying this progress:

---

6   Ibid., 295.
7   For Eucken's activism, see Meyrick Booth, *Rudolf Eucken: His Philosophy and Influence*. London: T. Fisher Unwin, 1913, 32.
8   Rudolf Eucken, "Against Pessimism." In *Collected Essays of Rudolf Eucken*. Ed. and trans. Meyrick Booth. New York: Charles Scribner's Sons, 1914, 170. The article first appeared in 1910.
9   Eucken, "The Reflection of the Age in its Concepts," ibid., 338. The article first appeared in 1893.

> The mechanism of the soul was at first spoken of as a simile, but the simile frequently overmastered the thought and drew the concepts within the circle of ideas of naturalism. In the contrary sense, concepts appear to be finally dismissed because there is no room for them in the sensuous reality. The rejection of metaphysics, teleology, and so forth, is largely to be explained in this way.[10]

Similar to Bergson, Eucken emphasized the spiritual life and its transcendental value:

> For the life of man does not exhaust itself in the life-impulse of the separate points. [...] life comes together to form a whole, and it is precisely this whole which we call *spiritual life*. In it there becomes visible a cosmic movement, an ascent of reality to a new stage far transcending the desire and capacity of the mere man.[11]

The holistic character of this vision should not escape us here. Eucken explicitly saw the spiritual life in terms of a dynamic of integration:

> Since here life does not proceed in relations from point to point, but is lived in the whole, and, moreover, always sets the individual in relation with the whole, it has also a different relationship with time and time events.[12]

Finally, against the pessimism of the age Eucken expressed the optimistic hope contained in the new mode of life:

> The complications of the age, reviewed from this standpoint, are realised to be indications of a great flux. [...] A joyful view of human affairs will then return [...].[13]

Eucken's *Lebensphilosophie* is notable for its direct and simplified style. He used the term "life," not in the biological sense but as an image critical of the degeneration and emptiness in the culture of the period, on the one hand, and as supporting dynamism and creativity, and furnishing human existence with content and meaning, on the other.[14] In 1908, the Nobel Prize Foundation appreciated the humanism of Eucken's thought and justified the decision to award him the literature prize with the following words:

> In recognition of his earnest search for truth, his penetrating power of thought, his wide range of vision, and the warmth and strength in presenta-

---

10 Ibid., 342.
11 Eucken, "Against Pessimism," ibid., 175. Italics in original.
12 Eucken, "The Problem of Immortality," ibid., 203. The article first appeared in 1908.
13 Eucken, "Against Pessimism," ibid., 171.
14 Herbert Schnadelbach, *Philosophy in Germany 1831–1933*. Trans. Eric Mathews. Cambridge: Cambridge University Press, 1984, 139.

tion with which in his numerous works he has vindicated and developed an idealistic philosophy of life.[15]

Bergson and Eucken's counter-positivist thought was marked by dualistic conceptions. They saw all phenomena as twofold relationships. The internal human factor, they argued, differs from, and is not analogously affected by the physical and social affairs that surround it. As far as human existence is concerned, they said, the measure of the discourse has to be "life," as it is intrinsically experienced, independent of positivistic reasoning. This framework reserved an internal space for the human being to autonomously experience life within a meaningful context.

The ideas of Bergson and Eucken were criticized by their contemporaries. John Dewey and Bertrand Russell were two of Bergson's main critics. Yet, hindsight suggests that the ideas of Bergson and Eucken which appeared before and during the first decade of the twentieth century conveyed a timely warning. Indeed, as Isaiah Berlin observes, even before World War I,

> [...] it became increasingly clear both to disinterested historical observers and still more to the victims of the new industrial age in Europe that the sum of human misery had not been appreciably decreased.[16]

The advent of the Great War raised fears of ever greater human suffering, and even the threat of extermination. The emerging cultural discourse came to involve questions about the value of human existence and its meaning. The war spelled out pessimistic views and the close of an age for European and Western critics. Views varied, but almost all accepted the diagnosis according to which something had gone wrong in modern Western attitude toward human life. Critics on the whole recognized the existence of a crisis, demanding new remedies. Oswald Spengler's title *The Decline of the West*[17] displays the extent of doubt. Dada, the artistic trend that called for creativity through total rejection, illustrates another radical aspect of the same critical pattern.[18] At the same time science was unceasingly evolving, though the commitments to it were not necessarily fully updated.

After the war ended the negative effects of modern life were fervently discussed in European intellectual circles; stressing the pace of life, social exploitation, emptiness, and desperation. Dichotomous contrasts imposing a superficial distinction between conceptions that actually complement each other surfaced, such as: spirituality vs. materialism; humanism vs. mechanism; subjectivism vs. objectivism; in-

---

15 *Nobel Prize Foundation Directory 1991–1992.* Stockholm: Sturetrycket AB., 1992, 120.
16 Isaiah Berlin, "Joseph de Maistre and the Origins of Fascism." *New York Review of Books,* (September 27, 1990), 58.
17 Published in summer 1918 but prepared before the war.
18 The group was established in Paris in 1919. For Chinese intellectuals familiar with that movement see Lee Leo Ou-fan, "Literary Trends I: The Quest for Modernity, 1895–1927." In *The Cambridge History of China.* Eds. John K. Fairbank and Denis Twitchett. Cambridge: Cambridge University Press, vol. XII, 1986, 496.

tuition vs. intellect; consciousness vs. knowledge; and internal vs. external. Once the "East vs. West" dichotomy joined the scene, one member of these pairs was associated with the East and its opposite with the West.

Chinese intellectual circles similarly wavered between dual distinctions, ascribing materialism, intellect and so on to the West. But an alternative tendency also appeared. Richard Wilhelm (1873–1930), the learned German sinologist who was personally associated with a number of Chinese intellectuals, maintained that the reaction to World War I in effect revived the original Chinese spirit.[19] In 1924 he observed that at a certain moment Chinese civilization seemed doomed to succumb "to the terrible jaws of the monstrous European mechanical [civilization] [...]." But the Great War, he believed, stimulated a counter movement.[20]

The attraction of some May Fourth intellectuals to the ideas of Bergson and Eucken is evident from the numerous articles on their thought, translations of their works, and the invitations to come and lecture in China, which they declined.[21] Two main reasons explain this attraction: the prestige their works had in Europe and in Japan,[22] and the apparent similarity to traditional Chinese categories of thought (discussed in chapter five). Despite these, quite likely, Bergson and Eucken would have remained marginal on the Chinese intellectual scene, had not World War I shattered confidence in positivist thinking in Europe itself. As a result idealist thought gained relevance and some Chinese intellectuals challenged Chinese scientism which at that time was the most prominent current of thought.

John Dewey and Bertrand Russell

Between 1919–1921, during the height of the May Fourth era, China hosted two outstanding Western philosophers. First came John Dewey who was welcomed in China by his former students at Columbia, among them Hu Shi (胡適 1891–1962) and Jiang Menglin (蔣夢麟 1886–1964). Dewey was invited by the Lecture Society

---

19 Wilhelm came to China originally to assist Ernst Faber. For Wilhelm's debt to Faber, see Ursula Richter, "Richard Wilhelm – Founder of a Friendly China Image in Twentieth Century Germany." In *Zhongyang yanjiuyuan. Jindaishi yanjiu suojikan* 中央研究院, 近代 史研究所集刊 (Academica Sinica, Bulletin of the Institute of Modern History), XX (June, 1990), 161.
20 Richard Wilhelm, "Intellectual Movements in Modern China." *Chinese Social and Political Science Review*, 8:2 (April 1924), 118.
21 *Minduo zazhi* 民鐸雜志 (Min-Toh Monthly) 3.1 (December 1921) was dedicated to Bergson. Zhang Dongsun translated *Creative Evolution* and *Matter and Mind* in 1919 and 1922. For Eucken's account of his relations with China and Japan, see Rudolf Eucken, *Rudolf Eucken: His Life, Works, and Travels*. Trans. Joseph McCabe. New York: Charles Scribner's Sons, 1922, 176–179, 204–205.
22 For Bergson and Eucken's wide popularity in early twentieth century Japanese intellectual circles see Gino K. Piovesana, *Recent Japanese Philosophical Thought: 1862–1962. A Survey*. Tokyo: Enderle Bookstore, 1968, 74–75. I am indebted to Prof. Sumio Ikeda for enlightening me about some facts on the reception of Bergson and Eucken's ideas in Japan.

(*Jiangxueshe* 講學社), whose chief sponsor was Liang Qichao and his Progressive Party (*Jinbudang* 進步黨), and remained in China from May 1919 to July 1921. The following lines from his *Lectures in China* illustrate the main message of his pragmatic philosophy:

> From time immemorial mankind has been subject to two errors, deficiency and excess. In times of crisis men have tended to be either too radical or too conservative. They have fallen into the trap of either-or, tending to regard everything they see as either good or bad. Yet our common sense and our everyday observation tell us that the problems of human life cannot be solved either by completely discarding our habits, customs, and institutions, or by doggedly hanging on to them and resisting all efforts to modify and reconstruct them.
>
> What mankind needs most is the ability to recognize and pass judgement on *facts* ... we must deal with concrete problems by concrete methods when and as these problems present themselves in our experience.[23]

Dewey upheld Experimentalism as "... a method of applying human action to creating a connection between the functions of the mind on the one hand and the facts of nature on the other."[24] The material and technological progress man achieves in this way, supposedly confirms his confidence in his intellectual capacities, and his critical thinking based on reason. Solving the problems of life will lead to a moral way of living. Life then will consist of new hope, new courage, and a new dimension of honesty.[25] Dewey thus established a linkage between material accomplishments which ensure scientific progress, and moral life.

In his lectures Dewey highlighted social living or what he called "the associated human living," meaning that a "human being lives in – and can live only in – some sort of association with other human beings."[26] This mode of life required the following essential factors: "... free and open communication, unself-seeking and reciprocal relationships, and the sort of interaction that contributes to mutual advantage."[27] This emphasis on associated living brings to mind the shift that Liang Qichao had suggested from the integration ideal to transpersonal inter-relatedness, the difference being that Dewey's model did not establish innate morality. Education was the cornerstone. Dewey advocated learning that would provide students with the tools to develop their intelligence. His educational program cultivated "conservation of culture through spoken and written language,"[28] and values such as open minded-

---

23 John Dewey, *Lectures in China, 1919–1920*. Eds. and trans. Robert W. Clopton and Ou Tsuin-chen. Honolulu: East-West Center, 1973, 53.
24 Ibid., 246.
25 Ibid., 243–244.
26 Ibid., 85.
27 Ibid., 92.
28 Ibid., 212.

ness, intellectual integrity, and accountability, to equip students with an experimental, critical, and scientific approach. He asserted that students who followed this program would eventually act as moral individuals in a moral society.[29]

Benjamin Schwartz observed that Dewey's

> [...] experimental method of science in its reliance on tentative hypotheses applied to the study of 'problematic situations' represented a rejection of all spiritual authority and all pre-established dogma – whether religious, political or metaphysical.[30]

This observation should be accepted, though with some reservations. Dewey did, in fact, acknowledge the value of tradition as the heritage of the past from which the present develops. He also argued that philosophy and not science should be held as the most complete system of knowledge. What is more, he said that "[...] it is in the spiritual realm that we locate the ultimate values of associated human living."[31] Nonetheless, Chinese intellectuals understood Dewey to say that traditional categories of thought should be replaced. He did, in fact, support rendering "science authoritative in control of human behavior."[32] Dewey seemed to them to support those who were against tradition and to reinforce the view of scientism.

Toward the end of 1920, while Dewey's influence was gathering momentum in Chinese intellectual circles, another prominent guest of the Lecture Society visited China. The renowned English philosopher, Bertrand Russell, accompanied by Dora Black, arrived shortly after a visit to Bolshevik Russia. He remained in China from October 1920 to July 1921, which, however, included a long period of illness. Two future supporters of metaphysics, Zhang Dongsun 張東蓀 (1886–1962) and Qu Shiying 瞿世英 (1900–1976), escorted Russell during his visit.[33]

Like Dewey, Russell stressed education. The objectives of education are the four values of vitality, courage, sensitivity, and intelligence. Jointly they form the foundation of the ideal individual's character in a healthy society.[34] In Russell's view, China's problems were generated by the inconsistency between Chinese culture and the nature of the Chinese people, on the one hand, and the actual economic and social situation, together with relations with Western civilization, on the other.[35] He

---

29 Ibid., 252–260.
30 Benjamin Schwartz, "Themes in Intellectual History: May Fourth and After." In *The Cambridge History of China* vol. XII. John K. Fairbank and Denis Twitchett, eds. Cambridge: Cambridge University Press, 1986, 424–425.
31 Dewey, *Lectures in China*, 173.
32 Ibid., 168.
33 Qu published articles that introduced Russell's ideas before and after his visit. For Zhang as one of Russell's Chinese escorts, see Susan P. Ogden, "The Sage in the Inkpot: Bertrand Russell and China's Social Reconstruction in the 1920s," *Modern China*, 16.4 (1982), 586.
34 Bertrand Russell, "The Aims of Education." In *Selected Papers of Bertrand Russell*. New York: Modern Library, 1927, 159–193.
35 Russell, "Chinese and Western Civilizations." In *Selected Papers of Bertrand Russell*, 208–224. A similar proposal was made by Gottfried Wilhelm Leibniz (1646–1716).

suggested an East-West reconciliation to solve these problems. The West excels, according to Russell, in the scientific approach to life, and the Chinese are best in conceptualizing the goals of life.[36] He said: "I wish I could hope that China, in return for our scientific knowledge, may give us something of her large tolerance and contemplative peace of mind."[37]

Chinese intellectuals found Russell's understanding of their problems somewhat puzzling. All around he was credited with the messages people actually wanted to hear. Supporters of tradition embraced his recognition of the spirituality of Chinese civilization; the proponents of science drew encouragement from Russell's anti-religious criticism which they found supportive for their arguments against tradition.[38]

Russell, the famed World War I pacifist, acknowledged the value of spirituality and supported the cause of morality and ethics. But in the early 1920's he also subscribed to the views of the empirical positivists. In a series of lectures delivered at Peking University, and published in 1921 under the title *The Analysis of Mind*, he said:

> The question whether it is possible to obtain precise causal laws in which the causes are psychological, not material, is one of detailed investigation ... It seems to be by no means an insoluble question, and we may hope that science will be able to produce sufficient grounds for regarding one answer as much more probable than the other ... Causal laws so stated would, I believe, be applicable to psychology and physics equally; the science in which they were stated would succeed in achieving what metaphysics has vainly attempted, namely, a unified account of what really happens [in the mind] ...[39]

These statements indicate that unlike Bergson who sought to establish the autonomy of the individual's mind, Russell tended to profess the attainability of a causal explanation.

Dewey and Russell differed in their impressions of China. One explanation for this involves the timing of their arrival in China.[40] Whereas the former was primarily struck by the enthusiasm of the intellectuals he found there, the latter expressed his admiration for the moral and ethical standards of Chinese culture.[41] Russell thought

---

36 Ibid., 219.
37 Ibid., 224.
38 D.W.Y. Kwok, *Scientism in Chinese Thought, 1900–1950*. New Haven: Yale University Press, 1965, 16, note 20. Raoul D. Findeisen finds that *The Prospects of Industrial Civilization* (1924), jointly written by Russell and Dora Black following their discussions of that topic during their stay in Beijing, suggested a position quite similar to that of the 1923 metaphysicians. See Findeisen, "Professor Luo. Reflections on Bertrand Russell in China." *Asian and African Studies* (Bratislava), 3.1 (1994), 15.
39 Bertrand Russell, *The Analysis of Mind*. London: George Allen and Unwin, 1921, 305–306.
40 R. D. Findeisen, "Vier westliche Philosophen in China," *Minima Sinica* 2 (1991), 1–36.
41 For Lu Xun's sarcastic remark about Russell's praise of the sedan-chair bearers who smiled at him, see Jonathan Spence, *The Gate of Heavenly Peace: The Chinese and Their Revolution 1895–1980*. New York: Penguin Books, 1981, 217.

it possible to preserve the existing foundations while making some adjustments for the sake of progress. His message seemed to support the substance-function (*tiyong*) formula, in his counsel to preserve China's accomplishments in the areas of morality and ethics, and simultaneously to adopt technology and the methods of science. He emphatically rejected mechanism. Dewey, on the other hand, was understood to support replacing the old categories of thought with new ones. Nonetheless, during their China stay, both rejected ascribing mere moral and spiritual connotations to the mind.

Dewey's and Russell's presence in China contributed to the reception of their ideas; this was an advantage that the ideas of Bergson and Eucken did not have. The former were able to offer judgments and notions concerning concrete problems encountered in China. With the latter the case was different.[42] Nonetheless, the ideas of Bergson and Eucken were available to Chinese intellectuals to interpret and use, as, in fact, they did in the 1923 controversy. Moreover, the philosophical trend to which Bergson and Eucken subscribed was soon re-represented in China by the visit of one of their contemporaries.

Hans Driesch

More than a year after both Dewey and Russell left China the philosopher and biologist Hans Driesch (1867–1941) arrived from Germany, remaining in China from October 1922 to June 1923.[43] As a biologist, Driesch's philosophical career had a positivist point of departure. Indeed, insofar as his early views are concerned, he subscribed to a dogmatic and mechanistic theory that did not acknowledge the existence of immaterial phenomena. But during the last decade of the nineteenth century he changed his views and argued that both nature and human life entail autonomous processes.[44] The Driesch who came to China had scientific achievements to his name, but subscribed to an anti-positivistic philosophy.[45] He lectured in China in either German or English, and the leading metaphysics supporter in the 1923 contro-

---

42 Although not a direct contact, mention should be made of the interview conducted by Zhang Junmai and Lin Zhijun with Bergson in Paris on May 26, 1921. See *Min-toh tsa-chih* 3.1 (December 1921). There is also the book co-authored by Eucken and Zhang. Rudolf C. Eucken and Carsun Chang (Zhang Junmai), *Das Lebensproblem in China und in Europa* (The problem of life in China and in Europe). Leipzig: Quelle and Meyer, 1922.
43 Eucken had first raised the name of Driesch as a possible candidate for a China lecture tour to Jiangxueshe 講學社 (Lecture society) representatives. Roger B. Jeans, *'Syncretism in Defense of Confucianism': An Intellectual and Political Biography of the Early Years of Chang Chunmai, 1887–1923*. Ph.D. Dissertation, George Washington University, 1974, 211–224.
44 Rudolf Otto, *Naturalism and Religion*. Trans. Arthur J. Thomson. London: Williams and Norgate, 1907, 266–268.
45 During his stay in China Driesch was regularly in touch with Richard Wilhelm who subscribed to similar ideas. See, Hans and Margarete Driesch, *Fern-Ost* (The Far East). Leipzig: Brockhaus, 1925, 203.

versy over the 'view of life', Zhang Junmai 張君勱 (1887–1965), who knew both languages, acted as simultaneous translator.[46]

Driesch delivered lectures on philosophical subjects in Nanjing for three months, and on the history of philosophy from Descartes to Kant for six months in Beijing. Upon demand, psychology was added, and eventually made the more lasting impression of his tour. Lecturing on the problem of the mind in Beijing, Driesch took issue with the earlier Russell lectures on the mind.[47] His psychology lectures culminated in the discussion on "The problem of freedom." The following is the gist of what he said:

> It is *only* under the *aspect of freedom* that consciousness becomes important. [...] No other aspect is imaginable under which consciousness might become really important; without this aspect [of freedom] we are forced to regard the world from the esthetic point of view exclusively, that is as a sort of mere theatrical performance [...]. And thus man may be a moral automaton! How to avoid this paradox I do not know![48]

Like Russell before him, Driesch was unable to define the mind's workings, but each approached the problem differently. Whereas the former viewed mind as something material, subordinated to causality, Driesch believed it possible to find a spiritual element within the mind associated with moral autonomy. Supporting the free will argument Driesch introduced a basic distinction between degrees of freedom. Bergsonian freedom, he thought, means that human action "[...] is neither determined by the medium, nor by the past history of the thing [person] in which it occurs, nor by the *essence* of that thing [person]." Driesch confined his own discussion of mental phenomena to a less radical definition which he associated with Kant and Spinoza, who, according to him, preserved the linkage between freedom and the essence of the self. In a way, this brings to mind Liang Qichao's attempt to reconcile the *tiyong* formula and the Kantian noumen-phenomena dichotomy (chapter two, 50). Driesch considered essence an *a priori* condition to autonomy and freedom.[49]

While Dewey and Russell appealed to a wide segment of the Chinese intellectual scene, Driesch spoke only to a narrow audience. The high tide of the May Fourth had subsided and philosophy was by now an established field of academic study. The sparser attendance at his lectures is perhaps an indication of the smaller support that talk about spiritual elements would have in the approaching 1923 controversy.[50]

---

46 Jeans, *Chang Chun-mai*, 446–464. For Chinese publication of the Driesch lectures, see *Dulishu jiangyanlu* (The Driesch lectures) 杜理舒講演錄. Trans. Zhang Junmai 張君勱 et al. Shanghai: Shangwu yinshuguan, 1923.
47 Like Russell's *Analysis*, the Driesch psychology lectures were later published. Driesch, *The Crisis in Psychology*. Princeton, NJ: Princeton University Press, 1925. The dialogue thus continued worldwide.
48 Ibid., 249, 252. Italics in original.
49 Ibid., 243.
50 For the Chinese iconoclasts, see Charlotte Furth, "Intellectual Change: from the Reform Move-

The majority of intellectuals regarded science as the method best-suited for emulation in order to achieve progress and to save China. Therefore, mysticism and spirituality, that people like Bergson, Eucken and then Driesch represented, were taken with an air of suspicion. The idealist trend seemed to disrupt the course of scientific progress. Furthermore, its ideas were easily associated with what most May Fourth intellectuals (even if still under its influence) abhorred most: Confucian ideas and Confucian modes of thought.

B. Resistance to Scientism in China: First Chinese Attempts to Reconcile Chinese and Western Ideas

Much as foreign ideas were involved in the Chinese resistance to scientism, an internal dynamic to this process was also evident. In 1919 and 1921, Liang Qichao and Liang Shuming published works marking the beginning of resistance to or rather attack on scientism.[51] Both expressed a strong commitment to Confucian traditions – and to a lesser degree to Buddhism – as the departure for their criticism of the positivist tendencies prevalent among their contemporaries. Their works re-examined the problem of individual autonomy together with questions of culture and civilization. Both used the ideas of Bergson and Eucken to support their arguments. Both also did not oppose science. They rather were concerned lest the function (*yong*) part of the *tiyong* formula would overwhelm the substance (*ti*) of Chinese culture. Accordingly, they sought ways to accept science but at the same time to secure the moral and spiritual values that science seemed to endanger.

The Reflections of Liang Qichao

At the end of April and the beginning of May 1919, the Versailles peace talks were not yet concluded. Liang Qichao was there as head of a semi-official delegation,[52] in addition to the geologist Ding Wenjiang 丁文江 (1887–1936) and Zhang Junmai – the leading participants in the controversy over the 'view of life' four years later.

---

ment to the May Fourth Movement, 1895–1920." In *The Cambridge History of China* vol. XII. John K. Fairbank and Denis Twitchett, eds. Cambridge: Cambridge University Press, 1986, 396–401; Kwok, *Scientism*, 11–15; and Chow Tse-tsung, *The May Fourth Movement: Intellectual Revolution in Modern China*. Cambridge, Mass.: Harvard University Press, 1960, 364.

51 Liang Qichao 梁啟超, "Ouyou xinying lu jielu" 歐游心影綠節錄 (Reflections on a trip to Europe). In *Yin bing shi zhuanji* 飲冰室專集 (Collected works of the Ice-Drinker's Studio). Lin Zhijun 林志均 (Lin Zaiping 林宰平), ed. Shanghai: Zhonghua shuju, vol. XXIII, 1936, 1–162. Hereafter *Reflections*. The relevant part of this discussion (pp. 1–38) was published in Shishi xinbao, March 1919. Liang Shuming 梁漱溟. *Dong Xi wenhua ji qi zhexue* 東西文化 及其哲學 (Eastern and Western cultures and their philosophies). Taibei: Liren shuju yinxing, 1983. Hereafter *Cultures*.

52 They were authorized to advise the formal Chinese delegates at the conference.

Aside from their function as observers, the delegates also traveled in war-torn Europe. Theirs was not a holiday excursion. They explored the culture of various states, they visited famous sights and met with intellectuals. The best known account of that journey appeared in Liang's *Reflections* and was intended as a window for viewing the state of Europe's civilization across the sea.

Liang's *Reflections* were apparently an attempt to probe the culture-civilization problem[53] in order to save China. For that purpose the text criticized Western civilization and tried to come to terms with its uses of science, and praised the spirituality of the East. It is not a systematic work. The exact meaning of the text is elusive; to uncover the message the ideas must be recombined and reordered. The following is an analysis of two principal parts of his *Reflections*. In one part, that is section number seven, he criticized the dream of the omnipotence of science (*kexue wanneng zhi meng* 科學萬能之夢).[54] In the other part, section thirteen, he referred to China's responsibility to involve herself in intercultural relationships, select the essential from the West, and provide the West with the assistance that it needs.[55]

Liang begins by suggesting that each person is ordinarily able "to calm the mind and determine destiny," namely, to internally realize himself and become involved in society. To contemporary European man, however, he observed, internal self realization was no longer available, the reason being his belief in "the dream of the omnipotence of science." The linkage between this belief in the "dream" and the injured capacity to calm the mind and determine destiny, this is the essence of Liang's criticism of the West.[56]

Liang based his account on the dualistic distinction, characteristic both of traditional Chinese thought and of Bergson and Eucken, between the exterior and the interior spheres of life (*waibu shenghuo* 外部生活 and *neibu shenghuo* 內部生活), as two complementary parts of a person.[57] In the last one hundred years, Liang explained, European existence had undergone a process of dramatic transformation that cannot be compared to anything experienced in the past. The magnitude of the scientific progress was too sweeping, the force too intense, and the tempo too abrupt. Consequently, the balance of life was upset at the expense of the interior sphere of life. Whereas the pace of exterior life was accelerated, the interior sphere of life failed to follow. The connection between them was severed.[58]

---

53 Generally, Liang used "civilization" (文明 wenming) when he wrote about the external relations with the non-Chinese world, and "culture" (文化 wenhua) for the internal relations. China was a civilization when it encountered the West, and a "culture" when her youth were called upon to reorganize their heritage. See Chang Hao, *Liang Ch'i-ch'ao*, 116.
54 Liang, *Reflections*, 10–12.
55 Ibid., 35–38.
56 Ibid., 10.
57 A. C. Graham, *Disputers of the Tao: Philosophical Argumentation in Ancient China*. La Salle: Open Court, 1989, 25.
58 Liang, *Reflections*, 10.

In the past, Liang maintained, three sources vitalized the European person's interior sphere of life. The feudal system established the normative relations between individual and society. Greek philosophy taught the profoundest principles of the universe and the purpose of human spirituality, including the moral standard for utmost goodness (*zhishan de daode biaozhun* 至善的道德標準). Christian religion accommodated the emotions (*qing* 情) and the will (*yi* 意), furnishing man with faith conducive to forming a linkage with transcendence (*chao shijie* 超世界). The interior sphere of life accordingly consists of knowledge, emotions, and will. Christianity contains the means to transcend the mere material existence, namely, to share religious experience or the life of faith. Man's original endowment consists of the innate virtues that enable him to attain spirituality.[59]

Moreover, Liang observes, neither the feudal system nor Greek thought or Christianity play a role today. The progress of science has disabled the interior sphere of life, and the exterior sphere has taken over. Philosophers today base their ideas on matter alone, are dedicated to science, and formulate an entirely materialistic and mechanistic 'view of life'. This view (scientism) ignores the difference between the interior and the exterior spheres of life, subordinating both indiscriminately to material determinism (*biran faze* 必然法則). As a result, the spiritual element which constitutes the working of the mind, is similarly categorized as a material phenomenon.[60]

Morality has suffered most. The causal law of matter, says Liang, is simply a "pre-determined destiny in disguise" (*bianxiang de yunming qianding* 變相的運命前定), a camouflaged determinism. Once mental phenomena and human spirituality become ordinary material phenomena, the will relinquishes its autonomy, and is no longer accountable for discriminating between right and wrong. The absence of moral standards to guide conduct has given rise to the current moral crisis. The individual has lost the capacity to determine his destiny. The decline of the West is essentially a moral one.[61]

As an alternative to morality, Liang continued, science cannot be trusted. The "scientific" truth we know today is false tomorrow. The illusion that science is dependable has caused people to be like a "ship lost in the sea without a compass." Liang associated with science the impending change in the concept of the context of human relationships, with no room for the transcendental. A materialistic and mechanistic 'view of life', formulated under the impact of scientific explanations, he cautioned, necessarily causes people to merely survive without ever being content. To survive, "people wrap noodles and run." That is all they can afford. Progress has not brought happiness but its opposite; therefore, all that remains is to hope for a future decline in the status of science.[62]

---

59 Ibid.
60 Ibid., 11.
61 Ibid.
62 Ibid. 12.

Liang was not really opposed to science. He rather wished only to indicate the consequences of its excessive use. However, one sentence included the phrase "the bankruptcy of science" (*kexue pochan* 科學破產). In the current intellectual atmosphere these characters caught the eyes of the advocates of scientism.[63] Instead of answering his specific accusations, they isolated "the bankruptcy of science" and presented it as the message of the whole article. Eventually, Liang's critics read his otherwise calm and sober, though occasionally somewhat emotional, examination of scientism, out of context. They ended up interpreting it for a total rejection of science. This case indeed may serve as an exercise in the politics of intellectual life.

From his anti-positivist position Liang depicted the damage to the interior and moral sphere of life as upsetting the balance of human existence. The cause of this imbalance was scientism and its materialistic and mechanistic 'view of life'. The *ti* was upset in favor of the *yong*. A possible cure for the situation would probably be the 'view of life' corresponding to the interior sphere. Nonetheless, Liang elsewhere explained more explicitly the aim of his criticism. This was primarily to praise the spirituality of Chinese civilization and to admonish China's young generation to shoulder the responsibility and to share their values with the rest of humanity. Liang defined the differences between Eastern and Western modes of thought as matters of orientation. In the West the orientation has always been "to bring the ideal to the reality." Conversely, the founding sages of Chinese thought, Confucius, Laozi, Mozi, and the Buddha, "always sought an adjustment between the ideal and its practical implementation." In other words, compared to the struggle to dominate the phenomenal world in the West, the Chinese are disposed to regard the particular self and the whole of society, the material and the spiritual, as forming one body.[64]

Liang exemplified the advantages that he associated with the Chinese *ti* by the following schools of thought: the pre-Qin philosophers, Tang thought, the Consciousness-Only (Yogacara) school, and Chan Buddhism. He enumerated four values: humanness (*ren* 仁); grace (*ci* 慈); wisdom (*zhi* 智); and goodness (*shan* 善). These values, especially humanness, so central to traditional Chinese thought, also impressed Russell as important in Chinese civilization a year later. Despite considering traditional values as valid in the present, Liang betrayed much concern about the actual decline of Chinese culture. In words that anticipated Hu Shi's call to "reorganize the national heritage," Liang appealed to China's "beloved youth" to acknowledge the merits of their traditional culture. He called for the founding of an intellectual project that would adopt Western methods of research to expand knowledge about Chinese culture and reach its true ideas. The next stage he estimated, involves "cooperation with others" and creation of a "new culture" (*xin wenhua* 新文化). Thereafter, Chinese youth would be required to share the merits of this culture with the rest of the world.[65]

---

63 Ibid.
64 Ibid. 36.
65 Ibid. 37–38.

The Cultures of Liang Shuming

The dramatic events of May 1919 diminished the impact of Liang Qichao's *Reflections* during the next two years. Meanwhile, however, similar ideas were being voiced in lectures by a Peking University professor, Liang Shuming. Though coming from a younger generation and a different educational background than Liang Qichao, he too ventured to reformulate the *tiyong* formula. Accommodating progress required science, but to avoid the negative effects of Western culture, China needed to preserve the moral and spiritual message of Confucianism.

Liang Shuming's parents appreciated Western learning and encouraged their son to study it. But in the same home he also witnessed the process that led his father, Liang Ji 梁濟 (1859–1918), to protest against the disintegration of the traditional order and the moral deterioration of the age by committing suicide.[66] Like many others of his generation, Liang Shuming read the new periodicals, memorized Liang Qichao's ideas, and was carried away by the nationalist ethos.[67] Still, watching the political process that followed the 1911 revolution, he reacted by considering culture and morality as a priority to national salvation. Subsequently he was led to Buddhism, but very soon he returned to Confucianism.[68]

In writing *Cultures*[69] Liang intended to offer a comprehensive diagnosis of the problem that China faced, which, he believed, was essentially a cultural question. He defined culture as the attitude people have toward that which was not accomplished by their will (*yiyu* 意欲).[70] Will is here understood as the spiritual and universal will, as in Schopenhauer.[71] Liang suggested three possible attitudes on the part of the individuals who live in each society, ranging from the basic to the advanced and to the perfect. First is the response to the primary material needs which drive the individual forward to utilize the environment. The second and more advanced attitude is acceptance of the given conditions. Being aware of the basic needs, the individual relinquishes the use of force and turns to search for balance and harmony between satisfying the immediate needs and attaining internal contentment. The society whose individuals have exhausted the first two stages eventually encounters the true and eternal problem: its individuals become aware of the world's temporality and the unavoidable extinction of the self. This realization leads to the third attitude, to

---

66 Lin Yu-sheng, "The Suicide of Liang Chi: An Ambiguous Case of Moral Conservatism." In *The Limits of Change: Essays on Conservative Alternatives in Republican China*. Ed. Charlotte Furth, ed. Cambridge, Mass.: Harvard University Press, 1976, 151–168.
67 Guy S. Alitto, *The Last Confucian: Liang Shu-ming and the Chinese Dilemma of Modernity*. Berkeley: University of California Press, 1979, 29–36.
68 Liang announced his return to Confucianism in March 1921.
69 Liang Shuming, *Cultures*, 1983.
70 Ibid., 28.
71 To Schopenhauer the Will is the fundamental metaphysical principle behind the entire phenomenal world. Arthur Schopenhauer, *The World as Will and Representation*. New York: Dover, vol. I, 1969, 110.

come to terms internally with the will itself.⁷² But can the individual be autonomous if the will has shed all goals? Liang's *Cultures* lacks a definite answer to this ambivalence concerning individual autonomy and the role of will.

To adapt his theory to historical reality, Liang suggested that these three attitudes correspond, respectively, to the cultures (and to the societies) of the West, to the Chinese and to the Indian. He then argued that, ultimately, the three attitudes represent stages which complement each other in a successive process of human development. Originally, instead of a uniform universal development, individuals in each different society reacted differently, leading to the formation of different cultures.⁷³ The correspondence between the second attitude and Chinese culture implied that Chinese culture was more advanced than the West. That Chinese culture was superior to Western was a highly unusual argument in Chinese intellectual circles at that period.

For Liang Shuming, the *ti* (spiritual substance) of China was interchangeable with Chinese culture. Yet, this culture remained open to interpretation. How did he conclude that Chinese culture is more mature and advanced than Western? How did he reconcile this conclusion with the opposite view, which was held by most intellectuals considering the situation around 1919–21? To answer these questions Liang went back to the original ideas of Confucius and the ancient sages. He found that they engaged in what he called metaphysical learning (*xingershang xue* 形而上學), which led to several valuable conclusions.⁷⁴ To him, metaphysics is the system of ideas that associate man with the original core which is inexpressible (*genben de difang jiushi wubiaoshi* 根本的 地方就是無表示), and is "[...] purposeless, [...] beyond consciousness and perception."⁷⁵ Against the material reality of the positivists, Liang proposed original core as the context of existence.

According to his interpretation, Confucianism contained a transcendental message – the true spirit of Chinese culture – which had been transmitted from antiquity. This message, he argued, should be isolated from the forms it assumed in later periods. The true spirit of Chinese culture is the value of integration (*diaohe* 調和), the solidarity of all beings and things as equals in a universal body.⁷⁶ It corresponds to the attitude required for the second stage in Liang's thesis of cultural development.

How is the individual to integrate with the whole? For that purpose Liang discussed the Mencian concept of human nature and the virtue of humaneness (ren 仁).⁷⁷ He believed that *ren* is neither based on reason nor concrete, as Hu Shi argued, but intuitive. Unlike thinking that is based on reason which inclines to selfish calculations, intuition directly connects with the individual's original goodness, push-

---

72 Liang Shuming, *Cultures*, 63–64.
73 Ibid., 64.
74 Ibid., 135.
75 Ibid., 141.
76 Ibid., 140.
77 Ibid., 149–155.

ing toward integration. The idea of linkage in Liang's thought postulates *ren* as an internal individual disposition to integrate with the whole. We have here a theory based on a mind-reality correspondence. The linkage between the individual's mind and the inexpressible original core is accomplished through the intuitive virtue of *ren*.

Due to his linkage with the ultimate context Liang's individual is also autonomous. In fact, autonomy is intrinsic to the idea of life. Chinese metaphysics, he maintained, focused on the concept of life (*sheng* 生), as constantly flowing change.[78] Like Bergson's flow of life, this 'life' that fills the whole universe is dynamic and creative. Using Bergson-like reasoning Liang maintained that life evades exact words and intellectual concepts which are essentially static and fixed. Life does not correspond analogously either to reason or to material causality.

Confucius, says Liang, was well aware that everything constantly transforms.[79] He therefore stubbornly resisted objective principles and absolute moral standards. Avoiding all rigid pronouncements that inevitably distort the *zhongyong* 中庸 idea of "[...] putting ideal sagely balance into actual kingly practice,"[80] in his conduct, thought, and judgement, Confucius used intuition to guide him toward achieving the goal of integration. According to Liang, the metaphysical position that relied on intuition and a non-utilitarian human capacity of effortlessly doing (*wu suowei erwei* 無所為而為) endowed Chinese culture with a significant advantage.[81]

At the same time, Liang attacked the May Fourth proponents of science and democracy. Survival was the goal of the Western attitude, he argued, which led to an intellectual and manipulative approach toward the phenomenal world. Seeking to dominate nature (*zhengfu ziran* 征服自然), this attitude brought about the emergence of science. The same attitude produced democracy. Science and democracy are good for the first stage of cultural development. They view the natural world as matter to be exploited. But to human relationships this attitude has brought painful consequences. Whereas knowledge, wealth, and comfort progressed immensely, spirituality suffered a critical blow. "Life became rich on the surface but extremely poor on the inside." Science and democracy therefore, reveal the deficiencies that define the conditions and the need for progress toward the Chinese way.[82]

Liang's thesis of cultural development pronounced Chinese values, considered by many as anachronistic, to remain relevant. He concluded that the first attitude, that of the West, although it satisfied basic needs, was only concerned with matter, thus setting concrete limitations on individual autonomy. On the other hand, the dis-

---

78 Ibid., 144–145.
79 Ibid., 144–149.
80 Andrew Plaks, "The Mean, Nature, and Self-Realization. European Translations of the Zhongyong." In *De L'un au Multiple* (From the one into the many): Translations From Chinese into European Languages. Viviane Alleton and Michael Lackner, eds. Paris: Fondation Maison des sciences de l'homme, 1999, 318.
81 Liang Shuming, *Cultures*, 159–160.
82 Ibid., 75, 211.

tinguishing quality of the third attitude is a turning inward, where the individual is autonomous. Bergson had argued and Schopenhauer before him, in fact the Buddhists even earlier, that matter limits the will, whereas only spiritually can the individual be free. The second attitude, that of Chinese culture, is the middle way between these two, a middle way between the inner and outer spheres of life, between material satisfaction and spiritual attainment. Liang's idea of individual autonomy is based on the same inner-outer differentiation which former Chinese thinkers, as well as men like Bergson, Eucken and Driesch proposed.

Although he attacked the proponents of science and democracy, Liang Shuming affirmed that China needed both. The correct development of a society is to progress from the first stage to the second and then to the third, in such a way that each stage is essential to the next. Science and democracy, which belong to the first stage, are therefore essential requirements if a healthy advance to the second stage is to take place. The far-reaching view of the ancient sages, however, had launched Chinese culture directly into the second stage, causing it to bypass essential steps of the correct road to progress.[83] To compensate for the loss caused by this untimely over-accomplishment, the present bearers of Chinese culture need to accept science and democracy completely, yet critically, and at the same time continue to pursue their original attitude.[84]

How to protect past achievements from negative effects once foreign elements are introduced? For that purpose Liang proposed to reorganize the *ti* of Chinese culture, classified now under what he termed the "life approach" (*rensheng taidu* 人生態度). He suggested that unyieldingness (*gang* 剛) should be the starting point of this approach.[85] The life approach is a pattern available to anyone ready to attend to his real internal direction. Each individual is expected to explore it according to his own measure of capacity. Liang introduced this life approach idea only toward the end of his *Cultures*.[86] Its content was not specified. But obviously he meant to include in it the metaphysical foundations mentioned above: the inexpressible original core, the *ren* linkage and the goal of integration. This approach now became a precondition to the absorption of the foreign influences.

What distinguished Liang from the main stream is that he sought ways to accept foreign ideas while preserving the spirit of Chinese culture. To that end he had to redefine the Chinese substance (*ti*), which he now reduced to a set of moral and spiritual values. Practical considerations dictated that a spiritual life approach should serve to filter the negative effects of the modernizing process. Through such a formulation Liang thought that China could avoid the negative effects of Western culture. This approach complemented Chen Duxiu's (1879–1942) call for science and

---

83 Ibid., 182, 236.
84 Ibid., 239.
85 According to Analects 5:11, a person whose virtue is so great that he does not give in to passions. According to *Mencius* 2A:2, it is the qi 氣 which is unyielding.
86 Liang Shuming, *Cultures*, 238.

democracy and Hu Shi's critical attitude. To be sure, science, democracy, and the critical approach, possessed merits of their own, but as long as they neglected the spiritual aspects of human existence, they were fundamentally deficient.

Conclusion

At the beginning of the twentieth century natural science presented an alternative concept of the phenomenal world, which aroused conflict among Chinese intellectuals regarding the nature of the mind-reality correspondence. Foreign sources contributed to both sides of the argument. On the one hand, the positivists proposed that everything, including mental processes, is matter. When Dewey spoke he was understood by most intellectuals to support the application of science to solving all the problems of life. He saw these problems in terms of concrete experience. Dewey associated the spirituality of being human exclusively to the mode he called the associated human living. Morality was however based on reason. Russell proposed in his lectures on the mind that in the near future mental phenomena would be explicable by causality.

On the other hand, Bergson, Eucken and Driesch believed that reality consists of more than mere matter. Bergson seemed to show that intellectual perception does not correspond to the phenomenal world as it is. To capture the flow of living reality, intuition is required. Eucken emphasized the spirituality of life when viewed as a whole, and the active role that the individual has to play in life. Driesch held that if mind is merely material and mechanical, that is, non-autonomous, then life is meaningless.

Liang Qichao in his *Reflections* and Liang Shuming in his *Cultures* saw the positivist arguments as an excessive accretion of the *yong* part of the *tiyong* formula and as threatening the substance (*ti*) of what it means to be human according to Chinese culture. According to Liang Qichao science ignored the differences between the exterior and interior spheres of existence. He based his argument for individual autonomy on the interior working of the mind, which science finds unintelligible. According to Liang Shuming, the phenomenal world must be apprehended in terms of an original non-explainable core in order to lead to a meaningful 'view of life'. Toward the goal of integration with the whole, reason, which leads to selfishness, will not do. Only intuition, which he associated with the value of humanness (*ren*) is useful toward that end.

Criticizing the culture of the West both Liangs indicated the downgrading of man's expectations from life to the level of mere survival. Liang Qichao admitted that in such areas as the accumulation of knowledge, wealth, and comfort, the West had indeed progressed considerably. He readily associated this progress with the development of science. But the rapid pace of the process and its all-pervasiveness disabled the interior sphere of life and ended in spiritual and moral neglect. Liang Shuming highlighted the deterioration in relations between human beings and the existential suffering that ensued. Both also thought that Chinese culture could avoid those pitfalls. Pursuing further the arguments that he raised in the *Essay* and the *Mirror*, Liang Qichao maintained in his *Reflections* that man has the spiritual resources which enable him to attain an internal balance with the exterior. Man has the innate moral excellence which makes Chinese culture a relevant resource for a universal recovery. Like in his earlier works he did not discuss integration with the whole but rather emphasized the social aspect of the individual. Here Liang Shuming, emphasizing the spirituality of individual life and the importance of the aspiration to merge with transcendence, differed from him.

Perhaps because Liang Shuming avoided an extensive and focused discussion of the "life approach," scholars have so far disregarded its value in the history of Chinese intellectual responses to encounters with foreign ideas. Two important points should be emphasized: the conditioning of the absorption of science and democracy by the earlier formulation of an "approach"; and the Confucian resoluteness at its center. These make the life approach an important landmark in the intellectual route that passed between Eucken's *Lebensanschauung* and the 1923 supporters of the 'view of life'.

Liang Qichao and Liang Shuming differed also in the way they arrived at their answers. The former championed mutual relations of individuals within society as leading to a universal recovery. The latter suggested a cultural model and a stage of temporary borrowing, regardless of any obligation toward foreign cultures. Yet both shared a dualistic view considerably influenced by Bergson and Eucken. Both emphasized values that have their origins in Chinese tradition. Regarding the link that associates the process of attaining progress while not abandoning tradition, Liang Shuming's call to adopt a life approach agreed with Liang Qichao's call to revitalize the Chinese heritage. Hu Shi's more critical efforts to find the roots of modern pragmatism in the ideas of Qing philosophers also shared the same concept, which is that tradition cannot be altogether abandoned.

CHAPTER FOUR

Arguments against Scientism

Early in 1923 Chinese advocates of positivism and those seeking a synthesis of idealist thought with the traditional concept of linkage, confronted one another on the problem of the 'view of life' during the science versus metaphysics controversy. That the supporters of metaphysics were not merely conservatives and traditionalists rejecting science and modern development emerges when the philosophical basis of their arguments is explored. What troubled them most about the position of the scientism proponents was the negation of the autonomous personality exercising free will, and the interpretation of the context of human relationships, thinking and knowing, that their views entailed. The supporters of metaphysics presented forceful ideas for the 'view of life' as well as arguments against scientism. This chapter deals with the latter.

While the controversy has been discussed in numerous studies,[1] the philosophical underpinning on which the arguments against science rested has not been sufficiently explored. These were based on three epistemological distinctions. The most fundamental among them involved the overall domain of relations between mind (consciousness) and reality.[2] The supporters of metaphysics divided this domain into two spheres: the "sphere of science," where sense perception and reason are valid, and its complement "sphere beyond science," which was the ground where the sup-

---

1 See the studies of D. W. Y., Kwok, *Scientism in Chinese Thought, 1900–1950*. New Haven: Yale University Press, 1965, and Charlotte, Furth, *Ting Wen-Chiang*. Cambridge, Mass: Harvard University Press, 1970. For more recent studies: Fung, Edmund S. K. *The Intellectual Foundations of Chinese Modernity; Cultural and Political Thought in the Republican Era*. Cambridge: Cambridge University Press, 2010. Wang Hui 汪晖, *Xiandai Zhongguo sixiang de xingqi* 现代中国思想的兴起 (The rise of modern Chinese thought). Beijing: Shenghuo dushu, 2003. Yang Guorong, "The Debate between Scientists and Metaphysicians in Early Twentieth Century: Its Theme and Significance." *Dao: A Journal of Comparative Philosophy* 2, 1 (December 2002): 79–95. Zhang Qing 張慶, *Zhongguo ershi shiji Zhongguo renshengguan lunzheng* 中國２０世紀中國人生觀論爭 (The Chinese view of life controversy in 20th century China). Guangzhou: Guangdong gaodeng jiaoyu chubanshe, 2000. Ye Qizhong 葉其忠 (Yap Key-chong), "1923 Nian 'Kexuan Lunzhan': Pingjia Zhi Pingjia 1923 年'科玄論戰'：評價之評價 (Revisiting Criticism of the 1923 'Debate on Science and Metaphysics.'). *Zhongyang Yanjiuyuan; Jindaishi Yanjiusuo Jikan* 中央研究院近代史研究所集刊 (Bulletin of the Institute of Modern History Academia Sinica) (Taipei) 26 (1996): 181–234.
2 The participants used mind rather than the perhaps more accurate consciousness. I will use mind in order to stay close to the sources. Similarly they used reality (shizai 實在) rather than the phenomenal world or other terms.

porters of metaphysics constructed the 'view of life' – the subject of the next chapter. How they negated the deterministic explanation of human behavior thus questioning the very basis of scientism, is the subject of this chapter.

The Problem

The resistance to scientism toward the end of 1922 may be termed Chinese anti-positivism to distinguish it from its European counterpart, and was reinforced by two major personages. One was the visiting German philosopher Hans Driesch. The other was Zhang Junmai, by that time known in intellectual circles mainly for his close relations with Eucken,[3] his acquaintance with Bergson's thought,[4] and his close ties with Liang Qichao's intellectual and political group. Zhang, who stayed in Europe between 1913–16 and 1919–22, brought back his eyewitness impressions of the troubled life in the West. Whereas Zhang assumed the role of the foreign-trained intellectual, Driesch was a foreign philosopher. The convergence of these two personalities on the Chinese intellectual scene created an extraordinary coincidence of anti-positivist forces, when together they launched a movement to resist scientism. Their program advocated the absorption of foreign ideas while maintaining the traditional core of the autonomous individual[5] and the regard for spirituality.

On February 14, 1923 an address given at Qinghua 清華 University in Beijing sparked the latent ferment in intellectual circles that had been present ever since the Chinese encountered foreign ideas. The speaker was Zhang Junmai, the audience consisted of students of science, and the topic was "The 'view of life'" (*rensheng guan* 人生觀) – a term that was extensively employed in Eucken's writings.[6] Zhang opened with an exposition of what he considered the presumptuous goal of science or, rather, scientism, to uncritically apply causality to all phenomena in the world. He warned that, when applied to mental phenomena, this goal implied the complete mechanization of the human being. Pointing out that causality was not valid in all spheres of reality and especially questionable in the sphere of human life, Zhang said:

---

3 Zhang studied under Eucken in Jena, between 1919–1922. Together they co-authored *Das Lebensproblem in China und in Europa* (The problem of life in China and in Europe). Leipzig: Quelle and Meyer, 1922.
4 Zhang and his friend Lin Zaiping (also known as Lin Zhijun, 1879–1960) interviewed Bergson in Paris in May, 26, 1921. *Minduo zazhi*, 3.1 (December, 1921), 10–14.
5 So far the discussion distinguished Western conceptions of individuals from Chinese conceptions of persons. Hereafter 'individual' is used for both.
6 The lecture was transcribed (zhuanlu 轉錄) in volume 272 of the *Qinghua Zhoukan* 清華週刊 shortly after the actual address had taken place. However much the printed version may vary from Zhang's lecture it was the former that mattered in the ensuing debate. Zhang never mentioned another version of his lecture.

> For a long time we have been reading and learning in the books of science that all phenomena in the world must have an explanation and that they are all ruled by the law of causality (*yinguo lü* 因過律). However, if we close our eyes and honestly reflect, we would have to admit that many problems are not that clear. Some questions do not belong to certain impressive philosophical theories but to daily life. One says this, the other says that, and no one can determine the categories of right and wrong, truth or falsehood. We ask what is it? The answer is: human life. Because human life is simultaneously perceived from different perspectives and non-identical points of view, views are not the same. Therefore among the most disputed problems in the world none can match the problem of the 'view of life'.[7]

Only implied in Zhang's speech, the key question of the controversy was more directly stated two months later in his ninety-eight-pages-long article: "Can science govern the 'view of life'?"[8] The problem he explored was whether science can adequately analyze, comprehend, and predict the experience of human life. Philosophically speaking, the question involved differing views about reality and mind and the correspondence between them. Like his opponents Zhang believed that the mind is reliable. The problem was rather whether the correspondence follows an analogous order, which makes mental phenomena completely intelligible to reason and therefore leads to determinism. Or are mind and reality related so that intuition can account for their correspondence, which allows for individual autonomy. The correct explanation depends on how human will is understood. Therefore, the main issue underlying the question of whether science can govern the 'view of life' was freedom of the will, or the nature of individual autonomy. The question was but a variation on the more familiar one: are human beings autonomous in their will, thought and actions, or are they – consciously or unconsciously – trapped in a system of causation and necessity.

The supporters of scientism believed that the answer to the key question is an emphatic Yes.[9] To Wu Zhihui 吳稚暉 (1865–1953), life is pure and simple desire; man is that animal with two hands and a large brain; senses, emotions, reason, mind, will, and soul; human beings manifest matter and energy, they are different from each other in degree and not in kind. Neither divinity nor spirit exist. The social and

---

7 Zhang Junmai 張君勱, "Rensheng guan" 人生觀 (The view of life). In *Kexue xuanxue lunzhanji* 科學玄學論戰集 (The controversy of science and metaphysics). Preface by Hu Shi 胡適 and Chen Duxiu 陳獨秀. Shanghai: Yadong shuju, 1923, 1. Hereafter *Controversy*.

8 Zhang Junmai, "Zai lun rensheng guan yu kexue bing da Ding Zaijun" 再論人生觀與科學 並答丁在君 (Another discussion of the 'view of life' and science and an answer to Ding Zaijun). *Controversy*, 46. As noted in chapter two, Dewey suggested to render science authoritative in control of human behavior. This article first appeared in May 1923. John Dewey, *Lectures in China, 1919–1920*. Eds. and trans. Robert W. Clopton and Ou Tsuin-chen. Honolulu: East-West Center, 1973, 168.

9 For the position of these participants see D.W.Y. Kwok, *Scientism in Chinese Thought, 1900–1950*. New Haven: Yale University Press, 1965.

moral order is based on three natural instincts: food, sex, and sociability. All behavior is grounded in these.[10]

To Hu Shi, the scientific 'view of life' is concrete, purely materialistic, and purely mechanistic. Causality may be a burden on human freedom, but it enables man to find the causes of effects and effects from causes; to explain the past, and envisage the future. Similarly, it enables man to make use of his intelligence, create new causes in the world and cause new effects. To be sure, cruelty and indifference are not necessary consequences of the struggle for survival. Scientism, to him, might even enhance the brotherhood between the individual and society. According to Hu, "The naturalistic view of human life" is in no way devoid of beauty, poetry and moral responsibility. It is rich with opportunities for fully putting into practice "creative intelligence."[11] These views by Wu and Hu represented the majority of Chinese intellectuals at that period.

The supporters of metaphysics, were, however, reluctant to abandon their traditional world-view based on the notion of the participation of man in the universal process (*tian ren heyi* 天人合一). Devoted to the linkage idea of Chinese tradition they sought a cross-cultural synthesis that accommodated new foreign ideas and yet remained faithful to a continuous traditional pattern. Aware of flaws in the structure of the scientific system, they raised doubts concerning scientism's boast of being all-encompassing, capable of answering the questions of total reality. Their response was a resounding no. They turned instead to the sources of the 'view of life' in the philosophical doctrines that inquires into ultimate and fundamental reality – metaphysics.

After Zhang's lecture was published in the *Qinghua Weekly* several days later, its contents became a hotly debated issue in Chinese intellectual circles. At a dinner party, Hu Shi and Ding Wenjiang notified Zhang that they would challenge him in *Endeavor* (*Nuli zhoubao* 努力周報). Shortly afterwards, articles appeared and addresses were delivered, constituting a separate discourse within the ongoing debates about the future course of Chinese culture initiated by Liang Qichao and Liang Shuming as discussed in chapter three. In the ensuing controversy, both camps took the opportunity to air their views and to advocate what they saw as the burning issues of the day.

---

10 Wu Zhihui, 吳稚暉, "Yi ge xin xinyang de yuyou guan ji rensheng guan" 一個新信仰的宇宙觀及人生觀 (A new belief in a cosmic view and the 'view of life'), Controversy, 489–654. See also Chow Tse-tsung, *The May Fourth Movement: Intellectual Revolution in Modern China*. Cambridge, Mass.: Harvard University Press, 1960, 337. This article appeared in parts in August, October 1923 and March 1924.

11 Source in Wu Zhihui, "Yi ge xin xinyang de yuyou guan ji rensheng guan." Hu Shi, "Kexue yu rensheng guan xu" 科學與人生觀序 (Introduction to science and the 'view of life'), *Controversy*, 1–42. See also Chow, *May Fourth Movement*, 336.

Views on Mind-Reality Correspondence

The proponents of scientism and metaphysics talked about several things simultaneously and not about science as such. In fact, in their arguments they confused science with the method of science and with its laws. Zhang Junmai opened his Qinghua speech about the 'view of life' with a positive description of science, its achievements and its ensuing popularity. He enumerated a few examples of what he called science:

> Science (*kexue* 科學) is constituted of demonstrated assumptions and general principles which are based on evidence. For example: two plus two equals four, the sum of three angles in a triangle equals two right angles, in mathematics; speed equals distance divided by time in physics; the formula of the constitution of water is H_2O, in chemistry.[12]

Zhang therefore, did not reject causality. But when the earlier quotation is taken into account, and as will be shown below, he meant to accord the exact sciences reduced validity. Causality did not embrace all of human life.

Ding Wenjiang, the leading speaker among the scientism supporters in the debate, referred to the purpose of science (*kexue de mudi* 科學的目的) and to the method of science (*kexue de fangfa* 科學的方法) in his rebuttal of Zhang's Qinghua address. The purpose of science is to banish subjective preconceptions in seeking the truth that everyone can agree upon. The method of science, according to Ding, was to sort out and to classify in detail the true facts from the complex of truth and false facts, then to detect the order in their relations and find the most simple and clear explanation to summarize these true facts.[13] Hu Shi, the man who pulled the strings behind the support of scientism in China at that period,[14] defined the method of science in an altogether different way. Although he backed Ding's attack against Zhang, he considered the method of science, in accordance with John Dewey, as a positive doctrine of experimental methodology.[15] No matter how varied their definitions, Hu, Chen Duxiu 陳獨秀 (1880–1942) and Wu, as well as the other supporters of scientism, agreed with Ding about a positivist view of the method of science that did not distinguish between living experience and the matter that the method deals with.

---

12 Zhang Junmai, "Rensheng guan," *Controversy*, 1.
13 Ding Wenjiang 丁文江, "Xuanxue yu kexue" 玄學與科學 (Metaphysics and Science), *Controversy*, 34. Originally published in April 12th.
14 Hu Shi recovered from illness during the greater part of that year. From his position behind the scenes he contributed one article and wrote the preface for the collected articles of the controversy at the end of that year.
15 Benjamin Schwartz, "Themes in Intellectual History: May Fourth and After." In *The Cambridge History of China*. John K. Fairbank and Denis Twitchett, eds. Cambridge: Cambridge University Press, 1986, vol. XII, 425.

On the side of the metaphysics proponents, Liang Qichao outlined his own definition of science, saying that "Analyzing the facts of experience and seeking the norm as close as possible to truth and correct for the same kind of things as well, this learning is called 'science.'"[16] Liang also mentioned Einstein's recent theory of relativism.[17] Another important participant was Zhang Dongsun 張東蓀 (1886–1962), who was well known for his efforts to introduce Western philosophy into China, and was at the time acting editor of *Current Affairs* (*Shishi xinbao* 時事新報), which carried most of the articles by the supporters of metaphysics.[18] In a note to Liang's article Zhang addressed the subject of the relativity of science.[19] Regarding Ding's definition of the purpose of science and its method, Zhang commented that what makes science is not the method, but the purpose.[20] Lin Zaiping 林宰平 (1879–1960), a lay Buddhist, joined the critics of the method of science saying that its validity holds true only under immutable, that is, unchanging, conditions. He characterized the objectivity of science by pointing out its impartiality: "Science itself is by no means inclined toward good or bad, [moreover] it does not take any credit for its usefulness in the accumulation of knowledge."[21] Qu Shiying 瞿世英 (1900–1976) preferred to analyze and divide science and its characteristics. He enumerated four constituents: the spirit of science, the approach that relies on evidence; the method of science, which uses experiment; the body of science; and its application, both of which result from experiment and application.[22]

Insofar as these attempts to understand what science is about were involved, disagreements occurred also among participants who belonged to the same side. Charlotte Furth is justified in pointing out the affinity between Hu, Wu, and Zhang Junmai's concepts of science.[23] The conflict was not in the definitions of science and its method but rather in the perspectives and intellectual tempers of the participants. In a wider sense, they had to cope with what Zhang Dongsun termed "the internal debate within philosophy."[24] The further they explored the limits of science and its method, the more the participants in the controversy were compelled to study the nature of knowledge and reason. Here, where the discussion moved into the field of theories of knowledge, the philosophical gap between the two sides came into view.

---

16 Liang Qichao 梁啟超, "Rensheng guan yu kexue" 人生觀與科學 (The 'view of life' and science), *Controversy*, 174. Originally published in May.
17 Ibid., 176. Afterwards Einstein was frequently evoked during the controversy.
18 Zhang Dongsun translated Bergson's works and escorted Russell during his visit to China.
19 Zhang Dongsun 張東蓀, "Dongsun an" 東蓀按 (Note by Zhang Dongsun), *Controversy*, 183. Originally published in May; see also his "Lao er wu gong" 勞而無功 (Wasted effort), *Controversy*, 324–325.
20 Zhang Dongsun, "Dongsun an" (Note by Zhang Dongsuni), *Controversy*, 183.
21 Lin Zaiping 林宰平, "Du Ding Zaijun xiansheng de 'Xuanxue yu kexue'" 讀丁在君先生 的'玄學與科學' (Criticizing Mr. Ding's article on Metaphysics and Science), *Controversy*, 238.
22 Qu Nong 菊農 (Qu Shiying 瞿世英), "Renge yu jiaoyu" 人格與教育 (Character and education), *Controversy*, 349.
23 Charlotte Furth, *Ting Wen-chiang*. Cambridge, Mass.: Harvard University Press, 1970, 126.
24 Zhang Dongsun, "Dongsun an," *Controversy*, 168.

The supporters of scientism (not including Chen Duxiu) did in fact acknowledge the existence of a certain unknown and unresolved dimension of reality.[25] They refused however, to admit its relevance to the context of human relationships, and insisted on considering known phenomena alone. Their disregard of that unknown dimension was of course not due to ignorance. Rather, they believed that the unknown dimension is neither related nor relevant to human experience.[26] Below I will refer to this position as "the claim of irrelevance."

The proponents of scientism therefore separated their discussion of reality from their views about its unresolved dimension. They nevertheless did discuss the epistemological process involved in the perception of the reality they were speaking about. According to Ding Wenjiang, before long the growing body of science with its steadily accumulating achievements will eliminate metaphysics altogether since, in any event, metaphysics is shrinking daily due to the increase in scientific discoveries. Using Kantian terms, he said that because of science, the phenomenal dimension is about to oust the nuomenal from the reality that is relevant to the context of human relationships. Ding based his argument on the contention that knowledge (*zhishi* 知識) is a rational process experienced in the mind by the brain, which processes sensations provided by sensory organs. What we know is provided by the data available to the senses, and knowledge belongs altogether within the framework of science; accordingly, "the content of the mind is entirely a matter of science."[27] Ding did not consider the possibility of innate perceptive categories, nor was he concerned with an internal moral standard. He claimed that an objective, all-embracing and uniform system of science is possible, and defined his scientific epistemology (*kexue zhishilun* 科學知識論) as "skeptical idealism" (*cunyi de weixinlun* 存疑之唯心論):

> Since they [scientific authorities such as Thomas Huxley, Charles Darwin, Herbert Spencer, William James, Karl Pearson, John Dewey, and Ernst Mach, who investigated philosophical questions] accept that sense-impression (*jueguan ganchu* 覺官感触)[28] is the only systematic mean of knowing things (*wuti* 物體), and that conceptions of things (*wuti de gainian* 物體的概念) are mental experiences (*xinli xianxiang* 心理現象), therefore it is idealistic; and since they acknowledge the limitation of sense-impression with regard to the existent world or the non-existent beyond it, therefore [they] are skeptical.[29]

---

25 For Furth's discussion of the epistemological views of the supporters of scientism, see Charlotte Furth, *Ting Wen-chiang*, especially 108–109.
26 The "beyond" should refer to what is inaccessible.
27 Ding Wenjiang, "Xuanxue yu kexue," *Controversy*, 23.
28 In translating of jueguan ganchu as 'sense-impression' I follow one of Ding's major sources, Karl Pearson, *The Grammar of Science*. London: Walter Scott, 1892, especially 50–53. There are more than a few statements in this source that closely resemble Ding's arguments.
29 Ding Wenjiang, "Xuanxue yu kexue," *Controversy*, 26–27.

Ding's fellow proponents of scientism, Wu Zhihui and Hu Shi, both of whom preferred mechanistic-materialistic explanations with Daoist-Buddhist overtones, did not support these philosophers.[30] But they agreed with Ding that the beyond is non-related and non-relevant to human existence. Wu upheld the uniformity of the natural world, within which man and his mind form no exceptions. His "complete" scientific theory of existence sounded unexpectedly idealistic at first. The universe is a dark chaotic whole, emanating from the infinite chaotic unity of time and space, although it consists of non-space and non-time as well. This universe also comprises rational and irrational elements, and being and non-being. It is a living universe. Wu introduced a positivist framework of the context of human relationships, positing this framework, however, within the transcendental context.[31] The claim of irrelevance sufficiently accommodated the epistemological views of Hu, Wu, and Ding.

But refusing to accept any notion of condoning a sphere beyond the reach of science, Chen Duxiu's position was more radical. In what became the aftermath of the controversy between Hu and Chen the latter argued that by eliminating even one part of reality from science and its method, Hu was just like Zhang Junmai.[32] Nevertheless, the point to emphasize here is that all four discussed human life in terms that were entirely accessible to science and its method.

Among the supporters of metaphysics, only Zhang Dongsun noticed the difference between the philosophers who engage in the epistemological discourse, and those who withdraw from epistemological discussions and try to deal with ontological problems.[33] The former, he wrote, are the Continental rationalists; the latter are the English and American analytic philosophers and their followers, recently joined by the Chinese supporters of scientism.[34] Zhang observed that this is a philosophical problem, and not a question of science against philosophy.[35] He then proceeded to expose a fundamental weakness in the arguments of the scientists, namely, the question of the reliability of intelligence (*zhihui* 智慧) itself.[36] He pictured science and its underlying rationality as a knife capable of cutting into all aspects of life, even the most mysterious ones, such as spirit, emotions and will. But one exception to

---

30 With the exception of Hu and Dewey.
31 Wu Zhihui, "Yi ge xin xinyang de yuyou guan ji rensheng guan," *Controversy*, 489–654. See also Chow, *May Fourth Movement*, 337.
32 Chen Zhongfu (Chen Duxiu), "Kexue yu rensheng guan xu" 科學與人生觀序 (Preface to the controversy over science and the 'view of life'). *Controversy*, 41. Chen's preface was followed by Hu's and each had another section where he answered the other's preface.
33 Zhang Dongsun, "Dongsun an," *Controversy*, 168. Charlotte Furth points out Zhang Junmai's failure to notice that distinction (see discussion below). Charlotte Furth, *Ting Wen-chiang*, 109–110. Zhang Dongsun is not mentioned in that connection.
34 Zhang Dongsun confused the schools and their views. I use here the correct order.
35 Zhang Dongsun, "Dongsun an," *Controversy*, 168.
36 When he spoke of intelligence he strongly alluded to both Russell and Dewey who were still very much present in Chinese intellectuals' minds.

this – the matter of the blade itself, the creative human intelligence, is beyond the reach of the scientific knife.[37]

Lin Zaiping did not acknowledge the distinction implied by the claim of irrelevance. He therefore insistently adhered to the Humean question of whether sense impressions are dependable.[38] He tried to integrate the Berkeleyan position that ideas are spirit and thus incapable of telling anything about the phenomenal world which is composed of matter, with the Buddhist notion that transient phenomena are devoid of concrete existence. Science based on the five senses cannot speak the language beyond sense perception (*ganjue* 感覺). Hence there is a break between the intentions of science and what it can deal with. Lin introduced his readers to a series of epistemological questions: 1) Can mental sensations be identical? 2) Except for mental sensations, or when there are no mental sensations, does objective reality exist? 3) What is memory? 4) What is the relation between the basic concepts of time and space in physics and in matter? He further expressed the following doubts: how and from where is knowledge derived; what is knowledge; and is the potentially knowable limited or unlimited? Finally he said: "of course no one can answer." His conclusion was not far from the observations of the philosopher Zhuangzi 莊子 (ca. 369–286 B.C.E.), who too had been aware of the problem of correlation between internal sensations and objective reality. Zhuangzi had a dream that he was a butterfly and upon waking did not know if he was Zhuangzi who dreamt that he was a butterfly, or a butterfly dreaming that he was Zhuangzi.[39] Lin introduced the same idea:

> If we ascribe to sense-impression the capacity to know things, then we cannot deny that the value of our mental reaction (*ganchu* 感觸) while we dream and while we are awake is not the same. This being the case, is scientific knowledge the same as what we know in a dream?[40]

Interestingly, Lin did not refer to Zhuangzi but to Russell, whom he cited: "We cannot view our knowledge while awake as better than while we dream."[41]

Zhang Junmai also ignored his opponents' claim of irrelevance, and its implications.[42] He agreed with Ding that data indeed flow through the senses to the mind and then knowledge is acquired. But regarding the internal process that generates knowledge in the mind his understanding differed. Zhang's process of knowledge was a Kantian process internally experienced by the mind, which is in itself inac-

---

37 Zhang Dongsun, "Lao er wu gong," *Controversy*, 333.
38 Lin Zaiping, "Du Ding Zaijun xiansheng de 'Xuanxue yu kexue'," *Controversy*, 213–221. Lin uses interchangeably perception, sense-impression, and other close variations of these terms.
39 *Zhuangzi duben* 庄子讀本 (Basic reader of Zhuangzi). Taibei: Sanmin shuju, 1988, 67.
40 Lin Zaiping, "Du Ding Zaijun xiansheng de 'Xuanxue yu kexue'," *Controversy*, 219.
41 Ibid.
42 Zhang's answer to Ding's "Discussing Scientific Knowledge," which introduced the idea of skeptical idealism, appeared under the title "So-called Scientific Knowledge" (suowei kexue de zhishilun 所謂科學的知識論). Zhang Junmai, "Zai lun rensheng guan," *Controversy*, 86–97. Originally published in August.

cessible to science. Illustrated with text and diagram, he introduced the Kantian nuomenon-phenomenon dualistic model of human knowledge and existence, concluding:

> Concerning causes and effects, science will do [...] but in case of living experiences such as remorse, love, mental responsibility, which belong to the moral dimension of spiritual devotion, no systematic explanation will do.[43]

Since reason cannot explain all of reality, other forms of knowledge should be consulted. One such form, he suggested, was intuition. By means of intuition we access and represent the content of the mind, including the spiritual element that the mental processes involve, thus making perceptions meaningful. The following propositions summarize Zhang's mind-centered epistemological argument: 1) Mind is the dominant factor in the perception of reality. 2) Mind in its entirety is inaccessible to science and reason.

The foundations of this approach, according to Zhang, are found in both East and West. The comparison that he had "longed to display for a long time" between the points of departure in the Western controversy of materialism and idealism, and a parallel debate in the history of Chinese thought, indicated that "both originated from the same mind and the same principle."[44] For comparison Zhang drew on Kant, Bergson, and Eucken and Confucius, Mencius, and others to whom he referred to as scholars who subscribed to the learning of principle (*lixue* 理學) in the Song-Ming period. All these sources agreed, he believed, about the correspondence between mind and reality (*shizai* 實在),[45] which involved, beside reason, a spiritual element as well. According to Zhang it is because of the spiritual element, the linkage, that the correspondence exists.[46]

Underlying the epistemological disagreement between the proponents of scientism and metaphysics was an essential difference in their conceptions of the context of human relationships. Ding's confidence in the future achievements of an all-embracing objective scientific system reveals the shared belief of his fellow supporters of scientism in the concept of a homogeneous world of phenomena. In Western thought this concept is based on the so-called "Platonic Ideal" and its claim that phenomena have but one homogeneous and unchanging substructure.[47] Its essential arguments, in the words of Isaiah Berlin are:

---

43 Ibid.
44 Ibid., 130–134. By the parallel debate he meant the Han Learning vs. Song Learning controversy at the beginning of the nineteenth century. On p. 136 Zhang Junmai further contended that this debate resembled the Western polemic concerning the mind being blank (tabula rasa) or not blank.
45 Ibid., 137.
46 For discussion of this linkage see chapter five.
47 Isaiah Berlin, "The Pursuit of the Ideal," *The Crooked Timber of Humanity*. Henry Hardy, ed. London: John Murray, 1990, 1–19.

> In the first place, that, as in the sciences, all genuine questions must have one true answer and one only, all the rest being necessarily errors; in the second place, that there must be a dependable path towards the discovery of these truths; in the third place, that the true answers, when found, must necessarily be compatible with one another and form a single whole, for one truth cannot be incompatible with another – that we know *a priori*.[48]

The concept of the homogeneity of all phenomena, we may add, presupposed a logical correlation between mind and reality. From his humanistic point of view, Berlin condemned this concept for leading to the belief in the possibility of a perfect world where mankind would be just and happy and creative and harmonious for ever. This belief calls for absolute solutions and has led humankind to adopt any and every means toward some goal seen as ideal.[49]

In apparent agreement with the concept of homogeneous reality, Ding Wenjiang, the leading proponent of the 'view of life' based on science, argued that the content of mind is totally a matter of science.[50] Wu Zhihui claimed that feeling, reason, mind, soul and will are all manifestations of energy, differing in degree yet certainly not in kind.[51] Hu Shi said that the "scientific 'view of life'" was purely materialistic and mechanical, and was dominated by causality.[52] Chen Duxiu maintained that "only material objective causality [...] can provide control over the 'view of life' [...] and is the absolute truth."[53]

Zhang Junmai's arguments against objectivism and homogeneity[54] were sharpened by Lin Zaiping, who challenged Ding's position:

> Dewey said that philosophy has the ambition to devise a methodological system [...] and here Ding's ambition is even greater. Wishing to unite everything by science he resembles a founder of religion. All religions aspire to unity and so does Ding. In the same way and with the same belief he wishes to push human life into a fixed pattern, to make the world a place where there is only one answer without exception. He uses science as a weapon to conquer the entire universe, the sun, the moon and the stars, and all the living beings below. And he dares to declare in a loud voice that whoever refuses to accept his science will turn into a dark evil demon (*xiemo waidao* 邪磨外道).[55]

---

48 Ibid., 5–6.
49 Ibid., 15.
50 Ding Wenjiang, "Xuanxue yu kexue," *Controversy*, p. 23.
51 Wu Zhihui, "Yi ge xin xinyang de yuzhou guan ji rensheng guan," *Controversy*, 510–511.
52 Hu Shi, "Kexue yu rensheng guan xu," *Controversy*, 13.
53 Chen Zhongfu, "Kexue yu rensheng guan xu," *Controversy*, 11.
54 For Zhang's basic arguments see next chapter.
55 Lin Zaiping, "Du Ding Zaijun xiansheng de 'Xuanxue yu kexue'," *Controversy*, 203. The last mentioned designation alludes to the way Ding referred to Zhang Junmai in his article.

By attacking the concept of homogeneous reality at the foundation of Chinese scientism, Lin showed, contrary to the arguments of the proponents of scientism, that this concept was in fact a statement of faith. Indicating that their thought fundamentally rested on faith and not on facts and proofs, Lin reversed the arguments of the supporters of scientism, exposed scientism as a religious doctrine, and labeled Ding a metaphysician.

Lin's propositions matched Zhang's and the others' subjectivism. They believed in the autonomy of each mind as well as in the heterogeneous nature of the context of human relationships, where various answers co-exist and interact. Though not yet sufficiently articulated, Zhang and his supporters could have agreed with the view that "[...] there are many different ends that men may seek and still be fully rational, fully men, capable of understanding each other and sympathizing and deriving light from each other."[56]

The Sphere of Science

The supporters of scientism assumed that unity of matter underlies reality. Science to them was a means to master reality. The supporters of metaphysics, on the other hand, held to the idea of a heterogeneous and dynamic context of human relationships. Zhang Junmai viewed the mind as not wholly rational, but as the sole mediation between the individual and the world of phenomena. He thus expressed a certain doubt regarding not only human communication, but he also doubted the reliability of reason even in the narrow sphere of the natural sciences. This is the problem Zhang set himself to solve when he defined the relations between mind and reality, the cognitive relations between the individual and reality outside himself: the "I" and the "non-I".[57]

Reality, according to Zhang, consists of two spheres. One is the firm and unvarying sphere where perception and reason are valid, the other is the sphere of life where relations are heterogeneous and dynamic, where man needs the " 'view of life'." He basically differentiated between self and other (non-I):

> The departure point of the 'view of life' is none other than the I and whatever that exists in my world which is not I. And in the sphere of the non-I there are diverse parts and kinds ...[58]

Driesch had introduced a very similar differentiation in his China lectures:

> Only if there is the 'I' on one side of reality and the 'other', which has a nature or essence of *itself*, on the other side, can there be a real meaning to the

---

56 Berlin, "The Pursuit of the Ideal," 11.
57 Zhang Junmai, "Rensheng guan," *Controversy*, pp. 1–4.
58 Zhang differentiated the non-I sphere into nine categories. Second footnote below.

question, whether I conceive the 'other' 'as it is' or in the form of mere symbols.[59]

Zhang further divided the "other" or the "non I" between two complementary spheres. "The sphere of science" was declared the valid range of perception and reason. "The sphere beyond science" required a 'view of life' that would be based on metaphysics.[60] The sphere of science is of a unified nature and is static; the sphere beyond science is dynamic and living. The axis separating these two spheres is constructed of five categories, each of which contains two complementary qualities: one belongs to the sphere of science, another to the sphere beyond it. For instance, objectivity belongs to science and subjectivity to the 'view of life', causality to science and free will to the 'view of life', and so on. The qualities that characterize and therefore mark the limit of the sphere where science is valid are: objectivity (*keguan* 客觀), logical method (*lunli fangfa* 論理方法), analytical method (*fenxi fangfa* 分析方法), causality (*yinguo lü* 因過律), and uniformity (*tongyi xing* 統一性).[61]

First, Zhang maintained, is objectivity as the source of science. A scientific law, once established, is valid and therefore accepted throughout the world. However, the province of science itself divides into the exact sciences and the social and human sciences. The near perfect objectivity of the natural sciences gradually disappears in the social and human sciences. Second, rationality is the exclusive instrument of science. Science is therefore governed by the logical method but is also restricted by it. Other means of conceptualizing such as intuitions and emotions are rejected. Third, by means of the analytical method, science sees only a narrow field of successive causes and effects while the complete picture remains concealed. Fourth, the law of causality is applicable to matter, but mental processes are inaccessible to it. Fifth, science basically asserts that reality is uniform and that comparison between objects that have similar aspects is possible. This promises some advantages but also has some limitations. Comparing one phenomenon with another, this is acceptable, but when dealing with human relations where spirit (*jingshen* 精神) is involved, then uniformity is unsound.

---

59 Hans A. E. Driesch, *The Crisis of Psychology*. Princeton, N.J.: Princeton University Press, 1925, 176. Italics in original.
60 Zhang further divided the sphere of the 'view of life': "The heart of the 'view of life' is the I. What the I faces is the non-I. The non-I further divides into various kinds ..." The classifications and some of their related attributes are: 1. Humankind: the greater, the smaller. 2. The other sex: respect, equality, free marriage, fixed (authoritarian) marriage. 3. Property: private, common. 4. The attitude towards the social system: conservatism, reformism. 5. The relations between inner spirit and external matter: material civilization, spiritual civilization. 6. The relations between the I and the greater body that the I belongs to: individualism, socialism. 7. Between the I and the others: egoism, utilitarianism. 8. The expectations of the I from the world: pessimism, optimism. 9. The belief of the I in the existence or non-existence of creation: theism, atheism; one god, many gods; single, all-encompassing (Babism). Zhang Junmai, "Rensheng guan," *Controversy*, pp. 1–3.
61 The qualities and their further elaboration are in ibid., 4–9.

The sphere of science was also discussed by Lin Zaiping. Responding to the claims of scientism he questioned whether predictability characterizes the natural order:

> In the little yard where I dwell, right now the leaves of the plum tree are falling on their own and white snowflakes cover the buds. No matter how long, sooner or later they are bound to germinate, never disappointing [...]. We assume that they will appear next year [...] but can we be certain? No one can be [absolutely] sure [...]. And the moon that I watch, in a thousand years, will it be the same? And the temperature, even if there was a [scientific] law it would be impossible to know [...] [therefore] all laws conform to probability [...] probability but not necessity.[62]

The wider the perspective, the smaller the idea of necessity. Lin argued for a broader perspective of time where perception and rationality are reduced and cannot be considered absolute.

The complementary aspect to the sphere of science is the point where science is no longer valid, which was the leading argument against scientism. For Zhang Dongsun, human intelligence, the blade of the knife itself, is beyond science (see above 84–85). Liang Qichao, while affirming that science can answer many questions of life, admitted that one small, though very important, aspect transcends science (*chao kexue* 超科學). In his words:

> In man's life it is difficult indeed to leave out the intellect (*lizhi* 理智), but it is also true that the intellect does not cover all internal content of life (*renlei shenghuo de quan neirong* 人類生活的全內容). Apart from the intellect there is something else, maybe the driving force of life, and that is 'emotions' (*qinggan* 情感). Emotions have few expressions, at least two of which carry some mystery (*shenmi xing* 神秘性), and these are 'love' (*ai* 愛) and 'beauty' (*mei* 美). In the 'kingdom of science', whatever it may be, Mr. Love and Mr. Beauty are not obedient [...]. They are inaccessible to science [...] and there is no doubt that this is one of the exceptional marvels of the 'view of life' [...]. Therefore, in the sphere of life where the intellect is involved we have to use science [...]. Concerning the sphere of emotions there are phenomena which are beyond science.[63]

Zhang Junmai introduced a different view:

> Science speaks about reasons and perceptions, but what about whatever is beyond that?[64] [...] To determine the individual's will and his attitude toward social development [...] this is the dream of science [...]. Science is fluent

---

62 Lin Zaiping, "Du Ding Zaijun xiansheng de 'Xuanxue yu kexue'," *Controversy*, 212–213.
63 Liang Qichao, "Rensheng guan yu kexue," *Controversy*, 178–179. Mr. Love and Mr. Beauty are certainly strong allusions to Chen Duxiu's earlier Mr. Science and Mr. Democracy.
64 Zhang Junmai, "Zai lun Rensheng guan," *Controversy*, 107.

about causality and perceptions but with regard to what is beyond them it is helpless [...]. Moreover, the foundations of science are not accessible to the ear and the eye. The logical discrimination between good or bad and between right and wrong has no standard. Beauty, sincerity, morality, dignity and belief have no form whatsoever.[65]

We notice here differences of approach. Where Liang differentiated in the context of human relationships between intellect and emotions, Zhang Dongsun distinguished between the function of intelligence (what its knife can cut) and the substance of intelligence – its own nature (the knife's blade). Neither function nor substance – knife or blade – are assigned priority. Zhang Junmai's distinction, which was also accepted by Lin, was different. Zhang's separation of the sphere of sense-perception and reason from that which is beyond it, defined the latter as the foundation of the former. Tracing the source of the immanent in transcendence he turned the context of human relationships into a sphere where rationality ceased to be dependable. Here, the supporters of metaphysics, except for Liang Qichao and Zhang Dongsun, arrived at a point of paradox, loosening their grip on reason.

Since the supporters of metaphysics aimed to explain metaphysics by means of rational arguments they were frequently destined to arrive at this paradox. Zhang thought that an all-encompassing rationality-intelligible substructure of the context of human relationships invited determinism. He therefore promoted intuition in order to preserve the autonomous element in man. To be sure, we have good reason to conjecture that the priority for intuition over reason was at least partly derived from Bergson. For Zhang it was Bergson who said: "Living activity (*huodong* 活動) and spontaneity (*zifa* 自發) are experienced by the mind where the so-called reality and so-called life is found."[66] It follows that intuition, which according to Bergson is more intimately linked with the experiences of the mind, has a more significant role in the mind's perception of the reality.

Aside from this disagreement, the proponents of metaphysics agreed on the division of the sphere of science and the sphere beyond science. As indicated above, the supporters of scientism (except Chen Duxiu) also accepted that ultimately reality should be divided between whatever is sense-perceived and rationally intelligible and that which is beyond, provided that the latter is admitted as irrelevant to the former. Chen Duxiu was the only participant who denied the existence of any "other" sphere.

The proponents of metaphysics furthermore agreed about the content of the sphere beyond science. Liang said that "except for the intellect there is something else, maybe the driving force of life." Zhang Junmai said in the opening lecture:

---

65 Zhang Junmai, "Kexue zhi pingjia" 科學之評價 (The value of science), *Controversy*, 310–311.
66 Zhang Junmai, "Zai lun Rensheng guan," *Controversy*, 109.

> For the sake of truth, when we close our eyes and reflect, we will have to admit that there is one kind of problem that [...] belongs to daily life [...]. The question is, what is it? The answer is, the life of man [...] who is living and different from dead material things which are easily associated by one set of measures.[67]

Matter, objectivity, and causality characterize that which is scientific valid, but the sphere beyond science is recognizable through its "life." This so-called "life," so central to vitalist philosophers like Eucken, Bergson, and Driesch, was considered by the supporters of metaphysics to be internal, spiritual, heterogeneous and dynamic. Transposing life to beyond science, the supporters of metaphysics neglected the effects of determinist factors in human life. Accordingly, they also negated the determinist explanation regarding mental processes and resisted any claim of life as predictable – a danger they had warned against at the beginning of the controversy. By discriminating between the sphere of science and the sphere beyond it, provided them with a basis for answering the key question of the controversy: since the 'view of life' is inherently beyond science, how can science govern the 'view of life'?

Our account of the metaphysicians' arguments against scientism would be incomplete without mentioning two other critical questions. One concerned the changing concepts of science. From Newton to Einstein historical evidence shows how key concepts of scientific knowledge have changed and been replaced by others. Both Zhang Junmai and Lin Zaiping pointed this out. These changes, they maintained, lead one to question the stability of natural laws.[68]

Another question concerns the problem of Creation. Zhang Junmai discredited Darwinism, the theory of evolution that cannot explain Creation.[69] And he inquired: what is matter and what is its origin? What is energy, and heredity, and what is the meaning of evolution? As long as the ultimate mystery has no answer, scientific knowledge is always partial and subject to doubt. Zhang quoted Arthur J. Thomson, the philosopher of science who said that identifying the progress of science reveals that it is regressive: "A small secret is solved, a great secret unfolds." The more science unveils the mysteries of the world, the more mystery there is.[70]

However, none of the participants dismissed science. Already in his Qinghua address, Zhang Junmai assigned an objective sphere to the exact sciences, stating that the senses absorb sensations which the intellect processes. In placing the sphere where science is valid within the framework of the relations between mind and real-

---

67 Zhang Junmai, "Rensheng guan," *Controversy*, 1–4.
68 Zhang Junmai, "Zai lun Rensheng guan," *Controversy*, 54; Lin Zaiping, "Du Ding," *Controversy*, 210.
69 Zhang Junmai, "Kexue zhi pingjia," *Controversy*, 312.
70 Zhang Junmai, "Zai lun Rensheng guan," *Controversy*, 100–103; Quote in English from Arthur J. Thomson, *Introduction to Science*. London: Williams and Norgate, 1911, 194–225.

ity Zhang allowed a restricted area where determinism provided legitimate and useful explanations. Others too affirmed the value of science. Zhang Dongsun criticized science but he also praised its wisdom, and called science an essential, and useful mode of thought.[71] Lin likewise affirmed a belief in science. According to him, Ding's words were not altogether wrong, rather the method and the attitude were unacceptable. Alluding to Hu Shi and to Dewey, Lin emphasized the indispensability of critical thought, calling on everyone to gather responsibly and present their views.[72] Qian Mu 錢穆 in his article "The Bystander's Comment,"[73] referred to the importance of science. He introduced Russell as someone whose brain has been "infected" by science, nevertheless, he exemplified that science coexists with humanity. "[...] his [Russell's] books forcefully profess to liberate mankind, urging to set everyone free at once; [Moreover,] unlike Ding whose science excludes everything else, [Russell's books] express views on various areas such as religion, literature and art."[74]

Conclusion

To contend with scientism the supporters of metaphysics had to formulate rational philosophical arguments against reason as the sole means for understanding all phenomena. They opposed those who maintained that mind consists of a principally intelligible material process by arguing that the mind does not correlate to objective reality. Zhang Dongsun objected that rational intelligence, the foundation of science, is incapable of investigating itself. Zhang Junmai argued that the internal process that generates knowledge in the mind is unintelligible to science. In its reliance on means such as objectivity, causality and reason, science is inapplicable to understanding the processes of the mind, which are subjective, freely willed and holistic. Lin Zaiping agreed, stating that mind follows an order which necessarily differs from objective reality. The claims against the correlation between mind and objective reality implied that the mental process involves a spiritual element.

The two sides in the controversy also disagreed in their concepts about the nature of the context of human relationships. Rejecting the claims of scientism for homogeneous reality Lin insisted that the world of human life is not a place where only one answer prevails. He and Zhang Junmai argued for a heterogeneous context of human relationships. Lin went a step further, stating that even the established natural laws of today cannot be tested for the future, nor can they be trusted absolutely.

---

71 Zhang Dongsun, "Lao er wu gong," *Controversy*, 333.
72 Lin Zaiping, "Du Ding Zaijun xiansheng de 'Xuanxue yu kexue'," *Controversy*, 239–240.
73 Qian Mu 錢穆, "Pangguanzhe yan" 旁觀者言 (The bystander's comment). In *Controversy*, 419–428. This article is included in Qian's *Zhongguo Xueshu Sixiangshi Luncong* 9 中國學術思想史論叢, 九 (Studies in the History of Modern Chinese Thought, 9). Taipei: Sushulou wenjiao jijinhui, 2000, 204–210.
74 Ibid., 426.

From the larger perspective of time passing, he concluded, science can talk about probabilities, but cannot predict the necessary. Lin, the two Zhangs, Liang and the other supporters of metaphysics agreed that there was a break between human life and the application of scientific explanations. The sphere of science, they argued, should be differentiated from the sphere of human relationships which is beyond science.

With these philosophical arguments against scientism, the supporters of metaphysics established a ground to distinguish between the essence of what it means to be human and the application of science. Recalling the *tiyong* formula of the late nineteenth century, in 1923 the cultural origin of the *yong* was no longer what intellectuals saw as the main point to emphasize. Science was no longer used to define all the West had to offer. The 1923 debaters saw science as a universally valid method of inquiry that belongs to and should be used by all mankind. Nonetheless, it was the question of life that must be at the center of discussion according to the arguments of the supporters of metaphysics. Regardless of its origins in the East or in the West, science was synonymous with the *yong*, but the question of the 'view of life' and what it means to be human requires an explanation that is not scientific.

CHAPTER FIVE

The View of Life Based on Metaphysics

The arguments against scientism paved the way for the 'view of life' arguments that were based on metaphysics. The following inquiry of this view is arranged in three parts. Apart from the philosophical argumentation against scientism, described in the previous chapter, the main speaker of the supporters of metaphysics, Zhang Junmai, saw another reason for assuming their particular position: he thought that the future would be the age of new metaphysics. How did he arrive at this conclusion? What were the implications of this supposition for his view? To answer these questions the first part will discuss his anti-positivist criticism, and his observations about contemporary currents in world thought.

Next follows an account of the framework of the 'view of life' presented by the supporters of metaphysics. As already observed by many scholars, the views as they were argued for in the heat of one year of strenuous debate were marked by a tendency to mix ideas unsystematically. My analysis of the arguments of the supporters of metaphysics attempts to arrange their view systematically, considering that the framework was not clearly stated but was nonetheless clearly implied. I begin with definitions of the 'view of life' by three of the supporters of metaphysics. Then I introduce what I will call the basic argument or the center of the 'view of life' position, the innate moral direction possessed by each individual, which everyone may use autonomously. Then follows "the sphere beyond science," and its five attributes, which complements the same number of attributes of "the sphere of science," introduced in the previous chapter. Together, the center and the attributes provide a framework for the 'view of life' based on metaphysics.

The third part will return to the larger context of the 'view of life' controversy, the question of culture that was raised earlier by Liang Qichao and Liang Shuming and other contemporary thinkers. The supporters of metaphysics welcomed the process of modernizing but, at the same time, they were concerned to preserve what it means to be human. Their arguments, as we saw earlier, continued to utilize dichotomizations (reminiscent of the *tiyong* formula in its philosophical meaning) and were now applied to the metaphysics-science dichotomy. To the extent that science was taken for the *yong*, the 'view of life' based on metaphysics was intended to serve as substitute for the *ti*. To determine the appropriate balance between them was the point.

The Age of New Metaphysics

Zhang Junmai launched the 'view of life' campaign early in 1923 on the basis of his observations both in Europe, especially in Germany where he stayed for five years, and in China. In fact, in his initiative to promote the 'view of life' discussion in China, the European post World War I cultural crisis certainly played a major role. Accordingly, the arguments against scientism also involved cultural, social and political criticism that considerably imitated the arguments of the European idealists against positivism. Describing what science had accomplished (*kexue zhi jieguo* 科學之結果), Zhang offered a dark picture of the situation in the West:

> [Regarding] the effects of science, the major accomplishment of science is the material civilization (*wuzhi wenming* 物質文明) in Western Europe [...]. Scientific knowledge is utilized and transformed into schemes for making profit; state policies motivate territorial expansion for the sake of wealth [...]. The focus is directed toward production and commerce [...] [commodities] are exported abroad while houses are ruined inside. Similarly, education concentrates on knowledge and militancy [...]. Knowledge is directed outward while an inward glance is avoided. In this way the industrial materialist and imperialist nations cannot hold out too long. Following the imperialistic race the [first] World War began.[1]

In this passage Zhang forged a linkage between the positivist application of science to all areas of life and a deterioration of the human condition in Western civilization. Some aspects of the modernizing process were not necessarily a blessing. He explicitly warned against installing wealth and power as the sole aim of the polity, a policy that would create unnecessary conflicts between states. "The greatest danger [we face] is the policy of wealth and power," he declared.[2] Similarly, he warned, this policy affects the life of the individual, turning people into means instead of ends. Corroborating Liang Qichao's earlier anti-positivistic sentiments, Zhang rejected determinism in human existence. The commercial and industrial race, he observed, benefits the national market, but sacrifices the family and ignores the individual, transforming people into machines. "People in the West are already discouraged by mechanism and competitiveness; we must prevent this from coming to China."[3]

Finding science inadequate to explain human life as a whole, Zhang suggested that metaphysics should take its place. He defined metaphysics as the search for the explanation that transcends the physical and sense-experienced world. Origins of

---

1. Zhang Junmai, "Kexue zhi pingjia," in *Kexue xuanxue lunzhanji* 科學玄學論戰集 (The controversy of science and metaphysics). Preface by Hu Shi 胡適 and Chen Duxiu 陳獨秀. Shanghai: Yadong shuju, 1923. Hereafter *Controversy*, 312–313.
2. Zhang Junmai, "Zai lun rensheng guan yu kexue bing da Ding Zaijun" 再論人生觀與科學並答丁在君 (Another discussion of science and the 'view of life' and an answer to Ding Zaijun [i.e. Ding Wenjiang]), *Controversy*, 124.
3. Ibid..

everything can all be traced back to metaphysical sources. Zhang maintained that whereas science is limited and narrow, metaphysics is boundless. Metaphysics' major virtue is that it is able to convey the truth of human existence.[4]

Zhang justified his support for metaphysics not only on philosophical grounds and considerations of values, but also because he considered metaphysics the contemporary tendency in world thought. Against Ding Wenjiang who depicted metaphysics as a ghost that had been deported from Europe and was secretly attempting to slink into China, Zhang argued to the contrary, that the status of metaphysics was on the rise. He enumerated several reasons for this:

> The explanations of the supporters of science [or scientism] regarding the relations between phenomena are insufficient to uncover the mystery of the beginning of the world. The dynamic affairs of society are beyond the reach of logic and [rigid] definitions. The limits of causality in explaining mental processes have driven philosophers to study freedom of the will. Disappointment with this world has led many to seek a link to that which is beyond forms. Religion is the medium to communicate with the beyond. There is the Christian revival, displayed in Eucken's thought, and the pragmatist explanation of religion's role, as in William James. In Europe of the last twenty or thirty years, there is a growing antagonism against mechanism, intellectualism, and determinism, and against false [pretentious and superstitious] religions.[5]

Accordingly, Zhang declared, the present age deserves to be named "The age of new-metaphysics" (*xin xuanxue shidai* 新玄學時代).[6] The age is witnessing an increase and growth in opposition to mechanism; in support for the individual's autonomy in human existence; and in the spread of the idea of free will.

To Zhang, "The age of new-metaphysics" will witness cooperation between scientific and metaphysical systems of knowledge. Despite their arguments against scientism, the supporters of metaphysics acknowledged the value of some aspects of science. At the same time, philosophy, art, and religion were introduced as systems of knowledge that benefit science.[7] To support their argument Zhang Junmai and Zhang Dongsun resorted to the ideas of the philosopher of science Arthur Thomson.[8] Thomson had indicated two aspects where philosophy aided science: science needs criticism, and science aims at bridging the gap between the worldviews of particular

---

4 Ibid., 103.
5 Ibid., 107.
6 The term xuanxue that literally means "Dark Learning" is associated with scholars of the Wei Jin period (220–420 A. D.) is used here perhaps as a Chinese alternative to the Western "metaphysics," otherwise referred to as "xingershang" 形而上.
7 Zhang Junmai, "Zai lun rensheng guan," *Controversy*, 100.
8 For Zhang Dongsun's reference to Thomson, see his "Lao er wu gong" 勞而無功 (Wasted effort). In Kexue xuanxue lunzhanji 科學玄學論戰集 (The controversy of science and metaphysics), *Controversy*, 320. Thomson was used to support the claims of the supporters of scientism such as Ding Wenjiang.

branches of science. According to Zhang, Thomson highlighted the unique capacity of art and religion, disciplines belonging to metaphysics, to mediate emotions and to approach the complexity which is reality:

> In the history of nature and man, science tried to provide an answer. But the world is so big and science so feeble and young, [...] the answer of science cannot satisfy [...]. There are things science cannot say, the answer is possible only through the emotion of poetry and religious faith.[9]

Recognizing that science is insufficient to provide a satisfactory 'view of life' philosophy, by means of his age of new metaphysics arguments Zhang conveyed the hope that modernity does not necessarily require for man to be treated as part of a machine. Once what he considered to be the implications of the metaphysical humanist outlook were accepted, the anti-positivist agenda could be realized. Therefore, Zhang concluded, "From the bottom of the sea of suffering caused by mechanism, man endeavors to recuperate and break out from the past. And there are those such as H. G. Wells and Thomson who blend science and metaphysics."[10] Thus the supporters of metaphysics introduced the 'view of life' based on metaphysics in order to offer an alternative grounding for a modern transformation that would challenge the positivist view.

The 'View of Life' Arguments

The 'view of life' based on metaphysics, has its source in what it presumes takes place within the individual self. According to Zhang Junmai:

> Since the formation of the view of life does not have objective categories to rely on, we can only turn inward and seek it inside the self (*wei you fan qiu zhi yu zi* 惟有反求之與自).[11]

Three participants, Zhang Junmai, Liang Qichao and the psychologist and philosopher Fan Shoukang 范壽康 (1896–1983) offered definitions, which shared a dualistic outlook on the 'view of life' position. Zhang's definition of the 'view of life' position associated a matter-spirit differentiation with the individual's concern for human society:

> I often wish to transform, to improve and to beautify the people and the things outside myself. Since ancient times and until the present age, this great question still involves the conflict between matter and spirit. When I observe,

---

9 Zhang Junmai, "Zai lun rensheng guan," *Controversy*, 101–103. Zhang was quoting from Arthur Thomson, Introduction to Science. London: Williams and Norgate, 1911.
10 Zhang Junmai, "Zai lun rensheng guan," *Controversy*, 107.
11 Zhang Junmai, "Rensheng guan" 人生觀 (The view of life), *Controversy*, 10.

appeal, hope and care for people and things outside myself, this is what is called the 'view of life'.¹²

Liang Qichao's definition echoed Zhang's matter-spirit differentiation, and also posited human life in relation to its ideal context:

> From within the world of matter (*wujie* 物界) and mind (*xinjie* 心界) man creates the combination which is called "human life." We employ a kind of "ideal" (*lixiang* 理想) to complement this life, and this is the so-called "view of life."¹³

Fan Shoukang suggested a "more precise" formulation:

> The 'view of life' creates a notion regarding an inner context, divided into the real and the ideal, but the emphasis is on the ideal.¹⁴

Different nuances in definitions of the 'view of life' notwithstanding, the 'view of life' position involved a single overriding quality, which Zhang characterized as the fundamental positive inclination toward the good:

> Human life takes place by combining matter and spirit; the good (*shan* 善) is all the spiritual phenomena, like law, religion, morality, art and so on; the bad (*e* 惡) is all the contact with matter, like falsity, lust and larceny. Recognizing the lack of harmony between matter and spirit, the greatest men of thought from time immemorial, who could not bear to see pain, silently concentrated and meditated, devotedly searching [for] the sake of the people. In our case [this search continued] from Confucius and Mencius to Lu-Wang, in Europe from Plato to Marx [...]. The goals of man have constantly changed [...]. But we must believe that the permanent tendency is toward the good and not toward the bad, to build and not to destroy.¹⁵

In the history of Chinese thought, the optimistic confidence about human nature, though implied in the *Analects*, was primarily developed by Mencius, according to whom it is natural to be good.¹⁶ Mencius formulated his human nature thesis around the idea that the beginnings of goodness are intrinsic to the mind. Wang Yangming elaborated this concept with his idea of the innate knowledge of the good (*liangzhi* 良知). Late Ming and Qing scholars further associated the concept with concrete

---

12 Zhang Junmai, "Zai lun rensheng guan," *Controversy*, 76.
13 Liang Qichao, "Rensheng guan yu kexue" 人生觀與科學 (The view of life and science), *Controversy*, 173.
14 Fan Shoukang 范壽康, "Ping suowei 'Kexue yu xuanxue zhi zheng' " 評所謂'科學與玄學之爭' (Criticizing the so-called 'Controversy over science and metaphysics'), *Controversy*, 459. Originally published July 10th, 1923. Fan's definition of the 'view of life' position is very similar to the definition of culture in Liang Shuming's *Cultures*, 28.
15 Zhang Junmai, "Zai lun rensheng guan," *Controversy*, 82.
16 *Mencius*, 6A:1–6.

ideas and practice. The supporters of metaphysics combined this tradition with their understanding of idealist moral thought. For that purpose Zhang resorted to the term *liangxin* (良心) which Liang Qichao had already used in his *Essay* (discussed in chapter two) where he discussed Kant. In chapter two we saw that *liangxin* means the inner independent element, the moral standard intrinsic to mind which is the essential substance of human relations.

Zhang distinctly highlighted *liangxin* as the overriding quality of the 'view of life' position, identifying it with Kantian and idealist concepts. *Liangxin*, said Zhang, echoing Liang Qichao, "... is the *categorical imperative* (*duanyan mingling* 斷言命令) in Kant's philosophy and the spiritual life in Eucken's thought."[17] He equated *liangxin* with ideas of Kant and Eucken, and he explained *liangxin* in Bergsonian terms as the autonomous individual who possesses intuition and free will (see discussion below). Zhang, like others before him, used terms that were rooted in Chinese philosophical tradition, and endowed the terms with new meanings according to the Mencius-Wang Yangming tradition.

Those in agreement with the *liangxin* concept included all the supporters of metaphysics except for Zhang Dongsun, who did not discuss it. During 1919–1921, Liang Qichao in his *Reflections* and Liang Shuming in his *Cultures* had warned against the tendency to lower man's expectations from life to mere survival. They did so by defending the ideal of spiritual attainments. Liang Qichao maintained a similar ideal by acknowledging the principle of *liangxin*; the person who aspires to goodness (*zhishan* 至善), he wrote, should keep a balance between what is external and internal, and should be attentive to his inner moral standard.[18] He also noted that, by means of the combination of knowledge, emotions and will, man can transform his life and attain a spiritual state.[19] Like Zhang who argued for the relationship between *liangxin* and free will, Liang Shuming had held that an inner moral standard guides human nature.[20]

Qu Shiying's article "Man's Character and Education" was rich in ideas that examined the question of the 'view of life' philosophy from an educational perspective. Autonomy, he wrote, is a major element in education. Education has a most significant role in instilling a purpose in life, while its main objective is to cultivate the mind's inner autonomy (*neixin ziyou* 內心自由). Qu differentiated between things which are moved by external causes and human beings who move themselves; things are dependent, but man has free will. He depicted autonomy as the flame of self-consciousness (*zijue* 自覺) that cannot be extinguished.[21] The individual envisaged by Qu relies on his self-conscious effort and autonomously determines

---

17 Zhang Junmai, "Zai lun rensheng guan," *Controversy*, 76–77. The italicized words appeared in English in Zhang's original text.
18 Liang Qichao, *Reflections*, 10–12.
19 Ibid.
20 Liang Shuming, *Cultures*, 80, 114–119.
21 Qu Shiying 瞿世英), "Renge yu jiaoyu" 人格與教育 (Character and education), *Controversy*, 345.

the course of his own life. Fan Shoukang, whose article set out to criticize both sides in the debate, specifically affirmed the idea of *liangxin*. He viewed *liangxin* as a central element underlying sensations, emotions, and will – the constituents of consciousness (*yishi* 意識). The roles of consciousness, said Fan, are to provide the individual with the ability to make moral judgments and to direct him toward doing what he considers to be good.[22]

Unlike Qu and Fan, Zhang Dongsun and Lin Zaiping concentrated on refuting the arguments of scientism and did not present constructive ideas for the 'view of life' position. Lin's arguments showed however, that he considered free will an indispensable element insofar as life's meaning and values are concerned. He attacked Ding Wenjiang's criticism of the *liangxin* concept, maintaining that *liangxin* should coexist with science.[23] Zhang Dongsun vowed to support the unpopular – metaphysics – side in the controversy."[24] However, he mainly wrote articles on epistemology, and consistently avoided questions of morality and culture. He remarked that Lin had done most of the work.[25]

In the previous chapter, we saw that according to the supporters of metaphysics, science belongs to the sphere of sense-perception and rationality. The 'view of life' philosophy belongs to "the sphere beyond science." Where objectivity, logical and analytical methods, and causality and the unity of the substructure (homogeneity) cease to be valid, there begins the sphere beyond science. Zhang Junmai enumerated five complementary attributes of this sphere, which form, he said, the axis of the 'view of life': subjectivity (*zhuguan* 主觀), intuition (*zhijue* 直覺), synthesis (*zonghe* 綜合), free will (*ziyou yizhi* 自由意志), and uniqueness (*dan yi xing* 單一性).[26] With the exception of intuition, all these, like the title "View of Life" (*rensheng guan*), were new or neologisms in Chinese thought, borrowed from Japanese.[27] In his Qinghua address in 1923, Zhang introduced these attributes in detail, followed by examples from the history of thought in both East and West. Apart from presenting the role, the value, and the character of the attributes, he also indicated the proximity of the sources that provide the content of the 'view of life' despite their origins in the West or in the East.

---

22 Fan Shoukang, "Ping souwei 'Kexue yu xuanxue zhi zheng'," *Controversy*, 469.
23 Lin Zaiping, "Du Ding Zaijun xiansheng de 'Xuanxue yu kexue'" 讀丁在君先生的'玄學與 科學' (Criticizing Mr. Ding's article on "Metaphysics and Science"), *Controversy*, 237–238.
24 Zhang Dongsun, "Lao er wu gong," *Controversy*, 318. In the years before the controversy Zhang was known for his support of the movement that sought to establish Confucianism as a religion. In later years he became a prominent philosopher known for his many contributions in the field of epistemology, contributing to social, moral, and political discussions. For a recent comprehensive study of Zhang Dongsun's thought see Yap Key-chong, *Western Wisdom in the Mind's Eye of a Westernized Chinese Lay Buddhist: The Thought of Chang Tung-hsun (1886–1962)*. Ph.D dissertation, University of Oxford, 1991.
25 Zhang Dongsun, "Lao er wu gong," *Controversy*, 318.
26 Zhang Junmai, "Rensheng guan," *Controversy*, pp. 4–9.
27 See Appendixes B, D, and E, in Lydia H. Liu, *Translingual Practice*. Xiong Yuezhi, *Xixue Dongjian*, 673–676.

Zhang contended that as an assortment of subjective ideas, the body of the 'view of life' embraces the thought of all the greatest philosophers of the West and of the East:

> Confucius advocated participation and activity while Laozi called for non-interference. Mencius talked about the inborn goodness of human nature while Xunzi argued that human nature is bad. Yang Zhu held to egoism and Mozi preached universal love. The moral obligation in the philosophy of Kant contrasted with Bentham's utilitarianism. Darwin [explained evolution] in terms of the struggle for survival and Kropotkin as mutual aid.[28]

Zhang argued that despite contrasts and contradictions, all kinds of ideas can be subsumed under the 'view of life'. Scientifically, they would not stand together because they are contradictory and would be dismissed. But the subjective perspective is not obliged to maintain objective standards; therefore, by virtue of their concern for human existence, such ideas all belong to the same body of views.

By means of intuition pure ideas originate in the mind. They are intuitive because in their incipient beginnings they are independent of intentional considerations. The teachings of Schopenhauer, Nicolai Hartmann, Johann Heinrich Lambert, Nietzsche, Hegel, Confucius, Mencius, Mozi, the Buddha and Jesus all originated in the individual *liangxin* (*zishen liangxin* 自身良心). Zhang emphasized the correlation between *liangxin* as an inner source of moral direction, and the value of moral ideas intuitively conceived by individuals. Since *liangxin* is charged with an absolute standard of morality, it follows that pure ideas without any extraneous intervention, emanating from the mind, are valuable. It was obvious to Zhang that the meritorious doctrines propagated around the world, as established models for all generations, demonstrate the intuitive way in which they were conceived and are innate.

The subjective ideas of the individual's 'view of life' are a synthesis – a structure that should not be dismantled. Once the synthesis is formulated, the motives and the causes leading to it cease to matter; what counts is the final result. Zhang cited some examples: an analysis of the Buddha's 'view of life' that called for liberating all living beings, shows that a major source is the Indian fondness for meditation, and the effect of the climate. Schopenhauer's personal dislike of women led him to some of his ideas. These apparently causal motives do not affect the value of the syntheses that Schopenhauer, the Buddha, and others eventually formulated, each in his own way. Zhang added that science is incapable of comprehending life in its entirety. Science provides knowledge, but only about parts of the complete 'view of life' synthesis. The true meaning of life is therefore beyond the reach of science and its analytic methods.

The fourth attribute of the 'view of life' is free will. The Qinghua address revealed that the only difference between free will and intuition was that the former was more oriented toward action and practice and less toward abstract thought.

---

28 Zhang Junmai, "Rensheng guan," *Controversy*, 5.

Zhang pointed out that founders of religions and fathers of thought who devoted themselves to goals concerning humanity, regardless of their personal needs and existential conditions, actively demonstrated the idea of free will. He asked four rhetorical questions: Why was the bed of Confucius never warm? Why did Mozi's stove not have a chance to blacken? Why did Jesus die on the cross? And why did the Buddha suffer physical tortures? These men are models of freely willed actions, they demonstrate the devotion and readiness of the individual to sacrifice all he has and even his life, for the sake of humanity. There is but one explanation: they derive free will directly from the *liangxin* of the self. Ordinary people demonstrate the same attribute when they reflect on universal human emotions and thoughts such as remorse, turn over a new leaf, and responsibility. Devotion, self-sacrifice and morality cannot be explained in terms of cause and effect. Accordingly, Zhang argued that *liangxin* dictated the achievements of great men like Confucius, Mozi, Jesus and the Buddha, and the force of free will helped to carry them out. Zhang's Qinghua address, while referring to the virtues of devotion and self-sacrifice, did not adequately explain the idea of free will. This was remedied in his later book-length article where he modified his explanation, presenting the levels of free will. Free will enables the individual to partake and be actively involved in the cosmological process. Moreover, free will is the power that enables man to transform society.

The free will attribute of the 'view of life' was directly derived from the ideas of Bergson and Eucken, and the intellectual justification was based on Bergson. According to Zhang, Bergson had argued:

> The consciousness of man incessantly transforms. Therefore, mental states constantly change and the self is different in every moment. Therefore, [mental phenomena] cannot be measured and cannot be explained by causality. Hence, the movement of mind is autonomous.[29]

Activism, another facet of the idea of free will, was a major contribution of Eucken. Lin Zaiping, who had met Eucken in Jena for several discussions, introduced the latter's idea of activism in the following words:

> There exists in the universe good and evil and the rest of things. In the world that is governed by disorder, man has the responsibility to stand in the midst of the good and the evil and determine a course of living.[30]

The fifth attribute of the 'view of life', individual uniqueness, largely paralleled the attributes of subjectivity and synthesis. Zhang specifically challenged the application of scientific disciplines and statistics to individuals and society. In his opinion, the scientific approach is incapable of recognizing the human being in his entirety, and thus comparison of individuals with each other will be erroneous. Regarding the human realm, the supporters of scientism who base their calculations on scientific data,

---

29 Zhang Junmai, "Zai lun rensheng guan," *Controversy*, 64.
30 Lin Zaiping, "Du Ding," *Controversy*, 234.

arrive at unreliable conclusions. To establish his claim of uniqueness, Zhang turned to the creative arts. The works of Goethe, Dante, Shakespeare and Richard Wagner, he declared, were achievements of men whose creativity cannot be scientifically explained. The uniqueness of each master precludes an evaluative grading among them. The diverse attributes that characterize human phenomena cannot be ranked and compared. Ancient China's sages gave priority to emotions and praised wisdom and courage. In the West, creativity and talent command respect. Man's unique character results from the fact that, from different subjective points of view, distinct attributes are valued, and this is what is called uniqueness.

To Zhang Junmai, scientific rationality is adapted to static states and is helpless in dealing with the incessant transformations of phenomena that have life. He sought to preserve the mind as not entirely intelligible to reason, thus emphasizing the individual's potential to independently and unpredictably transform himself. He therefore accepted Bergson's linkage between intuition and life which, in turn, affirmed individual uniqueness. The idea of individual uniqueness transposed the argument for heterogeneity from the claims about the phenomenal world (see discussion in chapter four) to the area of human relationships. This argument marked a change from the traditional Chinese view which did not explicitly recognize the uniqueness of each individual.

Inasmuch as the five attributes of Zhang's 'view of life' position, subjectivity, intuition, synthesis, free will and uniqueness are all linked to the concept of *liangxin*, we may rightly call *liangxin* "the center of the 'view of life'." In fact, through these attributes, *liangxin*, as a moral virtue that is realized in relationships among people, now assumed the function of the linkage between man and society as a whole. But this linkage was no longer entirely like its traditional counterpart. Throughout the development of Chinese thought, from Mencius to the Song, Ming and Qing masters, the linkage signified integration of the individual with the whole universe. The supporters of metaphysics, following the precedent of Liang Qichao in his *Essay* and *Mirror*, or perhaps Dewey's associated living, dropped the earlier cosmic implications, shifting their concern to the life of society in the world.

Liangxin now functioned as the unifying element of subjectivity, intuition, synthesis, free will and uniqueness and, because of the five attributes, *liangxin* elevated the individual to a higher, spiritual and moral mode of existence. By associating the attributes of the 'view of life' with a spiritual and moral ground, the *liangxin* linkage lent subjectivity, intuition, synthesis, free will and uniqueness a meaning they lacked as independent attributes. Moreover, as a function of *liangxin*, these attributes turned into a framework that emphasized morality, spiritual life and engagement in society.

At the risk of generalizing, I suggest that the supporters of metaphysics held the following 'view of life'. With *liangxin* as the center of the 'view of life', the subjective individual becomes an independent agent of his inner life, at whose heart a moral knowledge is formed. Intuition is a pure and direct form of communication between the individual's *liangxin* and his life experience. Without intuition, selfish calculations are likely to introduce external considerations into the course of thought and action. Intuition also is essential to individual creativity. Synthesis is the unifying and dynamic force of the ideas that the individual lives by. The association between free will and *liangxin* guarantees the autonomy of the individual and the capacity to overcome mental and physical obstacles, within himself and in society, while preserving the moral foundation of his thought and behavior. Uniqueness is the right of the individual to be different and to express himself as such, and remain moral through his linkage with *liangxin*. The unique individual regards himself and all other people as ends in themselves and not just means.

To illustrate the relations between *liangxin* and the attributes I furthermore suggest that the attributes of the 'view of life' based on metaphysics are not ordered successively in a series that begins in *liangxin*. Rather, the attributes should be regarded as constituting an encircling form around *liangxin*. The whole may be viewed as a ring – organized around *liangxin* – for the individual in his relations with both the external and the internal force of life. The structure that emerges resembles the pattern of self-cultivation or human attainment exemplified in the classical Confucian (Rujia 儒家) text of the *Daxue* (大學, The Great Learning), where the process of self-cultivation involves eight levels beginning with the inner dimensions of the individual person and proceeding to the broader interpersonal frame of the family and on to the realms of the kingdom and the world.[31] This and other resemblances between the 'view of life' based on metaphysics and foundations of Confucian thought need to be considered by students of the revival of Confucian ideas in the twentieth century.

On closer examination, the 'view of life' position favors the inward force of life.[32] This view suggests that the person look within himself and then, and in correspondence, concern himself with other human beings. The overemphasis on intuition, of which Liang Qichao and Zhang Dongsun are not guilty (see chapter four), conveys the same bias. The individual was encouraged to act intuitively, in accord with his own *liangxin*, but, apparently, without the need to consult his *liangxin*'s impulses as they related to the needs of other people.

Similarly, by relegating reason to a secondary role in constructing the context of human relationships, the supporters of metaphysics (see exceptions above) based the attempt to create the external world from within the mind on a not self-evident assumption. This assumption was actually the belief that truth is real and is somehow given within the mind.[33] Taking mind and reality as two sides of a dichotomy, they

---

31 The terminology used here draws heavily on Andrew Plaks, trans. and annotator, *Ta Hsüeh and Chung Yung (The Highest Order of Cultivation and On the Practice of the Mean)*. London: Penguin Books, 2003. See especially page 58.
32 Another point of resemblence. The *Daxue* model considers life and the world as structured in concentric circles that assign priority to the center and at the same time the center is conditioned by and attentive to the other spheres.
33 See Gabriel Motzkin's discussion of Continental philosophy in his *Time and Transcendence: Secular History, the Catholic Reaction, and the Rediscovery of the Future*. Dordrecht: Kluwer Academic Publishers, 1992, especially 14–15.

gave priority to mind – Liang and Zhang Dongsun were the only exceptions. They then went on to claim that reality is other than it appears to be. But assuming that mind is not divorced from reality, we know that if reality is other than it appears to be, mind too may be different from what it appears to be. Hence, one might also argue, that in view of their position toward reality, the supporters of metaphysics (with the exceptions noted above) located themselves on grounds no more secure than those they denied.

Regardless of these weaknesses, the supporters of metaphysics made a significant contribution by showing the questionable position of positivism and its concept of a homogeneous reality. They advocated instead a heterogeneous concept of the context of human relationships; they installed *liangxin* as the moral center of each individual; and they stipulated the five attributes. The 'view of life' based on metaphysics, encouraged the individual to confront the external states of life, to overcome obstacles and transform personal as well as social situations. In relation to his internal life, this individual is capable of acting in accordance with an internal virtue of moral direction and, with effort, attain to spiritual achievement by linking with society as a whole. The 'view of life' based on metaphysics highlighted the autonomy and morality of the individual and challenged determinism. The supporters of metaphysics worked in the direction of establishing the philosophical ground for free relationships in society.

The Question of Culture

Ethical concerns were at the center of the 'view of life' debate. Specifically, the problem revolved around the relations between autonomy and morality. A study of Hu Shi's introduction to the collected articles of the controversy reveals that he by no means opposed autonomy. Neither did the other supporters of scientism. From the perspective of the supporters of metaphysics, however, the positivist epistemology that Hu, like his fellow proponents of scientism, accepted, reduced man ethically to the same level as material things. A positivist interpretation of mental phenomena turned man into a mechanical agent of morality. If morality has no interior basis, no subjective nucleus, but is entirely learned or externally imposed, and if the will is not free but subordinated to the rules of causality, grave questions arise regarding moral responsibility and the possibility of moral accord.

Considering the divorce from autonomy and morality that the view of the supporters of scientism implied, the supporters of metaphysics concerned themselves with preserving what they now considered as the essence of what it means to be human.[34] Their approach is comparable to the substance-function (*tiyong*) formula.

---

34 In the book that Eucken and Zhang co-authored the German philosopher stressed the relations between moral action and the autonomy of man, which provides man with absolute meaning and dignity, and turns him into an end in himself and not merely the means. Eucken and Chang,

While the arguments against scientism placed limitations on the function (*yong*) part, the arguments for the 'view of life' philosophy discussed the philosophical meaning of the substance (*ti*). To be sure, Zhang Zhidong's well known association with this formula was adopted in order to ensure that China utilized foreign material products and technology while preserving its culture intact. He considered culture, of course, within the context of Chinese traditions, which included the three bonds system, the five relations and so on. Unlike the original *tiyong* approach, however, the supporters of metaphysics considered the substance in terms of what it means to be human. They focused on internal moral capacity and individual autonomy, and the implications of both on transpersonal inter-relatedness.

What is more, the entirely Chinese character of the substance, which Zhang Zhidong did not question, had by now been opened to foreign ideas. By reducing the traditional concept of integration to moral accord among people who relate to each other, thus eliminating the former cosmic implications of this goal, the supporters of the 'view of life' arguments also left much of the old metaphysics behind. At the same time, we note a considerable change in the terms of their discussion. Whereas human nature remained a central concern, concepts such as principle and material force had nearly disappeared. The discussion of human nature instead involved terms such as *liangxin*, the internal moral direction of the individual, which Zhang explicitly associated with Kant's Categorical Imperative and the "spiritual life" of Eucken. The attributes of this center of the 'view of life' – subjectivity, intuition, synthesis, free will and individual uniqueness, were also terms arrived at through attempts, of admittedly various degrees and also levels, of fusing or reconciling East and West ideas.

But that is not to say that the supporters of metaphysics were Westernized. It is true that they engaged in an intellectual discussion that closely paralleled the European idealist discourse, while their rivals' support of scientism paralleled European positivism. Yet, though they discussed contemporary European issues, both sides relied, for obvious reasons, on philosophical conceptualizations inherited from the past. They were, after all, products of a traditional education, and the inherited language of philosophy.[35]

The Han learning vs. Song learning polemic[36] that the controversy involved illustrates this aspect. The Han vs. Song learning controversy involved conflicting

---

Das Lebensproblem in China und in Europa (The problem of life in China and in Europe). Leipzig: Quelle and Meyer, 1922, 35.

35 Lin Yusheng, *The Crisis of Chinese Consciousness: Radical Anti-Traditionalism in the May Fourth Era*. Madison: University of Wisconsin Press, 1978, 28–29. Yu Yingshi 余英時, "Wusi yundong yu Zhongguo chuantong" 五四運動與中國傳統 (The May Fourth Movement and Chinese tradition). In *Qimeng de jiazhen yu juxian: Tai Gang xuezhe lun Wusi* 啟蒙的价值與局限：薹港學者論五四 (The limits and value of enlightenment: Scholars from Taiwan and Hong Kong studies of the May Fourth). Xiao Tingzhong 蕭廷中 and Zhu yi 朱藝, eds.. Shanxi: Shanxi renmin chubanshe, 1989, 74–85.

36 The polemic between Han Learning and Song Learning started in the seventeenth and eight-

views regarding the nature of moral behavior. Han learning scholars had promoted a theory of morality that was based on externally imposed "objective" rules of propriety. Song learning scholars, on the other hand, claimed that morality is primarily based on internal subjective attributes, and is only subsequently stabilized with the assistance of objectively given rules. According to Zhang Junmai, both schools have traits in common, both seek the Way, and represent the teachings of the ancient sages, but both also differ on the concept of the mind.[37] Regarding the concept of mind, Zhang sided with Song learning:

> The Song learning scholars viewed the mind as the pure medium that contains all things, therefore they industriously cultivated their minds. The Han learning scholars rejected this view, claiming that one has to write commentaries and name the things. But thinking about it, if the mind does not have the depth associated with it [by the Song learning scholars], then where do the commentaries and the names come from?[38]

Zhang specifically pointed out the importance ascribed to the cultivation of the inner life of the mind in Chinese thought and its effects:

> Since Confucius and through the scholars of the learning of principle (*lixuejia* 理學家) in Song, Yuan, and Ming, self cultivation of the inner life of the mind (*neixin shenghuo zhi xiuyang* 內心生活之修養) was emphasized, and this eventually led to the [idea of] spiritual civilization.[39]

Zhang singled out Song learning as the intellectual current that considered mind to include that which is beyond sense-perception and reason. Similarly, he emphasized the individual's capacity to link with a spiritual context. His view again reveals the extent to which his ideas represented an attempt of reconciling East and West ideas.

Observing the cultural dilemma of modern China during the period associated with the May Fourth Movement (roughly 1915–1923), the supporters of metaphysics sought to establish that the substance of their culture should be defined in terms of the 'view of life' philosophy. In their discussions they attempted to reconcile traditional Chinese thought and Western idealist sources. They explained autonomy using foreign arguments and they modified their traditional goal to transpersonal inter-relatedness rather than universal integration. But, like their ancestors, they were concerned that the individual should be autonomous to think, to will and to act in a moral way.

The 'view of life' controversy had significant implications regarding the question of the process of modernizing. The supporters of metaphysics approved of

---

eenth centuries. Whereas the latter was identified with inner moral self cultivation, the former was concerned with exegetical studies of traditional texts.

37 Zhang Junmai, "Zai lun rensheng guan," *Controversy*, 130–131.
38 Zhang Junmai, "Rensheng guan," *Controversy*, 136.
39 Zhang Junmai, "Zai lun rensheng guan," *Controversy*, 9–10.

modernity, including science. But they searched for a solution that would somehow embrace the technical and material aspects of modernity and individual uniqueness and autonomy. Regarding what it means to be human they applied a set of categories, essentially consisting of individual autonomy and innate morality, which had roots in their tradition but were modified to meet the changing needs of modern times.

Conclusion

Perhaps contending with other predictions about the future development of societies and ideas, Zhang Junmai argued that the world is approaching the age of new-metaphysics. This age will see the collaboration between science and metaphysics. At the same time, the limitations of science and the priority of metaphysics in understanding human life will be recognized. This will lead to a world where people are treated as ends and not as means, and to the realization of an anti-positivist agenda.

The 'view of life' controversy represented the culmination of May Fourth intellectuals' efforts to establish a philosophically grounded concept of individual autonomy. The 'view of life' based on metaphysics aimed to define what it means to be human in a way that matched the requirements of what was believed to be the age of new-metaphysics. The supporters of metaphysics based their view on the assumption according to which each individual's mind carries an inborn spiritual moral direction. They termed this individual moral center *liangxin*. All persons similarly share the attributes of the 'view of life' philosophy: subjectivity, intuition, synthesis, free will and individual uniqueness. Joined with the 'view of life' attributes, *liangxin*, the center of the view, autonomously links the individual with society as a whole. Transpersonal interrelatedness thus achieved implied a spiritual mode of existence, which goes beyond the limits of sense-experience and reason.

The process of knowledge and ethical theory were based on mind-centered assumptions. Like their science rivals these men sought an epistemological justification for allowing them to accept the world as objectively existing. Thus the debate between science and metaphysics was also a conflict between two claims for objectivity.[40] From the metaphysics' supporters point of view, a purely materialistic conceptualization of both the phenomenal world and mind neglected the deeper structure of meaning that associated life with spirituality. The claim of the scientist side for a homogeneous substructure of reality and for omnipotent reason, threatened to drain the meaning out of transpersonal interrelatedness and to render individual autonomy senseless.

The 'view of life' based on metaphysics was in effect an attempt to reconcile ideas across the cultures of China and the West. We saw in the last chapter that the

---

40 See discussion in Richard Rorty, *Objectivity, Relativism, and Truth: Philosophical Papers*. Cambridge: Cambridge University Press, vol. I, 1991, 35–45.

epistemological arguments against scientism, namely the vitalist distinction between the sphere of valid science and the sphere beyond it, were drawn from Western idealist sources. However, the core of the view was rather a mixture. The backbone was the commitment to the idea of an intrinsic element in man which when realized allows the person to interrelate with society as a whole. This idea contained traditional concepts such as innate moral knowledge and the goodness of human nature in Mencian theory, but without the cosmic implications. Mencius, Wang Yangming, and Song learning were reduced to moral accord among people who relate to each other within society.

CHAPTER SIX

Philosophical Continuities

After May Fourth, toward mid-twentieth century, philosophical assumptions concerning the context of human relationships, linkage, autonomy, and integration with the whole, continued to change. In fact, a second-phase of the 'view of life' controversy, in addition to other, no less relevant debates, was a part of the Chinese intellectual scene. This chapter carries the discussion forward, to the mid and late 1940s, by examining several ideas of Xiong Shili 熊十力 (1883–1968), Hou Wailu 侯外廬 (1903–1987) and Qian Mu 錢穆 (1895–1990) concerning the 'view of life'. For Xiong I use his major work, published in 1944, and his short review of it where he described the method of metaphysics.[1] For Hou I use his work on the history of Qing thought, published in 1944,[2] where he interpreted Qing thought through Marxist eyes and also reflected on recent intellectual issues. In 1946 Hou published the work that he co-authored with Luo Keting 羅克汀 (1921–1996) on the new philosophy, where he outlined his philosophical position for that period.[3] For Qian I use his first philosophical reflections which he published in 1948.[4] My investigation of these modern Chinese intellectuals and their ideas during the 1940s considers their hindsight thoughts and reminiscences on their intellectual activity during that period.[5]

---

1 Xiong Shili 熊十力, *Xin weishilun* 新唯識論 (New doctrine of Consciousness-only). Shanghai: The Commercial press, 1947. This final version was first published in March 1944. Xiong Shili 熊十力, "Lun xuanxue fangfa 論玄學方法" (Discussing the method of metaphysics). In *Zheli yu xinli* 哲理與心理 (The principle of knowledge and the principle of mind). Xie Youwei 謝幼偉, et al., eds. Shanghai: Zhengzhong shuju, 1948, 77–84.
2 Hou Wailu 侯外廬, *Zhongguo jindai sixiang xueshuo shi* 近代中國思想學說史 (History of modern Chinese learning). Chongqing: Chongqing shudian, 2 vols., 1944. This study of Qing thought should be seen against the context of works by scholars such as Zhang Taiyan, Liang Qichao, Hu Shi, Feng Youlan, Jiang Weijiao, and Qian Mu. His efforts to find traces of dialectical materialism date to his earlier works as well.
3 Hou Wailu and Luo Keting 羅克汀, *Xin zhexue jiaocheng* 新哲學教程 (The process of the new philosophy). Shanghai: Shanghai xinzhe shudian, 1946.
4 Qian Mu 錢穆, *Hushang xiansilu* 湖上閒思綠 (Quiet thoughts at the lake). Taibei: Dongda dushu gongsi yinxing, 1984, hereafter *HSXSL*.
5 Xiong Shili, *Shili yuyao chuxu* 十力語要初續 (Primary supplemented abstracts by Xiong Shili). Taibei: Hongshi chubanshe, 1982. Hou Wailu, *Ren de zhuiqiu* 韌的追求 (The stubborn quest). Beijing: Sanlian shudian chuban, 1985. Qian Mu, *Bashi yi shuangqin, Shiyou zayi* 八十憶雙親，師友雜憶 (Reminiscences of my parents at the age of eighty, Memories of teachers and friends). Taibei: Dongda tushu gongsi, 1992.

The years 1937–1945 are the time of the war of resistance against the Japanese. Recently John Israel described this period: "During wartime, with an enemy juggernaut threatening the very existence of Chinese civilization [...] [a principal purpose] was to preserve the nation's heritage [...]."[6] Aside from the threat of science, a new urgency was introduced into questions of what constituted this heritage. Thus the nature of that heritage and which parts of it were worth preserving remained crucial and controversial.

Another factor that should be taken into account is that after World War II Europe and Japan readily invoked cultural criticism. Xiong, Hou and Qian were concerned for China and the fate of its culture. Under intensifying pressure both at home and abroad, like the 1923 'view of life' debaters they probed into the question of what it means to be human, formulating syntheses that took up anew the 'view of life' problem. Without abandoning traditional categories of thought they formulated new syntheses of Chinese and foreign ideas. Their thought can be taken to represent three different currents that continue today: the "New Confucians" (*xin rujia* 新儒家),[7] the Marxists and the so-called New Leftists (xinzuopai 新左派), and those who would set Chinese philosophy within a broader framework of culture and history.

Xiong Shili

In 1944 Xiong Shili published the final version of his major philosophical work, *Xin weishilun*. Concerned as his 1923 predecessors with the problem of science vs. metaphysics, Xiong differentiates between two modes of the context of human relationships, that of sense-experience and reason which entails science, and the ultimate context of existence, which entails metaphysics. As his main contribution he contrasts the life governed by science to the life that is lived in accordance with the ultimate context of existence – the life that Tu Weiming has called authentic existence.[8]

Meaningful life, Xiong maintains, must correspond to the ultimate and spiritual rather than to material forms which are merely a partial dimension within the ultimate. He terms ultimate context of existence the original substance (*benti* 本體). He refers to the original substance as the ultimate origin of the myriad transformations that interrelates things and self into one.[9] This definition calls attention to the unceasing movement and change that characterize the original substance, its interrelating quality, and its transcendence.

---

6 John Israel, *Lianda: A Chinese University in War and Revolution*. Stanford: Stanford University Press, 1998, 142.
7 While Xiong did not define himself as a new Confucian, he was a forerunner of the trend that includes his students Mou Zongsan (1909–96) and Tang Junyi (1909–78), among others.
8 Tu Wei-ming, "Hsiung Shih-li's Quest for Authentic Existence." In Furth, ed., *The Limits of Change*, 242–275.
9 Xiong, "Lun xuanxue fangfa," 80.

Individuals relate to the original substance through their original mind (*benxin* 本心) and its corollary, intuitive knowledge (*xingzhi* 性智), the functional facet of the original mind.[10] Xiong writes that the original substance is in the individual's mind, and must be sought within oneself,[11] and he argues that the original substance in the mind is Wang Yangming's innate knowledge of the good. As Yu Yingshi observed, to Xiong, each individual has within himself a source of value and creativity which is also moral.[12] The original mind is essential to the function of knowing.

Xiong Shili's mind theory combines the Buddhist consciousness-only doctrine[13] and Bergson's theory of consciousness.[14] Bergson divided consciousness into intuition and intellect, claiming that intuition is better qualified to realize the living context of existence. Xiong adopts a similar division: intellectual knowledge (*liangzhi* 量智), which, according to the contemporary scholar, Liu Shu-hsien, "includes both the commonsensical and scientific ways of understanding which postulate a real, external world;"[15] and *xingzhi*, the intuitive knowledge that flows from within the depth of the individual's being. Xiong maintains that only intuitive knowledge correlates with the original substance. Thus intuitive knowledge "is self-illuminating and self-enlightening; it is the only origin of all our knowledge and it embraces all knowledge."[16]

Because every person has the original substance, the original mind, and their intuitive knowledge, everyone participates in the same ultimate context of existence. One needs only to realize this. Intuitive knowledge functions as the linkage between the self and the whole. Like Mencius, Xiong asserts that each individual internally possesses that which directly relates him to the whole. By means of intuitive knowledge, the person transcends the distinction between inner and outer, and forms one body with the whole universe. This, according to Xiong, is the union of heaven and man, the pivot of Chinese thought.[17] Insofar as this process is based on a mind-reality correspondence, the individual is subjectively autonomous in his efforts to realize integration with the whole.

Xiong recognizes, however, that the objective world of sense experience and reason exists. Perfect and pure as the original mind is, it still has to manifest itself through relative sense-experience. To this end he introduces the habitual mind (*xixin*

---

10 Ibid., 79.
11 Ibid.
12 Yu Yingshi, *Youji fengchui shuishanglin: Qian Mu yu xiandai zhongguo xueshu* 猶記風吹水上鱗：錢穆與現代中國學術 (Like wind over water: Qian Mu and modern Chinese learning). Taibei: Sanmin shuju, 1991, 71.
13 For the Consciousness-only doctrine see discussion on Zhang Taiyan in chapter 1.
14 For a discussion of the agreement and disagreement between the Consciousness-only doctrine and Xiong Shili's mind theory, see Tu Wei-ming, "Hsiung Shih-li's Quest for Authentic Existence," especially 264–268.
15 Liu Shu-hsien, "The Contemporary Development of a Neo-Confucian Epistemology," *Inquiry*, 14 (1971), 21.
16 Ibid.
17 Xiong, "Lun xuanxue fangfa," 81.

習心) and its corollary, intellectual knowledge (*liangzhi*).[18] Intellectual knowledge is used in science, creating the possibility of ordering the phenomenal world and its principles intelligibly.[19] Considering scientific investigations, political and economic affairs as matters belonging to the original substance that interrelates all things as one, Xiong argues that intellectual knowledge serves the purposes of intuitive knowledge. Whereas by means of intellectual knowledge alone a person is unable to relate to the original substance, still, this capacity to exhaust thought and learn about the phenomenal world, is indispensable.[20]

Though intellectual knowledge should by no means become separate from intuitive capacity, Xiong finds this hardly avoidable. According to him, intellectual knowledge is sense-dependent and as such directed toward outward phenomena. The senses, Xiong finds, tend to purposelessly follow external things. They may then become dissociated from their origin, the original substance. Therefore, by means of intellectual knowledge a person may construct a world that is exclusively material, thus losing contact with the original substance.[21] Xiong therefore criticizes the tendency to overestimate science-related intellectual knowledge, on the ground that it dissociates the individual from the mode of authentic existence.

To avoid this dissociation, intellectual knowledge has to coexist together with intuitive knowledge. Both are related to the original substance; the former through the habitual mind, the latter through the original mind. Contrary to the Consciousness-only theory that phenomena are temporary, tentative, transitory, and thus false, Xiong argues that phenomena which are associated with consciousness through this coexistence, are real, though in a ceaseless state of transformation. There is, however, a clear order of priority between the two forms of knowledge. When using both forms to complement each other, only intuitive knowledge can establish the great foundation of the world.[22] The nonscientific moral principles of intuitive knowledge should control intellectual knowledge, enforcing limits on its mode of application.[23]

Xiong Shili entitled his book *Xin weishilun*. "New" (*xin* 新) in the title signals his confidence about having persuasively redefined the essence of what it means to be human according to Chinese tradition, so that modern science would be compatible with its values. On the one hand, he argues for the preservation of the essence of Chinese metaphysics, which was for him the moral and spiritual linkage with the ultimate context of existence. On the other, he realizes that within certain limits science is necessary. However, although Xiong confirms the importance of both intui-

---

18 Liu translated this term as "wisdom or knowledge by measurement." Liu, "The Contemporary Development of a Neo-Confucian Epistemology," 21.
19 Xiong, "Lun xuanxue fangfa," 80.
20 Ibid.
21 Ibid.
22 Ibid.
23 Donald J. Munro, *The Imperial Style of Inquiry in Twentieth-Century China: The Emergence of New Approaches*. Ann Arbor: The University of Michigan, Center for Chinese Studies, 1996, 44.

tive and intellectual knowing, he stipulates the idea of original substance as something to be pursued for its own sake. To find the way of integrating with the ultimate context of existence, the person must adopt a standpoint from which his authenticity does not derive from a relation with mundane reality and society, but rather from a relation with his inner self. Yet, by turning inward, can the person avoid losing contact with society? To Xiong Shili, personal autonomy is not an objective condition, but is purely subjective and related to a person's original substance and intuitive knowledge. Yu Yingshi has critically pointed that this attainment is experienced by the individual within himself, and therefore it is elitist, only few in each generation can claim or be recognized to have realized it.[24]

Hou Wailu

During the mid-thirties Hou Wailu, who had been working on the translation of *Das Kapital* since 1927, commenced on his life project of accommodating the Marxist philosophy of dialectical materialism (*bianzhengfa weiwulun* 辯證法唯物論) to Chinese thought.[25] Dialectical materialism he wrote, "... scientifically explains the natural and social world ... providing the rules to understand the objective movement of things ..."[26] It is the culmination of a scientific philosophy (*kexue de zhexue* 科學的哲學), the highest accomplishment in intellectual history and the conclusion of human understanding.[27] Toward the end of his book on the new philosophy (1946), he offered the following utopian vision which can be taken as the goal of his efforts:

> ... in the great union (*datong* 大同) of the Communist society classes and the relations between them will disappear, there will be no more oppressive government ... Then idealism of itself will disappear, then men will have the life of mutual equality where "each does his best, and each takes according to his needs." Intellectual and physical work will no longer be distinguished; there will be no more social contradictions; and human society will live in peace with the natural world (*ziranjie* 自然界). Finally, mystic thinking will be entirely won over by science; and people will become the sovereigns of nature and society. This is the so-called "leap from the kingdom of necessity to the kingdom of freedom." Then the mystic philosophies will take their place in the history museum, and we will, in our leisure time, drop by to wonder at the infinite mysteriously absurd.[28]

---

24 Yu Yingshi, *Youji fengchui shuishanglin: Qian Mu yu xiandai zhongguo xueshu*, 74–77.
25 In this he continued the precedent by Guo Moro (1892–1978). Hou, *Ren de zhuiqiu*, 66.
26 Hou Wailu and Luo Keting, *Xin zhexue jiaocheng*, 5.
27 Ibid., 4.
28 Ibid., 292.

Searching for points of convergence between Marxist philosophy and the tradition of Chinese thought, Hou comes to distinguish early Qing philosophy from other phases of Chinese thought. The agenda of the seventeenth century philosophers appears most compatible with his "new philosophy" of dialectical materialism, and it is not surprising, therefore, that he associates their thought with the term "enlightenment" (*qimeng* 啟蒙).

Wang Fuzhi 王夫之 (1619–92), according to Hou, propounded a dynamic philosophy of thought and existence. Showing ambivalence regarding the problem of exercising autonomy (see discussion below), Hou couples Wang with Marx, saying that human beings create history and not the other way around.[29] He considers Huang Zongxi 黃宗羲 (1610–95) a social critic who stressed the centrality of capital in the economy, and who also denounced the order of feudal society.[30] Pan Yongwei's 潘用微 (fl. 1600) vision of a uniform universe preceded Wu Zhihui's 1923 view,[31] and Gu Yanwu 顧炎武 (1613–82) was a pioneer experimentalist.[32] Yan Yuan 顏淵 (1635–1704) established labor (*gongye* 功業) as the content of human affairs.[33] Rejecting subjectivism on "logical grounds," Yan surpassed the teaching of the former masters of the learning of principle (*lixue* 理學).[34] Hou's account of the seventeenth century philosophers particularly highlights ideas valued in dialectical materialism.

From his dialectical materialist perspective, Hou singles out the thought of Dai Zhen 戴震 (1723–77) for both approval and criticism. According to Dai Zhen, by means of intelligence man can arrive at the final immutable norm (*bu yi zhi ze* 不易之則).[35] Then the individual integrates with the whole. "Being unselfish, the desires all correspond to humanness, propriety, and righteousness; being impartial (*bu pian* 不偏), the emotions are inevitably mild and easy, altruistic and even. Having no delusion, knowledge becomes the so-called sagely wisdom."[36] According to Hou, Dai Zhen argued that without grasping the final unchanging norm, the person who seeks autonomy becomes the slave of nature rather than its master. Hou praises this line of thinking as compatible with modern science. Nonetheless, Dai Zhen, he argues, was a conceptualist (*guanzhaolun zhe* 觀照論者) who failed to recognize that a person's consciousness and objective reality are both matter. Hou argues that though Dai Zhen was not entirely mistaken, "... he was, however, only partially close to the truth (*zhenli* 真理)."[37] In this, Hou is motivated by Marxist considerations. Accordingly

---

29 Hou, *Zhongguo jindai sixiang xueshou shi*, 52.
30 Ibid., 104, 115.
31 Ibid., 162.
32 Ibid., 165.
33 Ibid., 239.
34 Ibid., 249.
35 See discussion of Dai Zhen in chapter one.
36 Cited in Qian Mu, *Zhongguo jin sanbainian xueshu shi* 中國近三百年學術史 (Chinese Learning in the Recent Three Hundred Years). Taibei: Taiwan shangwu, vol. I, 1995, 388.
37 Hou, *Zhongguo jindai sixiang xueshou shi*, 409.

he establishes the seventeenth rather than the eighteenth century as the period of enlightenment in Chinese thought. Unlike former critics, Liang Qichao and especially Hu Shi, Hou claimed that early Qing philosophers not only achieved the destruction of old ways of thinking but they also constructed the new.[38]

Hou repeatedly stresses the idea of a world in constant flux, a central concept in Chinese thought since antiquity. In his book on the new philosophy he associates the idea of constant flux with the concept of dialectical materialism, which, he says, significantly upgrades the traditional concept of constant flux.[39] On the one hand, Hou claims that all is matter.[40] On the other, the law of transformation is scientifically ascertainable by means of dialectical materialism.[41] The objective movement of things that results from internal negation progresses from the low to the high, from the simple to the complicated, and from social contradiction to freedom.[42] The problem of human nature in this view, is a historical and living discourse. Each period has its timely concept of human nature, which is subjected to the historical process of thought.[43] Discussing the underlying structure of both nature and society, dialectical materialism scientifically explains both the natural and the social world.

Epistemologically, Hou maintains that consciousness is a material phenomenon which reflects material and objective reality.[44] Our understanding of reality is therefore possible and reliable (*kenengxing he kekaoxing* 可能性和可靠性).[45] Consciousness is matter, which reflects objective reality, and reality is composed of matter, which transforms. Therefore, dialectical materialism, the science of this transformation, is completely authoritative concerning everything. Dialectical materialism is to Hou a substitute for metaphysics. This being so, writes Hou, the theory of Marx and Engels which is accurate in its explication of reality is omnipotent (*chuannengde* 全能的).[46] With this new philosophy, spirituality, subjectivity, and metaphysics, are no longer an issue.

Hou Wailu assumes a totally objective perspective to criticize Wu Zhihui and Ding Wenjiang, and the other proponents of science, for still wavering between materialism and idealism. In this respect, according to my discussion in chapter 4, he misreads Chen Duxiu. Admittedly, Hou observes, they laid the foundations for the propagation of science in China, which is the greatest accomplishment of the May

---

38 Ibid., 288.
39 Hou and Luo, *Xin zhexue jiaocheng*, 5.
40 Ibid., 26, 45.
41 Ibid., 222.
42 Ibid., 26, 45, 50.
43 Hou, *Zhongguo jindai sixiang xueshou shi*, 558. Hou regarded the question of human nature as the most important theme in the history of Chinese philosophy. But according to him, the masters were unable to provide an answer that was satisfying as the answer of dialectical materialism. *Zhongguo jindai sixiang xueshou shi*, 457.
44 Hou and Luo, *Xin zhexue jiaocheng*, 222–3.
45 Ibid., 222.
46 Ibid., 250.

Fourth Movement. But they were still insufficiently forceful, he writes.[47] He dismisses their claim that reality consists of a dimension which is unintelligible to science. Reformulating the arguments of the supporters of scientism, Hou contends that the world and its laws are knowable; knowledge is reliable; there is nothing that cannot be known; the unknown is merely not yet recognized, and in future, by means of science and its practice, everything will become known.[48]

Hou views the 1923 controversy from the perspective of a social critic. According to him, the city dwellers (the May Fourth intellectuals), confronting industrial progress, needed not only the natural sciences but also the means to rid themselves of the old feudal way of thought, resorting toward that end to materialist thought. Nonetheless, their concepts were only partly scientific, they still retained mystic elements, and believed they could study the subjective mind when in fact there is no such thing.[49] The major mistake of the 1923 scientists was that they failed to see that both reality and consciousness are objective and material.[50]

Like the positivists discussed in chapters three to five, Hou Wailu too believes in a homogeneous universe composed of matter. As other Marxists, he took it for granted that scientific inquiry understood matter as the underlying structure of reality. He therefore believes that knowledge (which is also material) of reality corresponds in fact to reality. The human being who is part of this universe obeys the same laws that govern matter. Hou's 'view of life' is accordingly mechanistic, following set and predictable patterns. Marxist epistemology, he believes, allows him to adopt a detached standpoint from which to gain an impartial, objective view of reality. Though he uses a different epistemological assumption for knowing objective reality, by stipulating a theory of knowledge Hou resembles Xiong Shili.

Did Hou Wailu's ideas during the forties still follow a pattern of linkage, autonomy, and integration? His utopian vision suggests that they did. His concept of linkage is productive work which improve one's own social consciousness. Quoting Marx (*Theses on Feuerbach*, no.6 and no.7), Hou writes that man is not merely an abstract concept but the product of social relations.[51] Indeed, the traditional concept of human nature is substituted by the nature that is determined by social and economic conditions. Through productive work and improving one's own social consciousness, he declares, man creates social life and establishes himself. By these means Hou's individual distinguishes himself from other beings and things, making mankind as the culmination of the world's evolution.[52]

Constantly improving one's own social consciousness, the person achieves autonomy. But Hou also seems to express an ambiguity regarding autonomy. Above

---

47 Ibid., 228.
48 Ibid., 27.
49 Ibid., 230.
50 Ibid., 231.
51 Ibid., 232.
52 Ibid., 256.

we observed that his 'view of life' was mechanistic. If it is incumbent on the individual to engage in productive work and improve his own social consciousness, how can he be autonomous? Regardless of this ambivalence Hou argues that through the linkage the autonomous person is able to eliminate transpersonal barriers and merge into the social whole. Society in its entirety is then integrated with the natural world. This sequence of linkage, ambiguous autonomy and integration with the whole, agrees with Hou's concept of a homogeneous substructure underlying reality, which proposes that there is one ideal for all of humanity.

Qian Mu

Writing his first collection of philosophical reflections in the summer of 1948, Qian Mu distinguished humanity from the ultimate context of existence and focused on society, discussing it in terms of history and culture. Unlike the ultimate and spiritual context that Xiong depicted, and unlike the reality unified by matter in motion and transformation that Hou introduced, Qian, perhaps after reading the lectures of John Dewey,[53] wrote about a world that consists of social relations. A lone individual, according to him, is spiritually deprived.[54] But when participating in society, the individual associates with history and culture, and then he distinguishes himself from other animate beings and phenomena of the world by attaining spirituality.[55]

The process that elevates the socially interrelating individual above mere matter starts with awareness (*juezheng* 覺證). Unlike matter, Qian argues, animate beings have consciousness (*zhijue* 知覺); but only human beings have a mind. Mind is distinguished from consciousness in that consciousness merely reflects external impressions, while the mind enjoys internal awareness. Internal awareness subsequently involves relations with other people. The individual's mind is variable, biased, imperfect, perishable, relative and finite. But within the mind resides human nature, and it is human nature that makes for the possibility of interrelating with others. Therefore, human nature is non-variable, non-biased, perfect, indestructible and everlasting. To substantiate this distinction between mind and human nature, Qian introduces the concepts of memory (*jiyi* 記憶) and what he calls speech and writing (*yuyan he wenzi* 語言和文字), namely, language.[56] Memory is the immaterial preservation of impressions in the mind. To the extent that memory is already a consciousness of past consciousness, he says, memory cannot be material.[57] Using

---

53 Qian, *Bashi huiyi*, 92.
54 Qian, *HSXSL*, 9.
55 Qian, *HSXSL*, chapter 1, pp. 1–3.
56 Dewey also spoke in China about the role of spoken and written language in conserving culture. The texts of his lectures circulated in Chinese periodicals and these were later translated back into English. John Dewey, *Lectures in China, 1919–1920*. Eds. and trans. Robert W. Clopton and Ou Tsuin-chen. Honolulu: East-West Center, 1973, 212.
57 *HSXSL*, 5–6.

memory to explain human spirituality was a new and ingenious contribution to the discussion of the 'view of life'.

Memory, however, Qian continues, does not function without language. As a medium of images, names and ideas, used to communicate between people, language introduces a spiritual dimension into human life. The physical body is merely a biological fact; the use of language which relates the individual with others informs him with a spiritual dimension. Spirituality to Qian is a direct attribute of social relations; it does not belong only to the individual. A person becomes endowed with a spiritual dimension when he uses language.[58] The intellectual knowledge that Xiong Shili described as serving the purposes of intuitive knowledge, according to Qian acquired through social interaction a spiritual dimension that exists within society and is extraneous to the individual. What to Xiong assists the function of substance is now both spiritual and concrete and requires social interaction.

Furthermore, says Qian, using language transforms images in the mind, which are spiritual, into the objective context within which human beings relate to one another. For once expressed, recorded language becomes collective memory and extends outside the individual; that is, it constitutes the context in which everyone participates. By introducing language, which involves the subjectivity of each individual, as the thread that interrelates all aspects of society, Qian contributed to the concept of heterogeneous context of existence that Lin Zaiping and the supporters of metaphysics upheld in the 1923 controversy. The linguistic fabric of existence is shared by each person according to his own subjective point of view.

Now, the usage of language which associates the individual with spirituality is synonymous with human nature. Like Zhu Xi, who argued that human nature is the principle (*li* 理) which the mind (*xin* 心) possesses, Qian identifies human nature with the use of language which originates in the mind. Equating human nature and the use of language, he creates a new meaning for the concept of integration, or, rather, eliminates transpersonal barriers. Human nature in this new formulation is not confined within the boundaries of the self, but is applied through a working system of words, a system by means of which individual minds interrelate (*guantong yu xin yu xin zhi jian* 貫通於心與心之 間). Qian strongly believes that the individual is inseparable from society as a whole. Going to the extreme Buddhist position, he declares that in this world there is no true instance of "my own thought" (*meiyou zhenzhende* [*wo de sixiang*] 沒有真真的 [我的思想]), no "my own," and no "[individual] self (*wo* 我)."[59] Like Liang Qichao before him and like the later supporters of metaphysics, Qian Mu affirms the idea of eliminating transpersonal barriers.

Goodness of human nature was also a consideration for Qian Mu. Enlarging on Mencius, he emphasizes the use of language as the application of the communicative capacity between people and identifies this as the goodness of human nature. Whereas Zhu Xi considered the communicative capacity of the mind to be the very

---

58 Ibid.
59 Ibid., 31.

essence of humanness (ren 仁), Qian associates the goodness of human nature, that is, the use of language, with the application of this capacity. The goodness of human nature is therefore not only that of the individual but an attribute of human beings collectively. Because they are a physical part of nature, he writes, each single person may have shortcomings. But how can the collective human nature of all people, who interrelate with each other, all be bad, that is, how can the history and the culture of all mankind all be bad? To focus on the individual, according to him, is to underestimate the great enterprise of human history and culture.[60]

Within this framework, the individual's nature is not limited to his own life span. By means of language, the person establishes links with the infinity of past, present and future. In Chinese thought, Qian writes, not soul (*linghun* 靈魂) but virtue, deeds, and words (*de* 德, *gong* 功, *yan* 言) are immortal. These three are held in common by the social community, transcending the existence of the individual.[61] Expanding on Hu Shi's idea of social immortality,[62] Qian therefore concludes that human nature, functioning by means of language, implies that the finite individual participates in the infinite and, furthermore, becomes in a sense immortal. The application of the goodness of human nature is infinite. Whereas the mind of the individual is perishable, the human nature that the individual realizes in social interaction persists forever in history and culture.[63] Therefore, unlike the religions of the West, which seek ultimate goodness in the external world, Confucians search for it internally in human nature, within the mind. The Confucian individual, whose human nature functions in social relations, achieved ultimate goodness within an infinite context.[64] Human nature as language locates life in a larger context, becoming the core of meaningful existence.

Within the context of history and culture, the individual is autonomous. He exercises his individual autonomy by using language to help conduct himself morally. According to Qian, the individual is the actor and the playwright of the life he lives.[65] Elsewhere, discussing human nature in Mencius, he applies the above mentioned consciousness and mind differentiation to the concept of human nature. The nature (*xing* 性) of all animate beings, he writes, is to obey external stimuli. Human beings, do not only respond to outside stimuli but also follow their moral human nature (*dexing* 德性), derived from within.[66] Nevertheless, he emphasizes that what he means by autonomy is not the autonomy of the individual of Western thought. The Western concept of autonomy does not require relationships between persons

---

60 Ibid., 2–3.
61 Ibid., 32.
62 Hu Shi 胡適, "San buxiu" 三不朽 (Three dimensions of immortality). In *Hu Shi Wencun* 胡適文存 (Hu Shi's collected works), vol. I, 1953, 693–702.
63 Qian, *HSXSL*, 121.
64 Ibid., 121.
65 Ibid., 32.
66 Qian Mu, "Bian xing" 辨性 (Discussing human nature). In *Zheli yu xinli*. Ed. Xie Youwei, 45–46.

and is therefore not real autonomy.[67] To Qian, the only true autonomy and the only mode of existence that is entirely human consists of the individual's independence in knowing and in his emotions.

Acknowledging the unknown, the individual overcomes the differentiation between self and things; then the individual is unconditioned in knowing and therefore autonomous.[68] Emotionally, according to Qian, we harmonize the accomplished with what is not yet accomplished or impossible to accomplish. Success or failure in accomplishments are external affairs and in this respect we are non-autonomous, but emotionally we follow that which is generated from within the mind. In wanting something we are emotionally autonomous; in despairing or expressing any other emotion, we are also autonomous.[69]

Qian Mu also addresses the problem of science and reason in their relationship to the 'view of life'. Reason alone, he writes, cannot explain human relations. Scientific thinking as a purely rational faculty (*chun lizhi* 純理智) dispassionately (*lengjing* 冷靜) seeks the truth. But the relations between persons are neither dispassionate nor purely rational. Accordingly, human life too is not entirely rational. Human life involves the movement of "warm blood" and the interaction of desires and emotions. How can dispassionate thinking and pure reason relate to this movement and interaction? The understanding of human life therefore cannot rely exclusively on dispassionate thinking and pure reason, for the entire truth about life cannot be revealed by these. If we eliminate vitality, emotions, desires and thoughts, and use only knowledge of science, we would talk about something other than life.[70]

Qian Mu contributes a good deal to the 'view of life' discussion. He does this by stipulating a connection between human nature and language, which he regards as spiritual because of memory and of the use of memory to create a society of individuals who relate with one another. Goodness exists when human beings live as a society and are engaged in personal relationships. Spirituality is impossible without practice; nor can it be experienced by the isolated individual. As a social being, the person is autonomous in acquiring knowledge and expressing his emotions. Language, moreover, provides an infinitely elusive context of subjective expression for each individual. The result is a heterogeneous society in which dispassionate reason is by no means omnipotent.

Conclusion

Xiong Shili, Hou Wailu and Qian Mu, each in his own way, offered new syntheses of Chinese thought and foreign ideas. Using categories of thinking that Chinese

---

67 Qian, *HSXSL*, 45.
68 Ibid., 46.
69 Ibid., 46–47.
70 Ibid., 65.

thinkers used in the past, their formulations affirm that a living society cannot eliminate recourse to its tradition. A close reading of these three views suggests that they borrowed distinct ideas found in association with Chinese tradition. Xiong Shili borrowed from Mencius and Wang Yangming the idea of the basic non-rational correlation between mind and transcendental reality. Hou Wailu justified Marxist philosophy with the ideas of the seventeenth century scholars who had sought to base their ideas on verifiable facts. Qian Mu read Zhu Xi's concept of human nature and humanness as the principle and essence of mind into his heterogeneous world of culture and history.

Furthermore, the three men continued to think in terms of linkage, autonomy and integration, or transpersonal interrelatedness. The individual, according to Xiong, is autonomous when he relates to the original substance or transcendence. "Authentic existence" required a similar relationship. The application of the linkage, though inseparable from social relations, was confined to the individual's subjective limits. Therefore the very few who apparently attained it are recognizable as a social elite. Hou, too, affirmed the individual autonomy of a person who chooses to engage in productive work and improve his own social consciousness. With this thought, perhaps too reminiscent of free will, Hou, by dropping all subjective implications, programs the individual, as it were, to exercise "autonomy" in preconditioned ways. According to Qian Mu, the individual realizes his autonomy, emotionally and intellectually, within the linguistic context of social relations. To use language and to morally interrelate with society transcends subjective boundaries, creating an autonomy that is available to all.

The differences among the three views revolve around the problem of what is the context of human relationships and how one lives in this context. To Xiong Shili, human relationships have a transcendental context, which is accessible to reason and sense-experience only through the mediation of intuitive knowledge. This context is dynamic and is in constant transformation. To Hou Wailu, the constant transformation of the context of human relationships is synonymous with reality, which involves only matter. This homogeneous reality is absolutely comprehensible to consciousness, which is matter as well. Qian Mu offers a middle way. Unlike Hou and Xiong, he confines his discussion to the context of social relations. This is the heterogeneous, because individually subjective, context of history and culture, which is accessible and knowable by means of language. This context is also in a constant state of transformation. Neither transcendental like Xiong's original substance, nor entirely material like Hou's, Qian Mu's context of human relationships emphasizes a spiritual quality. It avoids both the elitist implications of Xiong Shili's system and the homogeneity of Hou Wailu.

Conclusion

The discussions of the 'view of life' philosophy throughout the history of Chinese thought illuminate the search to adapt the meaning of being human to changing ideas about the context of human relationships. Before the twentieth century, the discourse on what it means to be human centered on the question of human nature. The Confucian masters used terms that correspond to the concepts of linkage, autonomy and integration. What is innate and what is not, and the course that action should take, were among the problems that remained controversial. Since the classical period the masters continuously reformulated their answers to cope with changing conditions, historical and intellectual. Zhu Xi sought to harmonize the person's inner endowments and their application, Wang Yangming regarded innate moral knowledge as trustworthy, and Early Qing thinkers critically stressed the concrete and the practical. The nineteenth century scholars further bequeathed their emphasis on concrete practice to the twentieth century intellectuals.

At the turn of the twentieth century, Christianity and especially natural science contributed new concepts and ideas that entered into discussions about culture and life. Liang Qichao, taking steps to introduce foreign ideas to his readers, considered the Confucian ideal of integration, which had involved cosmic implications, in terms that excluded those implications and focused on the area of human relationships *per se*. Scientism later suggested the homogeneous material and mechanistic context of human relationships. The 1923 supporters of the 'view of life', Liang included, countered this position, propounding the heterogeneous context of human relationships which is based on metaphysics. Marxism was already a dominant philosophical current during the forties, when Hou Wailu, like other dialectical materialists, argued for the constantly transforming material reality. Partly responding to this and partly to other challenges, Xiong Shili discussed the metaphysical context of "authentic existence," and Qian Mu introduced language as the context of the culture and the history of human relationships.

The modern search to adapt the meaning of being human to changing ideas about the context of human relationships was a syncretic process in that thinkers, like those discussed in this study, selectively borrowed new ideas in order to revitalize their ongoing dialogue with their own tradition. Changes during the twentieth century reflected the meeting with the West, but at the same time continued processes that were intrinsic to traditional thought, such as the practical tendency that had gained currency among nineteenth century scholars.

To better understand the dynamics both of the 'view of life' ideas and of the concepts of the context of human relationships, we turn now to look at these against the backdrop of the larger issues that occupied the minds of Chinese intellectuals in the twentieth century. The intellectual crisis that scholars today attribute to the consciousness of Chinese intellectuals,[1] was obviously a manifestation and at the same time a consequence of the deep national, political, economic and social wounds that China suffered in the course of "meeting" the West and of the decay of the imperial system. Twentieth century Chinese intellectuals, aware of this crisis, worked out various programs in answer to it. All those discussed in this study agreed that the process of modernizing should head the order of priorities. Two mutually complementary aspects of this process predominantly engaged their attention: nationalism and the New Culture agenda. "Nationalism" meant enhancing political, economic and social, as well as military strength within the state and outwardly. "New Culture" meant, among other things, revitalizing the meaning of being human and adapting this to correspond to the process of modernizing while still preserving the Chinese character. The dualistic relations between these two aspects continued the dualism of the *tiyong* formula. Whereas nationalism concerned the preservation of a politically distinct community, the New Culture agenda concerned the nature and the value of this community's life, that is, the essential justification for its existing at all.

Maintaining the balance between nationalist concerns and the cultural agenda remained, however, problematic. Around the turn of the twentieth century Chinese thinkers were only gradually realizing that the crisis demanded answers on the cultural level, where the 'view of life' philosophy mattered. Zhang Zhidong thought that Chinese culture, or what he called the spiritual essence (*ti*), could be preserved intact, implying that cultural change was not required. As far as what it means to be human was concerned, culturally, China was sufficiently "enlightened." Liang Qichao, however, already accommodated Western learning into the *ti*. Thereafter, intellectuals increasingly accepted the contention according to which nationalism and the New Culture agenda should proceed together as complementary aspects of the same goal, namely, the process of modernizing. In 1917, Hu Shi returned to China to invigorate the New Culture movement. By 1919, Mr. Science and Mr. Democracy were heralded as the saviors of the day. Meanwhile, the call for total Westernization increased in volume and intellectual tensions reached an unprecedented point. The 1923 'view of life' controversy actually put on stage the conflict between those who supported the pretensions of scientism to dominate the New Culture agenda, and their opponents, the supporters of metaphysics, who argued that scientism undermined the New Culture agenda.

Eventually, scientism triumphed in the May Fourth period, and the impact of Liang Qichao and his fellow supporters of metaphysics was played down, during the larger part of the twentieth century. This tendency corresponds to the way in which the balance between nationalism and the cultural agenda was upset, during the same period, in favor of the former (see discussion below). But the question arises, does this "failure" on the part of the supporters of metaphysics and the neglect on the part of historians imply that the cause of the 'view of life' based on metaphysics should

---

1 See in the introduction, especially pp. 4–5.

remain marginal, and philosophically disparaged? Can we say with Joseph Levenson that philosophically speaking the 1923 controversy was empty?[2] And can we follow his counsel and learn the history of this debate only from D.W.Y. Kwok, whose discussion was focused on the supporters of scientism?[3] The answers to these questions, I believe, should be negative.

Indeed, as observed by the supporters of metaphysics themselves, the marginalization of the 'view of life' position harbored some problematic implications as to the fate of the cultural agenda of twentieth century China. Considering the controversy, we find that the philosophical arguments leveled by the supporters of scientism against metaphysics correspond to positivism. They saw the world and the people living in it, including their mental processes, as homogeneous, material and mechanical phenomena. If we take into account that culture, in the words of Huang Chun-chieh and Erik Zürcher, is "... the womb of our being 'human', the universe of discourse in which our experience makes sense and distinguishes itself as humanly meaningful, not a mere spewing forth of animality,"[4] then, if, as positivists claim, life is merely matter and mechanisms, its value is no greater than that of any other thing. Scientism is, therefore, inconsistent with the project of New Culture, and arguably, the supporters of scientism were guiding that project, and with it, the whole process of modernizing, toward a deterministic and valueless dead-end.

In view of what has taken place in China during the twentieth century, the arguments of the supporters of metaphysics against scientism seem to have posed a timely warning against aberrations such as the Cultural Revolution that were still in the future. Scholars today are familiar with Li Zehou's 李澤厚 conclusion according to which, national salvation (*jiuwang* 救亡) eclipsed the project of "enlightenment" (*qimeng* 啟蒙), namely the New Culture agenda, that the May Fourth intellectuals had originally set forth.[5] Gan Yang 甘陽 further argues that these intellectuals became excessively attracted to absolute solutions and totalitarian ideologies.[6] The downgrading of the intellectual agenda of the supporters of metaphysics, I suggest, may be recognized as a corroboration of the truth of both these two observations.

---

2   See in the introduction, p. 2.
3   Ibid.
4   Huang Chun-chieh, Erik Zürcher, "Cultural Notions of Time and Space in China." In *Time and Space in Chinese Culture*. Huang Chun-chieh and Erik Zürcher, eds. Leiden: E.J.Brill, 1995, 4.
5   Li Zehou 李澤厚. *Zhongguo xiandai sixiangshi lun* 中國現代思想史論 (Discussion of modern Chinese thought). Anhui: Anhui wenyi chubanshe, 1994, 36. Quite a few writers use "enlightenment" for *qimeng*. Yet, considering the problematic usage of this term (enlightenment), I suggest "New Culture" which the intellectuals of that day employed. Recently, Robert Darnton warned against the inflated use of the term of enlightenment. See Robert Darnton, "George Washington's False Teeth." *New York Review of Books*, (March 27, 1997), 34–38.
6   Gan Yang 甘陽, "Ziyou de linian: Wusi chuantong de queshi mian" 五四傳：自由的理念-統之闕矢面 (The concept of liberty: A lacuna in the May Fourth tradition). In *Wusi: Douyuan de fansi* 多云的反思：五四 (Plural reflections on May Fourth). Lin Yusheng 林毓生 et al. eds. Hong Kong: Sanlian shudian, 1989, 70–71. I have substituted Gan Yang's "final solution" (appearing in English in the text) by the less misleading "absolute solution."

Those who marginalized the views of the metaphysics supporters regarded the cultural agenda too strongly in terms of nationalism and not as a value in itself, necessary to complement nationalist concerns. Those who were attracted toward total solutions eventually disregarded the arguments regarding the heterogeneous nature of the context of human relationships, and conceded the subjective complexity of individuals. After 1923, the 'view of life' based on metaphysics was therefore undervalued because of uncritical support for nationalist concerns and for total solutions. As a result the metaphysics' supporters' refutation of the homogeneous context of human relations – the philosophical grounding of claims for total solutions – as well as other aspects of their cultural agenda, remained largely unnoticed.

The works of the supporters of metaphysics are by no means unworthy of scholarly attention. The principal intellectuals discussed in this study tried to keep the project of the cultural agenda alive, during an age dominated by scientism. They did so partly by arguing against scientism and partly by arguing for the 'view of life' philosophy. Essentially they claimed that the human individual possesses spiritual and moral qualities which are subjective and accessible only to himself, and that there, within this subjective individual, starts social order. None of them rejected science itself. The arguments warning against scientism, or the use of science that is not balanced by humanistic values, can be traced to ideas that appeared in Faber's Chinese writings, and continued with Liang Qichao, Liang Shuming, the 1923 supporters of metaphysics, Xiong Shili and Qian Mu. Hou Wailu, who regarded the New Culture agenda only as a means toward nationalistic ends, is the exception. The same can be claimed with regard to subjectivity, and again, Hou is the exception. All of these also attempted to reconcile East and West philosophy, and none of them doubted that making China ready for the future required a process of modernizing.

Confidence in the subjective capacities of the individual originated long ago in the history of Chinese thought. In fact, since Mencius at least, it marked the ideas of the masters of Chinese thought regarding the question of what it means to be human. The masters discussed in chapter one suggested various changing formulations of the nature of these capacities and their application. But they agreed that world order starts with the individual who engages in self-cultivation. They based this on the assumption that each individual is in principle autonomously able to enact the linkage and achieve integration with the universe as a whole.

Substantiating the question of what it means to be human by stressing subjectivity represents a major pattern in the cultural agenda of twentieth century Chinese intellectuals. In the early 1900s Liang Qichao observed that "Today, when the Way is lost […]" social order should be based on the subjective moral knowledge that the individual autonomously exercises.[7] Though at that stage he did not yet mention "New Culture," his writings about "new people" and "new literature" were land-

---

7 Liang Qichao 梁啟超, "Deyujian" 德育鑑 (Mirror for Moral Cultivation), in *Yinbingshi zhuanji* 飲冰室專集 (Collected works of the Ice-Drinker's Studio). Shanghai: Zhonghua shuju, vol. XXVI, 1936, 27.

marks toward this end. On the level of ethics, he believed the philosophy of Kant enabled a dialogue with the Chinese concept of the person who autonomously chooses between moral alternatives. Whereas Ernst Faber emphasized a connection between the *noumenal* and reason, Liang, who was naturally more familiar with the *tiyong* formula, associated the *noumenal* with an innate spiritual and moral essence (*ti*), which he named *liangxin*. Another instance of his philosophical ingenuity can be seen in his reformulation of the Confucian goal of life. Reducing integration to transpersonal inter-relatedness, he modified the scope of the traditional goal of life. These two tenets that marked Liang's early thought represent a not yet sufficiently recognized contribution to a new beginning in the history of Chinese philosophy.

In 1919 Liang argued that the creation of a "New Culture," again constructed around the moral spiritual essence of Chinese thought, should be considered as partial fulfillment of China's responsibility toward humanity as a whole. To him, this project necessitated a challenge to the dream of the omnipotence of science. This dream, he felt, led people to overemphasize the role of science in all areas of life. As an alternative, he reinstated what he called the interior sphere of life and moral virtue, free will and spirituality, at the center of concern. In 1921 Liang Shuming joined him, arguing that life is a dynamic and creative force, incessantly flowing from within the person. Science and democracy are acceptable, he said, only when mediated through the life approach (*rensheng taidu*). Both implied in their arguments that to overemphasize nationalistic goals and the consequent scientism would reduce life to mere survival. They called for recognition of the urgent need for a complementary cultural agenda that would include the subjective and spiritual dimensions of life.

Toward the end of his *Qinghua* address (of February 14th 1923), Zhang Junmai associated the New Culture discussions with the question of the 'view of life'. He observed that his contemporaries were occupied with competing talks about New Culture, and that the fundamental question of the New Culture discussions was how to acquire the merits of Western culture and yet avoid its shortcomings. But, he realized, the axis of culture is the question of the 'view of life', and only after this question was decided could the Chinese resolve their position with regard to the combination of spiritual thought and materialistic method.[8] His arguments express the measure of readiness to welcome foreign ideas, and the need for Chinese culture to form a 'view of life' capable of critically supporting the selection of foreign influences according to its own criteria in order to modernize.

The 1923 controversy over the 'view of life' represents the culmination of the efforts of May Fourth intellectuals to determine the nature and the course of the New Culture agenda. Evidently, both sides of the polemic also shared the goals of nationalism and New Culture. They also recognized that the New Culture agenda could not be carried out without Western input, of whatever kind that might be. They also real-

---

8 Zhang Junmai, "Rensheng guan" 人生觀 (The view of life). In *Kexue xuanxue lunzhanji* 科學玄學論戰集 (The controversy of science and metaphysics). Preface Hu Shi 胡適 and Chen Duxiu 陳獨秀. Shanghai: Yadong shuju, 1923, 12.

ized that the present was anchored in the past. Both sides, furthermore, used Chinese philosophical concepts in pressing their arguments, having grown up within that tradition and having no other vocabulary but that of the Chinese philosophical conceptualization.

But they differed regarding the nature and the course of the New Culture agenda. When they focused their attention on the question of the 'view of life', both sides set human life as the criterion of the cultural agenda. Here the title itself and the very content of Zhang Junmai's opening lecture, *Rensheng guan*, had a crucial impact. The terminology necessarily determines the discourse; when *Lebensanschauung* is invoked, the subjective element is a given, because it is the human being who is at the center of philosophical concerns. To argue against scientism the supporters of metaphysics saw life as the experience of the individual. They insisted that life should be seen in its entirety and not as separate parts. Accepting Liang Qichao's *liangxin* center of the humane person, yet being more philosophically sophisticated, they defined the attributes of their new individual: subjectivity, intuition, synthesis, free will and uniqueness. The framework of the 'view of life' established the autonomous individual who can choose morally, and who rejects determinist explanations. The attributes and the center of the view also affirmed the ideal of transpersonal interrelatedness that Liang suggested in his earlier writings. The supporters of metaphysics further contributed to the project of modern Chinese philosophy, started earlier by Liang, by arguing for the heterogeneous context of human relationships. Remarkably, only Liang and Zhang Dongsun preserved a balance between reason and intuition, in their 1923 writings.[9]

The philosophy of the 'view of life' still appealed to thinkers during the forties. The thought of Xiong Shili represents an attempt, characteristic of both Confucians and Buddhists, to extend the subjective resources of the person, and the purposes of his self-cultivation program, beyond the limits of social relations. Hou Wailu approached the cultural agenda from the perspective of a dialectical materialist. Rejecting subjectivity, he nevertheless offered a humanist ideal of social equality which also supported the traditional ideal of integration. However, both adapted extreme positions involving speculative epistemological approaches; respectively, the original mind and the material consciousness. Eventually, Xiong's system harbored elitist implications, and Hou's conveyed ambivalence regarding individual autonomy.

Unlike Xiong and Hou, Qian Mu continued the ideas of Liang Qichao and the supporters of metaphysics by preserving and elaborating the ideal of transpersonal interrelatedness. To him, language informed the heterogeneous context of human relationships. Accordingly, this context is nothing but the culture and history of the human race. Qian stipulated human nature, in the specific sense of the use of language, as the distinctive feature of being human. He further regarded relations with other people as a manifestation of the goodness of human nature; not the individ-

---

9 In this respect, Zhang Junmai, who did not keep this balance, repeated an argument made by Liang Qichao in 1905, but not repeated in 1919 and 1923.

ual's goodness, but the goodness of humanity as a whole. Human nature, he thought, gains a spiritual attribute at the moment of being applied. Qian interpreted humaneness as the use of language which leads to transpersonal inter-relatedness. What is subjective to him is the individual's point of view and not the application of the spiritual and the moral which is shared by everyone.

The new Confucian perspective of Xiong Shili, the Marxist perspective of Hou Wailu, and Qian Mu's setting of Chinese philosophy within a broader framework of culture and history, well represent the mixture of philosophical thought that currently persists in Chinese intellectual circles. Among their other intellectual concerns, scholars such as Mou Zongsan, Li Zehou and Yu Yingshi, continue, like their predecessors, to reformulate ideas about what it means to be human. They arrive at new contributions by continuing the dialogue with the past – which to them includes foreign sources – and by interacting with other contemporary strands of thought. Li Zehou's synthesis of Marx, Kant and Chinese thought, is illustrative of this sort of development. It is especially interesting to trace the continuing dialogue between Chinese thinkers and the philosophy of Kant, whose ideas served as an intercultural bridge since the turn of the twentieth century in the case of Liang Qichao, and still earlier in that of Faber, whose contribution in this respect has not yet been fully recognized. Both Li and Mou, among others, base some of their major ideas on interpretations of Kant.

Recently we have been encountering articles and books about the "new discourse" of the 1978 post-Mao era after 1978. The new discourse, according to one source, is manifested in discussions concerning issues such as humanism, new Confucianism, the scientific method, and the need for cultural reconstruction.[10] The new discourse is by no means detached from Marxism, although subjectivity forms its crucial philosophical strand.[11] Lin Tongqi describes "the principle of subjectivity" in contemporary Chinese discussions as the endeavor to establish the human being as a subject and to view everything else as meaningful and valuable only by reference to that human being. The subjectivity trend also suggests perceiving "... humanity as a dynamic force, ... relying on some inner resource of its own ..."[12]

One can hardly miss the close affinities between this aspect of the contemporary trend and the 1923 'view of life' arguments. In agreement with the aforementioned observation of Li Zehou, this "revival" of the 'view of life' philosophy reveals the growing awareness in Chinese intellectual circles of the need to further pursue issues belonging to the cultural agenda that suffered for political reasons from a superficial mode of discussion after the forties. This is not the place for a philosophical comparison between the contemporary trend and the ideas of 1923. Nonetheless, the

---

10 Lin Tongqi, Henry Rosemont, Jr., and Roger T. Ames, "Chinese Philosophy: A Philosophical Essay on the 'State-of-the-Art'." *Journal of Asian Studies*, 54.3 (August 1995), 729.
11 Lin Tongqi, "Subjectivity: Marxism and 'The Spiritual' in China Since Mao." *Philosophy East & West*, 44.4 (October 1994), 609.
12 Ibid., 612.

contemporary cultural agenda, I believe, can profit by taking into account the point where it formerly, and perhaps prematurely, came into a halt, in the thought of the 1923 supporters of metaphysics, and later, in the thought of men like Xiong Shili, Hou Wailu and Qian Mu. The reemergence of the 'view of life' issues in the new discourse indicates that this philosophical concern still preserves its appeal and is relevant to Chinese intellectuals with humanistic persuasions.

In the 1923 'view of life' controversy, the supporters of metaphysics endeavored to refute the arguments of scientism. At the time, many if not most Chinese intellectuals considered them as irrelevant. Though thinkers during the forties continued to pursue the 'view of life' philosophy, this course of intellectual reflection remained marginal throughout most of the twentieth century. Recently, however, subjectivity, moral autonomy and spirituality, are resurfacing in discussions in Chinese intellectual circles. Regardless of changing fashions and times, human, or humane, life, should be considered a central concern. The 1923 supporters of metaphysics observed this responsibility during hard times. Though they were not philosophically consistent in all their arguments, their attempts to reconcile Eastern and Western ideas established a new beginning of Chinese philosophy. Today, while the cultural agenda has not yet reached a stable course, their formulations that safeguarded the spiritual moral essence of Chinese thought through the transformations of modern Chinese history are as relevant as ever and deserve a reappraisal.

Bibliography

CHINESE SOURCES

Chen Zhongfu 陳仲甫 (Chen Duxiu 陳獨秀), "Kexue yu rensheng guan xu" 科學與人生觀序 (Preface to the controversy over science and the view of life). In *Kexue xuanxue lunzhanji* 科學玄學論戰集 (The controversy of science and metaphysics). Preface Hu Shi 胡適 and Chen Duxiu. Shanghai: Yadong shuju, 1923, 1–12.

Ding Wenjiang 丁文江, "Xuanxue yu kexue" 玄學與科學 (Metaphysics and science). In *Kexue xuanxue lunzhanji* 科學玄學論戰集 (The controversy of science and metaphysics). Preface Hu Shi 胡適 and Chen Duxiu 陳獨秀. Shanghai: Yadong shuju, 1923, 15–44.

Fan Shoukang 范壽康, "Ping souwei 'Kexue yu xuanxue zhi zheng'" 評所謂'科學與玄學之爭' (Criticizing the so-called 'Controversy over science and metaphysics'). In *Kexue xuanxue lunzhanji* 科學玄學論戰集 (The controversy of science and metaphysics). Preface Hu Shi 胡適 and Chen Duxiu 陳獨秀. Shanghai: Yadong shuju, 1923, 455–478.

Gan Yang 甘陽, "Ziyou de linian: Wusi chuantong de queshi mian" 自由的理念：五四傳統之闕矢面 (The concept of liberty: A lacuna in the May Fourth tradition). In *Wusi: Douyuan de fansi* 五四：多云的反思 (Plural reflections on the May Fourth). Lin Yusheng 林毓生 et al. eds. Hong Kong: Sanlian shudian, 1989, 62–81.

He Lin 賀麟, "Kangde Hei-ge-er zhexue dongjianji" 康德黑格尔哲學東漸記 (The introduction of Kant and Hegel's philosophy in the East). *Zhongguo zhexue* 中國哲學, vol. II (April 1981), 343–387.

Hou Wailu 侯外廬. *Zhongguo jindai sixiang xueshuo shi* 中國近代思想學說史 (History of modern Chinese learning). Chongqing: Chongqing shudian, 2 vols., 1944.

——. *Ren de zhuiqiu* 韌的追求 (The stubborn quest). Beijing: Sanlian shudian chuban, 1985.

—— and Luo Keting 羅克汀. *Xin zhexue jiaocheng* 新哲學教程 (The process of the new philosophy). Shanghai: Shanghai xinzhe shudian, 1946.

Hu Songping 胡頌平, ed. *Hu Shizhi xiansheng nianpu changpian chugao* 胡適之先生年譜長編初稿 (An extended preliminary record of Mr. Hu Shi's chronological biography). Taipei: Lianjing chuban gongsi, 10 vols., 1973.

Hu Shi 胡適, "San buxiu" 三不朽 (Three dimensions of immortality). In *Hu Shi Wencun* 胡適文存 (Collected essays of Hu Shih). Taibei: Yundong, vol. I, 1953, 693–702.

——, "Kexue yu rensheng guan xu" 科學與人生觀序 (Introduction to science and the view of life). In *Kexue xuanxue lunzhanji* 科學玄學論戰集 (The controversy of science and metaphysics). Preface Hu Shi 胡適 and Chen Duxiu 陳獨秀. Shanghai: Yadong shuju, 1923, 1–42.

——, "Jige fanlixue de sixiangjia" 幾個反理學的思想家 (Some thinkers who opposed the learning of principle). In *Hu Shi Wencun* 胡適文存 (Collected essays of Hu Shih). Taibei: Yundong, vol. III, 1953, 53–107.

——. *Dai Dongyuan de zhexue* 戴東原的哲學 (The philosophy of Dai Dongyuan). Taibei: Taiwan shangwu yinshuguan, 1996.

Hua Zhi-an 花之安 (Ernst Faber). *Taixi xuexiao* 泰西學校 (Western schools). Shanghai: Shangwu yinshuguan chengyin, 1897.

—. *Zi Xi cu Dong* 自西徂東 (From West to East) (English title: Civilization, East and West: The Fruits of Christianity Compared with Those of the Chinese Religion). Hong Kong: Zhonghua yinwu zongju, 1884.

—. *Xinghai yuanyuan* 性海淵源 (Inquiry of theories of human nature). Shanghai: Guangxuehui yin, 1893.

—. *Jingxue bu yan jing* 經學不厭精 (The classics are not contrary to Christianity) (English title: An Examination of the Thirteen Classics and the Development of Confucianism). Shanghai: American Presbyterian Mission Press, 1898.

Huang Kewu 黃克武, "Liang Qichao yu Kangde" 梁啟超 與康德 (Liang Qichao and Kant). In *Zhongyang yanjiuyuan. Jindaishi yanjiu suojikan* 中央研究院，近代史研究所集刊 (Academica Sinica, Bulletin of the Institute of Modern History), vol. XXX (1998), 101–148.

Jiaohui xinbao 教會新報 (Church News).

Li Zehou 李澤厚. *Zhongguo xiandai sixiangshi lun* 中國現代思想史論 (Discussion of Modern Chinese Thought). Anhui: Anhui wenyi chubanshe, 1994.

Liang Qichao 梁啟超, "Jinshi diyi dazhe kangde zhi xueshuo" 近世第一大哲康德 之學說 (The doctrine of Kant, the greatest philosopher of modern times) In *Zichan jieji xueshu sixiang pipan cankao ziliao* 資產階級學術思想批判參考資料 (Reference material for criticizing capitalist thought). Beijing: Shangwu yinshuguan, vol. VIII, 1960, 1–20.

—, "Deyujian" 德育鑑 (Mirror for moral cultivation), in *Yinbingshi zhuanji* 飲冰室專集 (Collected works of the Ice-Drinker's Studio). Shanghai: Zhonghua shuju, vol. XXVI, 1936.

—, "Ouyou xinying lu jielu" 歐游心影綠節錄 (Reflections on a trip to Europe). In *Yin bing shi zhuanji* 飲冰室專集 (Collected works of the Ice-Drinker's Studio). Lin Zhijun 林志均 (Lin Zaiping 林宰平), ed. Shanghai: Zhonghua shuju, vol. XXIII, 1936, 1–162.

—, "Rensheng guan yu kexue" 人生觀與科學 (The view of life and science). In *Kexue xuanxue lunzhanji* 科學玄學論戰集 (The controversy of science and metaphysics). Preface Hu Shi 胡適 and Chen Duxiu 陳獨秀. Shanghai: Yadong shuju, 1923, 171–184.

Liang Shuming 梁漱溟. *Dong Xi wenhua ji qi zhexue* 東西文化及其哲學 (Eastern and Western cultures and their philosophies). Taibei: Liren shuju yinxing, 1983.

Lin Zaiping 林宰平, "Du Ding Zaijun xiansheng de 'Xuanxue yu kexue'" 讀丁在君先生的'玄學與科學' (Criticizing Mr. Ding's article on "Metaphysics and science"). In *Kexue xuanxue lunzhanji* 科學玄學論戰集 (The controversy of science and metaphysics). Preface Hu Shi 胡適 and Chen Duxiu 陳獨秀. Shanghai: Yadong shuju, 1923, 201–240.

Minduo zazhi 民鐸雜誌 (Min-Toh Monthly), vol. 3.1 (December 1921).

Mou Zongsan 牟宗三. *Zhongguo zhexue shijiujiang* 中國哲學十九講 (Nineteen lectures on Chinese philosophy). Taibei: Xuesheng shuju, 1997.

Peng Shaosheng 彭紹升, "Yu Dai Dongyuan shu" 與戴東原書 (A letter to Dai Dongyuan). In Hu Shi 胡適, *Dai Dongyuan de zhexue* 戴東原的哲學 (The philosophy of Dai Dongyuan). Taibei: Taiwan shangwu yinshuguan, 1996, 339–342.

Qian Mu 錢穆, "Pangguanzhe yan" 旁觀者言 (The bystander's comment). In *Kexue xuanxue lunzhanji* 科學玄學論戰集 (The controversy of science and metaphysics). Preface Hu Shi 胡適 and Chen Duxiu 陳獨秀. Shanghai: Yadong shuju, 1923, 419–428.

—, "Bian xing" 辨性 (Discussing human nature). In *Zheli yu xinli* 哲理與 心理 (The principle of knowledge and the principle of mind). Ed. Xie Youwei 謝幼偉, et al. Shanghai: Zhongzheng shuju, 1948, 41–76.

—. *Hushang xiansilu* 湖上閒思綠 (Quiet thoughts at the lake). Taibei: Dongda dushu gongsi yinxing, 1984.

—. *Bashi yi shuangqin, Shiyou zayi* 八十憶雙親，師友雜憶 (Reminiscences of my parents at the age of eighty, Memories of teachers and friends). Taibei: Dongda tushu gongsi, 1992.

—. *Zhongguo jin sanbainian xueshu shi* 中國近三百年學術史 (Chinese learning in the recent three hundred years). Taibei: Taiwan shangwu, 2 vols, 1995.

—. *Zhongguo sixiangshi* 中國思想史 (History of Chinese thought). Taibei: Xuesheng shuju yinxing, 1995.

—. *Zhongguo Xueshu Sixiangshi Luncong* 9 中國學術思想史論叢, 九 (Studies in the History of Modern Chinese Thought, 9). Taipei: Sushulou wenjiao jijinhui, 2000.

Qu Nong 菊農 (Qu Shiying 瞿世英), "Renge yu jiaoyu" 人格教育 (Character and education). In *Kexue xuanxue lunzhanji* 科學玄學論戰集 (The controversy of science and metaphysics). Preface Hu Shi 胡適 and Chen Duxiu 陳獨秀. Shanghai: Yadong shuju, 1923, 337–354.

Sishu duben 四書讀本 (Basic reader of the Four Books). Xie Bingying 謝冰莹, ed. Taibei: Sanmin shuju, 1988.

Tan Sitong 譚嗣同, "Shang Ouyang Banjiangshi shu" 上歐陽瓣疆師書 (Letter to Ouyang Banjiang shu), *Tan Sitong quanji* 譚嗣同全集 (Complete works of Tan Sitong). Beijing: Xinhua shuju, 1954, 316–29.

—. *Renxue* 仁學 (An Exposition of Benevolence). Chinese text in Chan Sin-wai, trans., *An Exposition of Benevolence: The Jen-hsueh of T'an Ssu-t'ung*. Hong Kong: The Chinese University Press, 1984.

Tang Jian 唐鑒, "Zhiyu shuo" 窒欲說 (On the control of desires). In *Tang Queshen gongji* 唐確慎公集 (A collection of Tang Jian), *Sibu beiyao* 四部備要. Taibei: Zhonghua shuju, book 2, 1972, 24–26.

Wang Guowei 王國維, "Lun jinnian xueshujie" (On the recent world of learning) 論今年之學術界, in *Wang Guantang quanji* 王觀堂全集 (Collected works of Wang Guantang), vol. V, 1767–1770.

Wang Hui 汪暉, *Xiandai Zhongguo sixiang de xingqi* 现代中国思想的兴起 (The rise of modern Chinese thought). Beijing: Shenghuo dushu, 2003.

Wanguo gongbao 萬國公報 (The Globe Magazine).

Wu Zhihui, 吳稚暉, "Yi ge xin xinyang de yuyou guan ji rensheng guan" 一個新信仰的宇宙觀及人生觀 (A new belief in a cosmic view and the view of life). In *Kexue xuanxue lunzhanji* 科學玄學論戰集 (The controversy of science and metaphysics). Preface Hu Shi 胡適 and Chen Duxiu 陳獨秀. Shanghai: Yadong shuju, 1923, 489–654.

Xiong Shili 熊十力. *Xin weishilun* 新唯識論 (New doctrine of Consciousness-only). Shanghai: The Commercial press, 1947.

—, "Lun xuanxue fangfa 論玄學方法" (Discussing the method of metaphysics). In *Zheli yu xinli* 哲理與心理 (The principle of knowledge and the principle of mind). Xie Youwei 謝幼偉, et al., eds. Shanghai: Zhengzhong shuju, 1948, 77–84.

—. *Shili yuyao chuxu* 十力語要初續 (Primary supplemented abstracts by Xiong Shili). Taibei: Hongshi chubanshe, 1982.

Xiong Yuezhi 熊月之. *Xixue Dongjian yu wan Qing shi hui* 西學東漸与晚清社會 (The dissemination of Western learning and late Qing society). Shanghai: Renmin chubanshe, 1994. *Xunzi yuezhu* 旬子約注 (Xunzi). Taibei: Shejie shuju, vol. II, 1958.

Ye Qizhong (Yap Key-chong) 葉其忠, "1923 Nian 'Kexuan lunzhan': pingjia zhi pingjia 1923 年'科玄論戰': 評價之評價 (Revisiting criticism of the 1923 'Debate on science and metaphysics.'). *Zhongyang Yanjiuyuan; Jindai Shi Yanjiusuo Jikan* 中央研究院；近代史研究所集刊 (Bulletin of the Institute of Modern History Academia Sinica) (Taipei) 26 (1996): 181–234.

Yu Yingshi 余英時. *Zhongguo jindai sixiangshi de Hu Shi* 中國近代思想史上的胡適 (Hu Shi and the history of modern Chinese thought). Taibei: Lianjing chubansheye gongsi, 1984.

—. *Zhongguo sixiang chuantong de xiandai quanshi* 中國思想傳統的現代詮釋 (Interpretation of the tradition of thought in modern China). Taibei: Lianjing chuban shiye gongsi, 1987.

—, "Wusi yundong yu Zhongguo chuantong" 五四運動與中國傳統 (The May Fourth Movement and Chinese tradition). In *Qimeng de jiazhen yu juxian: Tai Gang xuezhe lun Wusi* 啟蒙的价值與局限：臺港學者論五四 (The limits and value of enlightenment: Scholars from Taiwan and Hong Kong studies of the May Fourth). Xiao Tingzhong 蕭廷中 and Zhu yi 朱藝, eds. Sahnxi: Sahnxi renmin chubanshe, 1989, 74–85.

—. *Youji fengchui shuishanglin: Qian Mu yu xiandai zhongguo xueshu* 猶記風吹水上鱗：錢穆與現代中國學術 (Like recording the wind blowing the water on the unicorn: Qian Mu and modern Chinese scholarship). Taibei: Sanmin shuju, 1991.

Zhang Dongsun 張東蓀, "Dongsun an" 東蓀按 (Note by Zhang Dongsun). In *Kexue xuanxue lunzhanji* 科學玄學論戰集 (The controversy of science and metaphysics). Preface Hu Shi 胡適 and Chen Duxiu 陳獨秀. Shanghai: Yadong shuju, 1923, 167–169, 180–184.

—, "Lao er wu gong" 勞而無功 (Wasted effort). In *Kexue xuanxue lunzhanji* 科學玄學論戰集 (The controversy of science and metaphysics). Preface Hu Shi 胡適 and Chen Duxiu 陳獨秀. Shanghai: Yadong shuju, 1923, 317–336.

Zhang Hao (Chang Hao) 張灝, "Zhongguo jindai sixiangshi de zhuanxing shidai" 國近代思想史的轉型時代 (The age of transition in modern Chinese intellectual history). *Ershiyi shiji* 二十一世紀, vol. 52 (April 1999), 29–39.

Zhang Junmai 張君勱 et al, trans. *Dulishu jiangyanlu* (The Driesch lectures) 杜理舒講演錄. Shanghai: Shangwu yinshuguan, 1923.

—, "Rensheng guan" 人生觀 (The view of life). In *Kexue xuanxue lunzhanji* 科學玄學論戰集 (The controversy of science and metaphysics). Preface Hu Shi 胡適 and Chen Duxiu 陳獨秀. Shanghai: Yadong shuju, 1923, 1–14.

—, "Zai lun rensheng guan yu kexue bing da Ding Zaijun" 再論人生觀與科學並 答丁在君 (Another discussion of science and the view of life and an answer to Ding Zaijun). In *Kexue xuanxue lunzhanji* 科學玄學論戰集 (The controversy of science and metaphysics). Preface Hu Shi 胡適 and Chen Duxiu 陳獨秀. Shanghai: Yadong shuju, 1923, 45–142.

—, "Kexue zhi pingjia" 科學之評價 (The value of science). In *Kexue xuanxue lunzhanji* 科學玄學論戰集 (The controversy of science and metaphysics). Preface Hu Shi 胡適 and Chen Duxiu 陳獨秀. Shanghai: Yadong shuju, 1923, 307–316.

Zhang Qing 張慶, *Zhongguo ershi shiji Zhongguo renshengguan lunzheng* 中國２０世紀中國人生觀論爭 (The Chinese view of life controversy in 20th century China). Guangzhou: Guangdong gaodeng jiaoyu chubanshe, 2000.

Zhang Taiyan 章太炎, "Wushen lun" 無神論 (Discussing atheism). In *Zhangshi congshu* 章氏叢書 (The collected writings of master Zhang). Hangzhou: Zhejiang tushuguan, 3:2, 1919, 1–10.

—, "Bianxing" 辨性 (On human nature), in *Zhangshi congshu* 章氏叢書 (The collected writings of master Zhang). Hangzhou: Zhejiang tushuguan, 2:15, 1919, 148–162.

—, "Jianli zongjiao" 建立宗教 (On establishing religion), in *Zhangshi congshu* 章氏叢書 (The collected writings of master Zhang), 3:2, 1919, 10–30.

Zhongguo zhexueshi jiaoxue ziliao zaoji 中國哲學史教學資料造輯 (Selected sources for the study of the history of Chinese philosophy). Ed. the philosophy department at Beijing University. Beijing: Zhonghua shuju, vol. II, 1982.

Zhuangzi duben 莊子讀本 (A Zhuangzi reader). Taibei: Sanmin shuju, 1988.

WESTERN SOURCES

Alitto, Guy S. *The Last Confucian: Liang Shu-ming and the Chinese Dilemma of Modernity*. Berkeley: University of California Press, 1979.
Bellah, Robert N. *Beyond Belief: Essays on Religion in a Post-Traditional World*. New York: Harper and Row, 1970.
Bergson, Henry. *Creative Evolution*. Trans. Arthur Mitchell. New York: The Modern Library, 1944.
—. *Time and Free Will: An Essay on the Immediate Data of Consciousness*. Trans. F.L. Pogson. New York: The Macmillan Publishers, 1950.
Berlin, Isaiah, "Joseph de Maistre and the Origins of Fascism." *New York Review of Books*, (September 27, 1990), 57–64.
—, "The Pursuit of the Ideal." In *The Crooked Timber of Humanity*. Henry Hardy, ed. London: John Murray, 1990, 1–19.
Berling, Judith A., "When They Go Their Separate Ways: The Collapse of the Unitary Vision of Chinese Religion in the Early Ch'ing." In *Meeting of Minds: Intellectual and Religious Interaction in East Asian Traditions of Thought*. Irene Bloom and Joshua Fogel, A., eds. New York: Columbia University Press, 1997, 209–237.
Bernstein, Richard J. *Praxis and Action: Contemporary Philosophies of Human Activity*. Philadelphia: University of Pennsylvania Press, 1971.
Bloom, Irene, "On the Abstraction of Ming Thought: Some Concrete Evidence from the Philosophy of Lo Chin-shun." In *Principle and Practicality*. Irene Bloom and Wm. Theodore de Bary, eds. New York: Columbia University Press, 1979, 69–113.
—, "On the Matter of the Mind: The Metaphysical Basis of the Expanded Self." In *Individualism and Holism: Studies in Confucian and Taoist Values*. Donald J. Munro, ed. Ann Arbor: University of Michigan Center for Chinese Studies, 1985, 293–330.
—, "Fundamental Intuitions and Consensus Statements: Mencian Confucianism and Human Rights." In *Confucianism and Human Rights*. Wm. Theodore de Bary and Tu Weiming, eds. New York: Columbia University Press, 1998, 94–116.
Booth, Meyrick. *Rudolf Eucken: His Philosophy and Influence*. London: T. Fisher Unwin, 1913.
Chan, Wing-tsit, trans. *Instructions for Practical Living and other Neo-Confucian Writings by Wang Yang-ming*. New York: Columbia University Press, 1963.
—, "The Concept of Man in Chinese Thought." In *Neo-Confucianism, Etc.: Essays by Wing-tsit Chan*. Hong Kong: Oriental Society, 1969, 117–185.
—, trans. and comp. *A Source Book in Chinese Philosophy*. Princeton. N.J.: Princeton University Press, 1973.
Chang Hao. *Liang Ch'i-ch'ao and Intellectual Transition in China, 1890–1907*. Cambridge, Mass.: Harvard University Press, 1971.
—. *Chinese Intellectuals in Crisis: Search for Order and Meaning, 1890–1911*. Berkeley: University of California Press, 1988.
—, "Some Reflections on the Problems of the Axial-Age Breakthrough in Relation to Classical Confucianism." In *Ideas Across Cultures: Essays on Chinese Thought in Honor of Benjamin I. Schwartz*. Paul A. Cohen and Merle Goldman, eds. Cambridge, Mass.: Council on East Asian Studies, Harvard University, 1990, 17–31.
—, "Confucian Cosmological Myth and Neo-Confucian Transcendence." In *Cosmology, Ontology, and Human Efficacy*. Richard J. Smith and D.W.Y. Kwok, eds. Honolulu: University of Hawaii Press, 1993, 11–33.
—, "The Intellectual Heritage of the Confucian Ideal of Ching-shih." In *Confucian Traditions*

in East Asian Modernity: Moral Education and Economic Culture in Japan and the Four Mini-Dragons. Tu Wei-ming, ed. Cambridge, Mass.: Harvard University Press, 1996, 72–91.

Chen Chi-yun, "Liang Ch'i-ch'ao's 'Missionary Education': A Case Study of Missionary Influence on the Reformers." *Papers on China*, vol. XVI, 1962, 66–125.

Chen Xiaomei. *Occidentalism: A Theory of Counter-Discourse in Post-Mao China.* Oxford: Oxford University Press, 1995.

Ching, Julia, "Chu Hsi on Personal Cultivation," In *Chu Hsi and Neo-Confucianism.* Wing-tsit Chan, ed. Honolulu: University of Hawaii Press, 1986, 273–291.

Chiu Hansheng, "Zhu Xi's Doctrine of Principle." In *Chu Hsi and Neo-Confucianism.* Wing-tsit Chan, ed. Honolulu: University of Hawaii Press, 1986, 116–137.

Chiu Wei-chun. *Morality as Politics: The Restoration of the Ch'eng-Chu Neo-Confucianism in Late Imperial China.* Ph.D. dissertation, Ohio State University, 1992.

Chow Kai-wing, "Purist Hermeneutics and Ritualist Ethics in Mid-Ch'ing Thought." In *Cosmology, Ontology, and Human Efficacy.* Richard J. Smith and D.W.Y. Kwok, eds. Honolulu: University of Hawaii Press, 1993, 179–204.

Chow Tse-tsung. *The May Fourth Movement: Intellectual Revolution in Modern China.* Cambridge, Mass.: Harvard University Press, 1960.

Cohen, Paul A., "Christian Missions and Their Impact to 1900." In *The Cambridge History of China.* John K. Fairbank, ed. Cambridge: Cambridge University Press, vol. X, 1978, 543–90.

Darnton, Robert, "George Washington's False Teeth." *New York Review of Books*, (March 27, 1997), 34–38.

de Bary, Wm. Theodore, "Neo-Confucian Cultivation and the Seventeenth-Century Enlightenment." In *The Unfolding of Neo-Confucianism.* W.T. de Bary, ed. New York: Columbia University Press, 1975, 1–38.

Dewey, John. *Lectures in China, 1919–1920.* Robert W. Clopton and Ou Tsuin-chen, eds. And trans. Honolulu: East-West Center, 1973.

Driesch, Hans A. E. *The Crisis of Psychology.* Princeton, N.J.: Princeton University Press, 1925, 176.

— and Margarete Driesch. *Fern-Ost* (The Far East). Leipzig: Brockhaus, 1925.

Dumont, Louis, "A Modified View of Our Origins: The Christian Beginnings of Modern Individualism." In *The Category of the Person: Anthropology, Philosophy, History.* M. Carrithers, S. Collins, and S. Lukes, eds. Cambridge: Cambridge University Press, 1985, 93–122.

Eber, Irene, "Hu Shih and the Controversy on Chinese Culture and Western Civilization." *East Asian Occasional Papers* (II). Harry, J. Lamley, ed. Honolulu: University of Hawaii Press, 1970, 29–45.

Elman, Benjamin. *From Philosophy to Philology: Social and Intellectual Aspects of Change in Late Imperial China.* Cambridge, Mass.: Harvard University, Council on East Asian Studies, 1984.

—. *Classicism, Politics and Kinship: The Ch'ang-chou School of New Text Confucianism in Late Imperial China.* Berkeley: University of California Press, 1990.

—, "The Revaluation of Benevolence (Jen) in Ch'ing Evidential Research." In *Cosmology, Ontology, and Human Efficacy.* Richard J. Smith and D.W.Y. Kwok, eds. Honolulu: University of Hawaii Press, 1993, 59–80.

Eucken, Rudolf C., "Against Pessimism." In *Collected Essays of Rudolf Eucken.* Meyrick Booth, ed. and trans. New York: Charles Scribner's Sons, 1914, 169–178.

—, "The Reflection of the Age in its Concepts." In *Collected Essays of Rudolf Eucken.* Meyrick Booth, ed. and trans. New York: Charles Scribner's Sons, 1914, 327–351.

—, "The Problem of Immortality." In *Collected Essays of Rudolf Eucken*. Meyrick Booth, ed. and trans. New York: Charles Scribner's Sons, 1914, 193–210.
— and Carsun Chang (Zhang Junmai). *Das Lebensproblem in China und in Europa* (The problem of life in China and in Europe). Leipzig: Quelle and Meyer, 1922.
—. *Rudolf Eucken: His Life, Works, and Travels*. Joseph McCabe, trans. New York: Charles Scribner's Sons, 1922.
Faber, Ernst. *Socialismus oder die Lehre des Philosophen Micius* (Socialism or the teaching of the philosopher Mo Zi). Elberfeld: R.L. Friderichs, 1877.
—. *Introduction to the Science of Chinese Religion. A Critique of Max Muller and other Authors*. Hongkong: Lane, Crawford and Co., 1879.
Fass, Joseph, "The Introduction of Kant's Ideas into Japan and its Historical Prerequisites." *Asian and African Studies* (Bratislava), vol. XX (1984) 111–118.
Findeisen, Raoul D., "Vier westliche Philosophen in China," *Minima Sinica* 2 (1991), 1–36.
—, "Professor Luo. Reflections on Bertrand Russell in China." *Asian and African Studies* (Bratislava), 3.1 (1994), 10–33.
Fröhlich, Thomas, "Das Grosse Ich: Religion, Evolution und Entpolitisierung bei Liang Qichao (1873–1929)" (The great self: religion, evolution and de-politization in Liang Qichao). *Oriens Extremus*, 41.1 (1998/99), 193–210.
Fung, Edmund S. K. *The Intellectual Foundations of Chinese Modernity; Cultural and Political Thought in the Republican Era.* Cambridge: Cambridge University Press, 2010.
Furth, Charlotte. *Ting Wen-chiang*. Cambridge, Mass.: Harvard University Press, 1970.
—, "Intellectual Change: from the Reform Movement to the May Fourth Movement, 1895–1920." In *The Cambridge History of China*. John K. Fairbank and Denis Twitchett, eds. Cambridge: Cambridge University Press, vol. XII, 1986, 396–401.
Graham, Angus C. *Disputers of the Tao: Philosophical Argumentation in Ancient China*. La Salle: Open Court, 1989.
Huang Chun-chieh, Erik Zürcher, "Cultural Notions of Time and Space in China." In *Time and Space in Chinese Culture*. Huang Chun-chieh and Erik Zürcher, eds. Leiden: E. J. Brill, 1995, 3–14.
Huters, Theodore, "A New Way of Writing: The Possibilities for Literature in Late Qing China, 1895–1908." *Modern China*, 14.3 (July, 1988), 243–276.
Isay, Gad C., "A Missionary Philosopher in Late Qing: Ernst Faber (1839–99) and his Intercultural Synthesis of Human Nature," *Sino-Western Cultural Relations Journal*, 23 (August 2001), 22–49.
—, "Religious Obligation Transformed into Intercultural Agency. Ernst Faber's Mission in China," *Monumenta Serica*, Vol. 54, 2006, 273–287.
Israel, John. *Lianda: A Chinese University in War and Revolution*. Stanford: Stanford University Press, 1998.
Jeans, Roger B. *'Syncretism in Defense of Confucianism': An Intellectual and Political Biography of the Early Years of Chang Chun-mai, 1887–1923*. Ph.D. dissertation, George Washington University, 1974.
Kubin, Wolfgang, "On the Problem of the Self in Confucianism." In *Confucianism and the Modernization of China*. Silke Krieger and Rolf Trauzettel, eds. Mainz: Hase and Koehler Verlag, 1991, 63–95.
Kwok, D.W.Y. *Scientism in Chinese Thought, 1900–1950*. New Haven: Yale University Press, 1965.
Kwong, Luke S.K. *T'an Ssu-t'ung, 1865–1898: Life and Thought of a Reformer*. Leiden: E.J. Brill, 1996.
Lee Leo Ou-fan, "Literary Trends I: The Quest for Modernity, 1895–1927." In *The Cam-

bridge History of China. John K. Fairbank and Denis Twitchett, eds. Cambridge: Cambridge University Press, vol. XII, 1986, 452–505.
—, "Modernity and its Discontents: The Cultural Agenda of the May Fourth Movement." In *Heritage of China: Contemporary Perspectives on Chinese Civilization*. Paul S. Ropp, ed. Berkeley: University of California Press, 1990, 158–177.
Levenson, Joseph R.. *Confucian China and Its Modern Fate: A Trilogy*. Berkeley: University of California Press, 1968.
Lin Tongqi, "Subjectivity: Marxism and 'The Spiritual' in China Since Mao." *Philosophy East & West*, 44.4 (October 1994), 609–646.
Lin Tongqi, Henry Rosemont, Jr., and Roger T. Ames, "Chinese Philosophy: A Philosophical Essay on the 'State-of-the-Art.'" *The Journal of Asian Studies*, 54.3 (August 1995), 727–758.
Lin Yu-sheng, "The Suicide of Liang Chi: An Ambiguous Case of Moral Conservatism." In *The Limits of Change: Essays on Conservative Alternatives in Republican China*. Charlotte Furth, ed. Cambridge, Mass.: Harvard University Press, 1976, 151–168.
—. *The Crisis of Chinese Consciousness: Radical Anti-Traditionalism in the May Fourth Era*. Madison: University of Wisconsin Press, 1978.
Locke, John. *An Essay Concerning Human Understanding*. Ed. P.H. Nidditch. Oxford: Oxford University Press, 1975.
Liu Lydia H.. *Translingual Practice: Literature, National Culture, and Translated Modernity – China, 1900–1937*. Stanford: Stanford University Press, 1995.
Liu Shu-hsien, "The Contemporary Development of a Neo-Confucian Epistemology." *Inquiry*, 14 (1971), 19–40.
Marchant, Leslie R.. *Ernst Faber's Scholarly Mission to Convert the Confucian Literati in the Late Ch'ing Period*. N.P.: University of Western Australia Center for East Asian Studies, 1982.
McMorran, Ian, "Wang Fu-chih and the Neo-Confucian Tradition." In *The Unfolding of Neo-Confucianism*. W.T. de Bary, ed. New York: Columbia University Press, 1975, 413–468.
Meissner, Werner. *Philosophy and Politics in China: The Controversy over Dialectical Materialism in the 1930s*. Richard Mann, trans. London: Hurst and Company, 1990.
Metzger, Thomas A.. *Escape From Predicament: Neo-Confucianism and China's Evolving Political Culture*. New York: Columbia University Press, 1977.
Motzkin, Gabriel. *Time and Transcendence: Secular History, the Catholic Reaction, and the Rediscovery of the Future*. Dordrecht: Kluwer Academic Publishers, 1992.
Munro, Donald J. *The Concept of Man in Early China*. Stanford: Stanford University Press, 1969.
—, ed. *Individualism and Holism: Studies in Confucian and Taoist Values*. Ann Arbor: University of Michigan, Center for Chinese Studies, 1985.
—. *Images of Human Nature, A Sung Portrait*. Princeton, N.J.: Princeton University Press, 1988.
—. *The Imperial Style of Inquiry in Twentieth-Century China: The Emergence of New Approaches*. Ann Arbor: The University of Michigan, Center for Chinese Studies, 1996.
Ng On-cho, "Toward an Interpretation of Ch'ing Ontology." In *Cosmology, Ontology, and Human Efficacy*. Richard J. Smith and D.W.Y. Kwok, eds. Honolulu: University of Hawaii Press, 1993, 35–58.
Niebuhr, Reinhold. *The Self and the Dramas of History*. New York: Charles Scribner's Sons, 1955.
—. *The Nature and Destiny of Man. Human Nature*. New York: Charles Scribner's Sons, vol. I, 1964.

Nobel Prize Foundation Directory 1991–1992. Stockholm: Sturetrycket AB, 1992.

Ogden, Susan P., "The Sage in the Inkpot: Bertrand Russell and China's Social Reconstruction in the 1920s." *Modern China*, 16.4 (1982), 529–600.

Otto, Rudolf. *Naturalism and Religion*. Arthur J. Thomson, trans. London: Williams and Norgate, 1907.

Pearson, Karl. *The Grammar of Science*. London: Walter Scott, 1892

Peterson, Willard J., "Confucian Learning in Late Ming Thought." In *The Cambridge History of China*. Denis Twitchett and Frederick W. Mote, eds. Cambridge: Cambridge University Press, vol. VIII, 1998, 708–788.

Piovesana, Gino K.. *Recent Japanese Philosophical Thought: 1862–1962*. A Survey. Tokyo: Enderle Bookstore, 1968.

Plaks, Andrew H., "The Mean, Nature, and Self-Realization. European Translations of the Zhongyong." In De L'un au Multiple (From the one into the many): Translations From Chinese into European Languages. Viviane Alleton and Michael Lackner, eds. Paris: Fondation Maison des sciences de l'homme, 1999, 313–331.

—, trans. and annotator, *Ta Hsüeh and Chung Yung* (The Highest Order of Cultivation and On the Practice of the Mean). London: Penguin Books, 2003.

Reed, Edward S., "The Separation of Psychology from Philosophy: Studies in the Sciences of the Mind 1815–1879." In *Routledge History of Philosophy: The Nineteenth Century*. C. L. Ten, ed. London: Routledge, vol. VII, 1994, 297–356.

Richter, Ursula, "Richard Wilhelm – Founder of a Friendly China Image in Twentieth Century Germany." In *Zhongyang yanjiuyuan. Jindaishi yanjiu suojikan* 中央研究院, 近代史研究所集刊 (Academica Sinica, Bulletin of the Institute of Modern History), vol. XX (June, 1990), 153–181.

Rorty, Richard. *Objectivity, Relativism, and Truth: Philosophical Papers*. Cambridge: Cambridge University Press, vol. I, 1991.

Routledge Encyclopedia of Philosophy. Edward Craig, gen. ed. London: Routledge, 1998.

Russell, Bertrand, "The Aims of Education." In *Selected Papers of Bertrand Russell*. New York: Modern Library, 1927, 159–193.

—, "Chinese and Western Civilizations." In *Selected Papers of Bertrand Russell*. New York: Modern Library, 1927, 208–224.

—. *The Analysis of Mind*. London: George Allen and Unwin, 1921.

Scalapino, Robert and George T. Yu. *Modern China and Its Revolutionary Process*. Berkeley: University of California Press, 1985.

Schopenhauer, Arthur. *The World as Will and Representation*. New York: Dover, 2 vols, 1969.

Schrag, Calvin O. *The Self after Postmodernity*. New Haven: Yale University Press, 1997.

Schnadelbach, Herbert. *Philosophy in Germany 1831–1933*. Eric Mathews, trans. Cambridge: Cambridge University Press, 1984.

Schwartz, Benjamin I., "Themes in Intellectual History: May Fourth and After." In *The Cambridge History of China*. John K. Fairbank and Denis Twitchett, eds. Cambridge: Cambridge University Press, vol. XII, 1986, 406–450.

—. *The World of Thought in Ancient China*. Cambridge, Mass.: Harvard University Press, 1985.

—. *In Search of Wealth and Power: Yen Fu and the West*. Cambridge, Mass.: Harvard University Press, 1964.

Shek, Richard, "Testimony to the resilience of the mind: the life and thought of Peng Shaosheng (1740–1796)." In Richard J. Smith and D.W.Y. Kwok, eds. *Cosmology, Ontology, and Human Efficacy*. Honolulu: University of Hawaii Press, 1993, 81–113.

Spence, Jonathan. *The Gate of Heavenly Peace: The Chinese and Their Revolution 1895–1980*. New York: Penguin Books, 1981.

Stevens, Wallace. *Collected Poems*. New York: Alfred A Knopf, 1954.
Tang Jun-i, "Liu Tsung-chou's Doctrine of Moral Mind and Practice and his Critique of Wang Yang-ming." In *The Unfolding of Neo-Confucianism*. W.T. de Bary, ed. New York: Columbia University Press, 1975, 305–332.
Teng Ssu-yu and John K. Fairbank, eds. *China's Response to the West*. Cambridge, Mass.: Harvard University Press, 1965.
Thomson, Arthur J.. *Introduction to Science*. London: Williams and Norgate, 1911.
Tillich, Paul. *The Dynamics of Faith*. New York: Harper and Brothers Publishers, 1957.
Tu Wei-ming, "Hsiung Shih-li's Quest for Authentic Existence." In *The Limits of Change: Essays on Conservative Alternatives in Republican China*. Charlotte Furth, ed. Cambridge, Mass.: Harvard University Press, 1976, 242–275.
Wilhelm, Richard, "Intellectual Movements in Modern China." *Chinese Social and Political Science Review*, 8:2 (April 1924), 110–124.
Wilhelm, Hellmut, "Chinese Confucianism on the Eve of the Great Encounter." In *Changing Japanese Attitudes toward Modernization*. Marius Jansen, ed. Princeton, N.J.: Princeton University Press,1965, 283–310.
Yang Guorong, "The Debate between Scientists and Metaphysicians in Early Twentieth Century: Its Theme and Significance." *Dao: A Journal of Comparative Philosophy* 2, 1 (December 2002): 79–95.
Yap Key-chong. *Western Wisdom in the Mind's Eye of a Westernized Chinese Lay Buddhist: The Thought of Chang Tung-hsun (1886–1962)*. Ph.D dissertation, University of Oxford, 1991.
Yu Ying-shih, "The Radicalization of China in the Twentieth Century." In *China in Transformation*. Tu Weiming, ed. Cambridge, Mass.: Harvard University Press, 1994, 125–157.

Index

age of new-metaphysics 93, 94, 95, 96, 107
autonomy 4, 6, 9, 10, 12, 14, 16, 17, 20, 21, 22, 24, 31, 33, 34, 35, 36, 41, 42, 45, 46, 47, 48, 49, 50, 51, 53, 54, 62, 64, 65, 67, 70, 71, 73, 77, 86, 95, 98, 103, 104, 106, 107, 109, 113, 114, 116, 119, 121, 123, 128, 130

Bentham: Jeremy 100
Bergson: Henri VII, 53, 54, 55, 56, 57, 58, 59, 62, 63, 65, 66, 71, 72, 73, 74, 76, 80, 84, 89, 90, 101, 102, 111, 135
Berlin: Isaiah 58, 84, 85, 86, 135
Black: Dora 61, 62
Bloom: Irene 13, 16, 17, 20, 135
Bodhisattva 27, 49
Buddha 25, 26, 68, 100, 101
Buddhist 26, 27, 28, 32, 44, 45, 46, 49, 54, 80, 82, 83, 99, 111, 118, 140
Busse: Ludwig 43

Cai Yuanpei 31
Categorical imperative: *daode zhi faling* 48–51, 98, 105
causality 49, 64, 71, 73, 76, 77, 79, 85, 87, 89, 90, 91, 95, 99, 101, 104
Chan Buddhism 68
Chang Hao 4, 5, 9, 10, 11, 23, 25, 26, 27, 44, 66, 134, 135
Chen Duxiu 6, 72, 77, 79, 81, 82, 85, 88, 89, 94, 115, 127, 131, 132, 133, 134
Chen Li 10, 23, 28
Cheng Yi 13, 14
Cheng-Zhu 14, 22, 23
Confucian 1, 2, 3, 6, 7, 8, 10, 11, 12, 13, 14, 15, 16, 17, 18, 19, 22, 23, 24, 26, 28, 33, 34, 35, 40, 41, 43, 46, 48, 50, 54, 65, 69, 74, 110, 111, 112, 119, 123, 127, 129, 135, 136, 138, 139
Confucianism: New 4, 6, 9, 15, 16, 22, 23, 24, 32, 63, 69, 70, 99, 129, 132, 135, 136, 137, 138, 140

Confucius 2, 3, 11, 12, 21, 22, 26, 68, 70, 71, 84, 97, 100, 101, 106

Dai Zhen 10, 20, 22, 28, 114
Dante: Alighieri 102
Darwin: Charles 44, 81, 100
de Bary: W. T. 16, 17, 19, 135, 136, 138, 140
determinism 53, 54, 56, 67, 77, 89, 91, 94, 95, 104
Dewey: John VII, 53, 58, 59, 60, 61, 62, 63, 64, 73, 77, 79, 81, 82, 85, 91, 102, 117, 136
Deyujian 32, 44, 126, 132
Dialectical materialism: bianzhengfa weiwulun 8, 113, 114, 115
Ding Wenjiang 65, 78, 79, 81, 85, 94, 95, 99, 115, 131
Driesch: Hans VII, 53, 63, 64, 65, 72, 73, 76, 86, 87, 90, 134, 136

Einstein: Albert 80, 90
Engels: Friedrich 115
epistemological 7, 13, 37, 42, 75, 81, 82, 83, 84, 107, 108, 116, 128
Eucken: Rudolf C. VII, 53, 54, 55, 56, 57, 58, 59, 63, 65, 66, 72, 73, 74, 76, 84, 90, 95, 98, 101, 104, 105, 135, 136, 137
Experimentalism 60

Faber: Ernst VII, 26, 31, 32, 33, 34, 35, 36, 37, 38, 39, 40, 41, 42, 43, 44, 47, 49, 50, 51, 53, 59, 126, 127, 129, 131, 137, 138
Fan Shoukang 96, 97, 99, 131
Fang Dongshu 22
Furth: Charlotte 64, 69, 75, 80, 81, 82, 110, 137, 138, 140

German 1, 4, 31, 32, 33, 34, 36, 43, 59, 63, 76, 104
Goethe 102

Graham: A. C. 11, 66, 137
Great Learning: Daxue 15, 29
great union: datong 46, 113
Gu Yanwu 114

Haeckel: Ernst 56
Han learning 105, 106
Hartmann: Nicolai 100
Hegel: G. W. F. 32, 45, 100, 131
Heinrich: Johann 100
Hou Wailu VIII, 109, 113, 115, 116, 120, 121, 123, 126, 128, 129, 130, 131
Hu Shi 6, 8, 20, 28, 49, 59, 68, 70, 73, 74, 77, 78, 79, 82, 85, 91, 94, 104, 109, 115, 119, 124, 127, 131, 132, 133, 134
Hua Zhi-an *See* Faber Ernst
Huang Zongxi 114
human nature: xing 7, 12, 13, 14, 20, 23, 24, 27, 28, 29, 31, 32, 33, 34, 35, 39, 41, 42, 46, 50, 70, 97, 98, 100, 105, 108, 115, 116, 117, 118, 119, 120, 121, 123, 128, 132, 134
humanism 45, 57, 58, 129
humanity 9, 11, 23, 27, 41, 42, 55, 68, 84, 91, 101, 117, 127, 129
Huxley: Thomas 53, 81

Inoue Tetsujirō 43
integration 9, 10, 12, 13, 15, 16, 17, 18, 19, 20, 21, 23, 25, 26, 28, 33, 40, 41, 42, 47, 50, 57, 60, 70, 71, 72, 73, 74, 102, 105, 106, 109, 111, 116, 117, 118, 121, 123, 126, 127, 128
interrelatedness 16, 21, 28, 47, 49, 50, 60, 105, 107, 121, 127, 128, 129

James: William 81, 95
Japan 1, 4, 23, 32, 43, 59, 110, 136, 137
Jiang Menglin 59
Jiao Xun 10, 20, 21, 22, 25, 28

Kang Youwei 42
Kant: Emmanuel VII, 4, 31, 32, 33, 36, 38, 42, 43, 44, 45, 46, 47, 48, 49, 50, 51, 53, 64, 84, 98, 100, 105, 127, 129, 131, 132, 137
Kierkegaard: Søren 40
Kropotkin: Pyotr Alexeyevich 100
Kubin: Wolfgang 16, 137

Kwok: D. W. Y. 2, 5, 10, 62, 65, 75, 77, 125, 135, 136, 137, 138, 139

Lambert: Johann Heinrich 100
Laozi 68, 100
Lebensanschauung 1, 56, 74, 128
Lebensphilosophie 57
Levenson: Joseph R. 2, 3, 125, 138
Li Zehou 8, 125, 129, 132
Li Zhi 17, 35
Liang Ji 69
Liang Qichao VII, 1, 6, 31, 32, 33, 39, 41, 42, 44, 45, 46, 48, 49, 53, 60, 64, 65, 69, 73, 74, 76, 78, 80, 88, 89, 93, 94, 96, 97, 98, 102, 103, 115, 118, 123, 124, 126, 128, 129, 132, 137
Liang Shuming VII, 6, 53, 65, 69, 70, 72, 73, 74, 78, 93, 97, 98, 126, 127, 132
liangxin 43, 48, 50, 98, 99, 100, 101, 102, 103, 104, 105, 107, 127, 128
Liangzhi 12, 14
Lin Zaiping 65, 76, 80, 83, 85, 88, 90, 91, 99, 101, 118, 132
linkage 9, 10, 11, 12, 13, 14, 17, 18, 19, 20, 21, 23, 25, 27, 28, 29, 33, 34, 37, 41, 42, 47, 50, 51, 60, 64, 66, 67, 71, 72, 75, 78, 84, 94, 102, 103, 109, 111, 112, 116, 117, 121, 123, 126
Liu Zongzhou 19
Locke: John 37, 138
Lotze: R. H. 37
Lu Xiangshan 13, 14
Luo Keting 109, 113, 131
Lu-Wang 14, 20, 43, 97

Mach: Ernst 53, 81
Marx: Karl 40, 97, 114, 115, 116, 129
May Fourth 1, 2, 4, 5, 6, 8, 54, 59, 61, 64, 65, 71, 78, 79, 82, 105, 106, 107, 109, 116, 124, 125, 127, 131, 134, 136, 137, 138, 139
McMorran: Ian 19, 138
memory 83, 117, 118, 120
Mencius 2, 3, 11, 12, 14, 19, 48, 50, 72, 84, 97, 98, 100, 102, 108, 111, 118, 119, 121, 126
metaphysics 2, 7, 28, 49, 54, 55, 57, 61, 62, 63, 70, 71, 75, 77, 78, 79, 80, 81, 82, 84, 86, 87, 89, 90, 91, 92, 93, 94, 95, 96, 97,

98, 99, 102, 103, 104, 105, 106, 107, 109, 110, 112, 115, 118, 123, 124, 125, 126, 127, 128, 130, 131, 132, 133, 134
missionaries 2, 26, 33, 42
morality 2, 11, 12, 23, 28, 35, 48, 50, 53, 54, 62, 63, 67, 69, 73, 89, 97, 99–102, 104, 106, 107
Mou Zongsan 110, 129, 132
Mozi 25, 40, 41, 42, 68, 100, 101
Mr. Beauty 88
Mr. Democracy 5, 124
Mr. Love 88
Mr. Science 5, 88, 124

neisheng waiwang 23
New Citizen 44
New Culture Movement 2, 5
New Text: Jinwen 22, 28, 136
New Youth: magazine 1
Newton: Isaac 90
Ng: On-cho 18, 19, 138
Nietzsche: Friedrich 100

Onishi Hajime 48

Pan Yongwei 114
Pearson: Karl 54, 81, 139
Peng Shaosheng 10, 20, 28, 132
Piovesana: Gino K. 43, 44, 59, 139
positivism 54, 55, 56, 75, 76, 94, 104, 105, 125
positivist 6, 43, 53, 54, 58, 59, 63, 65, 68, 73, 76, 79, 82, 93, 94, 96, 104, 107
principle: li 3, 13, 14, 17, 21, 22, 23, 25, 28, 29, 34, 37, 45, 48, 69, 84, 98, 105, 106, 109, 114, 118, 121, 126, 129, 131, 132, 133

Qian Mu VIII, 20, 21, 22, 23, 24, 91, 109, 111, 113, 114, 117, 118, 119, 120, 121, 123, 126, 128, 129, 130, 132, 134
Qu Shiying (Junong) 61, 80, 98, 133

Reflections VII, 9, 39, 62, 65, 66, 69, 73, 74, 98, 132, 135, 137
religion 20, 22, 32, 40, 45, 63, 95, 132, 135, 137, 139
Ruan Yuan 10, 20, 21, 22, 23, 28

Russell: Bertrand VII, 53, 58, 59, 61, 62, 63, 64, 68, 73, 80, 82, 83, 91, 137, 139

sagehood 40
Schopenhauer: Arthur 40, 69, 72, 100, 139
Schwartz: Benjamin I. 9, 11, 12, 31, 48, 61, 79, 135, 139
scientism VII, 2, 5, 53, 62, 65, 75, 77, 78, 123, 125, 137
self-knowledge 35
setting the world in order: jingshi 22, 28, 31
Shakespeare: William 102
Song learning 3, 22, 23, 24, 28, 105, 106, 108
Spencer: Herbert 44, 81
Spengler: Oswald 58
spirituality 21, 33, 34, 50, 51, 54, 58, 62, 65, 66, 67, 68, 71, 73, 74, 76, 107, 115, 117, 118, 120, 127, 130
substance and function: tiyong 3, 4, 7, 31, 47, 50, 51, 63, 64, 65, 69, 73, 92, 93, 104, 105, 124, 127

Taizhou school 17
Tan Sitong 25, 26, 27, 28, 133
Tang Jian 10, 23, 24, 28, 133
Thomson: Arthur J. 63, 90, 95, 96, 139, 140
ti 3, 4, 6, 7, 31, 47, 51, 65, 68, 70, 72, 73, 93, 105, 124, 127
Tillich: Paul 39, 140
Timothy: Richard 43
tiyong see substance and function
Tongzhi restoration 3
total Westernization 8, 124
Tu Weiming 5, 110, 135, 140

vital force: qi 13, 14, 17, 19
von Koeber: Raphael 43

Wagner: Richard 102
Wang Fuzhi 19, 114
Wang Gen 17
Wang Ji 17
Wang Yangming 13, 14, 15, 17, 32, 44, 45, 46, 47, 48, 50, 97, 98, 108, 111, 121, 123
Wei Yuan 4, 42
Wells: H. G. 96

Wilhelm: Helmut 24, 59, 61, 63, 139, 140; Richard 59
Williamson: Alexander 26
World War I 6, 55, 58, 59, 62, 94
World War II 8, 110
Wu Zhihui 77, 78, 82, 85, 114, 115, 133

Xiong Shili VIII, 109, 110, 111, 112, 116, 118, 120, 121, 123, 126, 128, 129, 130, 133
Xunzi 12, 100, 133

Yan Fu 31
Yan Yuan 19, 20, 114
Yogacara 27, 44, 45, 68
yong 3, 4, 6, 31, 47, 65, 68, 73, 92, 93, 105
Young: J. Allen 43

Yu Yingshi 5, 14, 49, 105, 111, 113, 129, 133

Zeng Guofan 10, 23, 24, 28
Zhang Dongsun 59, 61, 80, 82, 83, 88, 89, 91, 95, 98, 99, 103, 104, 128, 134
Zhang Junmai 63, 64, 65, 76, 77, 79, 80, 82, 83, 84, 85, 86, 88, 89, 90, 91, 94, 95, 96, 97, 98, 99, 100, 101, 102, 106, 127, 128, 134, 137
Zhang Taiyan 25, 26, 27, 28, 109, 111, 134
Zhang Zai 13, 14, 15, 19
Zhang Zhidong 3, 51, 105, 124
Zhou Dunyi 15
Zhu Xi 3, 13, 14, 15, 16, 34, 118, 121, 123, 136
Zhuangzi 83, 134